How are religious ideas represented, acquired and transmitted? Confronted with religious practices, anthropologists have typically been content with sociological generalisations, informed by vague, intuitive models of cognitive processes. Yet modern cognitive theories promise a fresh understanding of how religious ideas are learnt; and if the same cognitive processes can be shown to underlie all religious ideologies, then the comparative study of religions will be placed on a wholly new footing. The present book is a contribution to this ambitious programme. In closely focused essays, a group of anthropologists debate the particular nature of religious concepts and categories, and begin to specify the cognitive constraints on cultural acquisition and transmission.

Cognitive aspects of religious symbolism

Cognitive aspects of religious symbolism

edited by
Pascal Boyer
King's College, Cambridge

CAMBRIDGE
UNIVERSITY PRESS

Published by the Press Syndicate of the University of Cambridge
The Pitt Building, Trumpington Street, Cambridge CB2 1RP
40 West 20th Street, New York, NY 10011–4211, USA
10 Stamford Road, Oakleigh, Victoria 3166, Australia

First published 1993

Printed in Great Britain at the University Press, Cambridge

A catalogue record for this book is available from the British Library

Library of Congress cataloguing in publication data

Cognitive aspects of religious symbolism / edited by Pascal Boyer.
    p.   cm.
Includes bibliographical references.
ISBN 0–521–43288–X
1. Religious thought. 2. Symbolism. 3. Cognition. 4. Ritual.
I. Boyer, Pascal.
BL85.C63 1992
291'.01–dc20 92–15803 CIP

ISBN 0 521 43288 X hardback

CE

Contents

Contributors

Scott Atran
 CREA, Ecole Polytechnique, Paris

Maurice Bloch
 Department of Anthropology, London School of Economics

Pascal Boyer
 King's College, University of Cambridge

Michael Houseman
 Laboratoire d'Ethnologie, University of Paris, Nanterre

Roger Keesing
 Department of Anthropology, McGill University, Montreal

J. D. Keller
 Department of Anthropology, University of Illinois, Urbana Champaign

E. Thomas Lawson
 Department of Religion, Western Michigan University, Kalamazoo

F. K. Lehman (U Chit Hlaing)
 Department of Anthropology, University of Illinois, Urbana Champaign

Carlo Severi
 College de France, Paris

Christina Toren
 Department of Human Sciences, Brunel University, London

Part I

Cognitive processes and cultural representations

In these introductory essays, the issues treated in the volume are placed in the wider framework of anthropological research. The first chapter considers the various questions a cognitively oriented framework is supposed to deal with, and the differences in methods and concepts between cognitive theories, on the one hand, and other types of anthropological models, on the other. Atran's paper describes in detail the contribution of past cognitive anthropology ('ethnosemantics') to the understanding of symbolism. In his view, early studies in cognitive anthropology did not produce satisfactory models of cultural knowledge and its transmission, mainly because it was based on inadequate psychological models. Atran's essay also outlines the research programme of a more sophisticated approach to cultural representations, which would integrate recent advances in theories of cognitive development.

1 Cognitive aspects of religious symbolism

Pascal Boyer

In the vast anthropological literature devoted to religious behaviour and discourse, one particular domain is relatively neglected: that of the psychological, more precisely of the cognitive dimensions of religious behaviour. This is particularly surprising now, in view of the enormous development and complexification of 'cognitive' science, that is, the heterogeneous cross-breeding of theories and hypotheses put forward in linguistics, psychology, artificial intelligence and philosophy. The aim of this introductory essay is both to account for this state of affairs and to suggest some directions of investigation in the cognitive study of religious symbolism.

The term 'symbolism' is particularly difficult to define. As Sperber points out (1975b: 2), the domain is construed either as the mental minus the rational or the semiotic minus language. A theoretical difficulty is thus reified as a real domain of thought and action, which justifies Gellner's wry comment (1987: 163), that 'in social anthropology ... if a native says something sensible it is primitive technology, but if it sounds very odd then it is symbolic'. I will deal presently with the important problems involved in delineating the domain of 'religious symbolism', more specifically with the ambiguities of the very notion of 'symbolism'. At this stage, however, the term should be understood, in a fairly straightforward way, to denote the ideas, beliefs, actions and interaction patterns which concern extra-human entities and processes. In this domain of cultural interaction, certain conceptual domains, concerning for example, ancestors, spirits, gods, sacrifice, etc., stand out as especially difficult to describe in a precise and explanatory way.

The main point of a *cognitive* framework is to explain the recurrent properties of religious symbolism by giving a precise answer to the following questions: what are the mental representations and processes involved in religious beliefs, discourse and actions? How are these representations acquired and transmitted? As we will see, there are few satisfactory answers to these questions in cultural anthropology. The aim of this introduction is to explain this state of affairs, describe the problems involved and suggest some possible directions for research. I will start with a description of the strategic position of a cognitive study of religion, that is, a review of the general assumptions upon which such a study is based (part I). As will become obvious, most of these assumptions are of a 'reactive' nature. They are the outcome of a dissatisfaction with the hypotheses and theories put forward in non-cognitive frameworks. This is why part I includes a very brief, and slightly polemical account of the state of the art in non-cognitive frameworks. The conclusion is that treating the cognitive aspects of religions as immaterial, or considering that a few *ad hoc* principles are all that is required in this domain, can lead to serious problems, notably to rather implausible anthropological descriptions. This is why we will have to examine in more detail, in part II, a framework which does see cognitive processes as crucial to the understanding of cultural knowledge, namely the sub-discipline called 'cognitive anthropology', which grew out of American 'ethnosemantics' and 'ethnoscience'. Modern cognitive anthropology makes use of psychological findings and hypotheses in its descriptions, and therefore represents a step in the right direction. Cognitive anthropology, however, has seldom ventured into the complicated problems posed by traditional religion. It is therefore legitimate to ask to what extent cognitive-anthropological methods and hypotheses are equipped to deal with religious symbolism (part II). It is necessary, in particular, to understand exactly what makes the domain of symbolism special, what cognitive processes make it particularly difficult to describe in the terms of cognitive anthropology, before developing a renewed, psychologically plausible description of religious symbolism. Part III will identify the main domains on which such a renewed anthropology of religion should focus. These can be summarised as a series of three crucial problems concerning (1) the representation of knowledge in religious matters, (2) the acquisition of religious knowledge and (3) the representation of ritual action and interaction. This final section will go beyond present areas of research and suggest some directions of research.

The background: cognition in classical theories of religion

Let me begin with a general description of what a cognitive study of religion aims to do. The main differences between a cognitive theory and other anthropological frameworks concern not only the repertoire of specific answers given to anthropological questions, but also the manner in which these questions are posed, and what sort of evidence counts as relevant towards their solution. In other words, we are dealing here with different axioms as much as different theorems. The easiest way to explain exactly how cognitive frameworks, at least in an ideal intellectual world, differ from the rest, is to use a series of nested disjunctions. At each disjunctive point, we will see that having a cognitive framework implies making a choice that some other anthropological framework has either refused or neglected. In the following sections, however, the skeleton will be fleshed out with illustrations taken from actual anthropological theories.

The type of framework that is put forward in this volume can be characterised by the answers given to a series of five crucial questions, concerning the nature of the enterprise, the nature of the data and the type of generalisations it tries to capture,[1] as follows:

1 An account of religious phenomena is either of an *interpretative* or of an *explanatory* nature. In other words, it aims either at giving an intuitively satisfactory rendering of religious phenomena, or else at relating their recurrent properties to some general, explanatory principles. In this case the second alternative is chosen, which leads to another question:

2 The theory may postulate that cultural phenomena belong to a special level of reality, quite autonomous from their realisation in individual people's minds, discourse or action. Or alternatively, as in this book, the theory is based on the premise that religious phenomena consist of nothing other than special configurations and distributions of people's ideas, discourse and actions. This leads to a third choice:

3 In providing a repertoire of explanatory principles which account for the recurrent properties of religious phenomena, the framework must determine whether these recurrent features have anything to do with universal properties of the mind–brain. Many anthropological frameworks are founded on the idea that cognitive properties are irrelevant. Our framework, being based on the opposite stance, is then faced with a simple methodological question:

4 The relevant properties of human minds can be approached either, in a somewhat speculative and *ad hoc* manner, by just formulating what seems to emerge from cultural data, or else by confronting such data with independent hypotheses formulated in other disciplines concerned with the human mind, notably in psychology. The choice is between the optimistic assumption that cultural data are firm enough to be the basis of specific psychological hypotheses, and the more sober idea that they provide a series of interesting problems, in which general psychological hypotheses can be tested, and which they can in turn illuminate. Choosing the latter

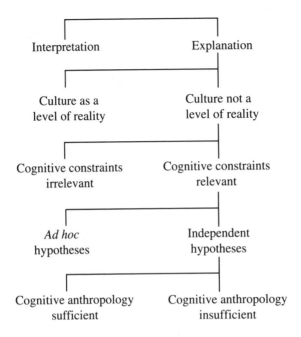

Figure 1.1   Five choices in the study of religious symbolism

option leads us to a new choice, this time elicited by the existence of a specific sub-discipline in cultural anthropology:

5 The choice is whether the models and hypotheses developed in 'cognitive anthropology' are relevant to the description of religious symbolism. Cognitive-anthropological models were developed in order to account for people's representations of practical domains of knowledge, such as animal and plant species or other observable features of the everyday world. The problem, then, is to understand to what extent the type of knowledge structures encompassed under the vague term 'religious symbolism' are fundamentally different from those relevant in everyday knowledge. The answer given in this volume is a qualified one, although most authors tend to insist on the differences, and therefore on the need for special models of religious symbolism.

The series of choices can be represented as a disjunctive tree (see fig. 1.1). In the following pages, I will provide a more detailed justification for these choices, in a brief presentation and evaluation of alternative anthropological accounts of religion. I should stress again that what follows is in no sense a classification of theories of religion. The point of the presentation is purely pragmatic, to serve as a clear presentation of what cognitive theories are about, by showing what background they stand up against.[2] Also, I must indicate that the point of such explanations is not to suggest that the cognitive framework is the only rational option, but to show more precisely what this option consists of, why it is worth pursuing and in what ways it is different from other frameworks.

Hermeneutics and naturalised anthropology

Let me first consider the interpretative or hermeneutic viewpoint. It is based on the idea that cultural phenomena are of a special kind, and cannot be subjected to the type of causal explanation that is manifestly successful in the natural sciences. The explanatory point of view, on the other hand, starts from the idea that social and cultural phenomena are firmly grounded in natural properties, such as the properties of human minds, those of the ecological milieux in which human groups live and so on. The main tenet of the interpretative stance is the idea that *meaning*, understood here in a very general sense, is not amenable to the same descriptions as physical phenomena. Geertz, for instance, argues that the study of cultural systems should be 'not an experimental science in search of law but an interpretive one in search of meaning' (1973: 5). The general study of religion, then, should be nothing other than an attempt to make the general feature of religious phenomena understandable, that is, intuitively 'meaningful' to readers.[3]

The hermeneutic stance is based on the fundamental premise that phenomena of meaning cannot be the object of explanation because they cannot be causally related to other, notably physical phenomena (Lawson & McCauley 1990: 17). Against this framework, the 'naturalised' view of cultural phenomena is based, precisely, on the assumption that 'meanings', or in less metaphysical terms, thought events and processes, are the consequence and manifestation of physical phenomena. They are therefore amenable to causal descriptions. Obviously, there is nothing new in this assumption, which is at the basis of most anthropological theories, from Durkheimian symbolism or Tylorian intellectualism to Marxist analyses of ideology or cultural 'superstructures'. What is special about the cognitive framework is that it introduces new arguments in defence of that assumption. The cognitive study of cultural phenomena is only a distant echo, in the field of anthropology, of the greater changes introduced by cognitive science in the domains of philosophy and psychology. It may be of help to indicate, very briefly, in what manner these changes make it possible to reconsider questions of cultural 'meaning'.

That human thought is ruled by general principles, that it does not consist in a random succession of chaotic mental events, has always been a truism of psychology. The connection, however, between such regularities or principles and the properties of human brains was incomprehensible, not only in its specific details, but also in principle. It therefore led to the quasi-mystical assumption of a special 'essence' for thought processes. What is new about the cognitive science 'paradigm' is that it makes at least the *principle* of the connection intelligible, by observing that the rule-directed manipulation of tokens of abstract symbols by machines of whatever nature (mechanical, electronic or biological) can simulate some regularities of thought processes. In other words, the shift to a 'physicalist' or materialist interpretation of cognition is made possible, because cognitive science has at least a minimal 'causal story' to explain how thought processes can be actualised in material processes, as well as some practical implementations of that story.[4]

The development of cognitive science has a practical moral for anthropologists. It shows that there is no reason to think that phenomena of 'meaning' should require a special essence, a special domain in which causal laws are irrelevant. If thought processes in general are rooted in physical brain processes, this should apply equally well to the special sub-category of thought processes, studied by anthropologists. However, making this inference seems to imply that the cultural phenomena are indeed just a special category of cognitive processes, that they consist in thoughts. This is where anthropologists may argue that the phenomena they deal with are *not* just a sub-class of cognitive processes, that they comprise a special domain, that of 'cultural' realities, which are not of a psychological nature; in other words, that cultural meaning is not cognitive meaning. This is why we must discuss the second 'choice' of the disjunctive tree, namely the idea that the study of cultural objects does not need a special 'level of reality'.

Cultural objects and their psychological 'reduction'

There are two main arguments against the idea of 'psychologising' culture, of considering cultural phenomena as a sub-category of psychological phenomena. The first one is the true observation that the 'cultural' realities studied by anthropologists include many objects and processes which are not at all of a psychological nature. For instance, the fact that rice crops have a certain yield, given ecological conditions and the techniques used, certainly has important effects on local 'cultural' phenomena, although the constraints here are clearly not psychological. This, of course, is trivially true; no reasonable anthropological paradigm has ever tried to deny or even minimise such effects.

Even if this elementary point is granted, it is still possible to deny the relevance of cognitive considerations, on the assumption that even such phenomena as religious ideas or ritual systems are not psychological in nature. This is the essence of the second argument, to the effect that anthropological enquiries concern 'cultural systems' or 'meaning systems', independently of their realisation in actual minds. This idea is pervasive, though often in an implicit and vague form, in anthropological theories. There is no space here for a general survey of all frameworks based on such assumptions, the most prominent of which being, of course, the Durkheimian notion of 'collective representations'.[5] I will focus here on more recent exponents of the idea of 'culture' as an autonomous level of reality, for their ideas will lead us directly to a clear formulation of the cognitive stance. D. Schneider, for instance, has presented a clear and explicit formulation of a pervasive way of treating cultural data, in which their abstracted form, as presented in ethnographic descriptions, exists in its own right, as it were, on a specifically cultural level of reality. Schneider thus makes a distinction between objective 'cultural' levels of meaning and what he calls a 'normative' system, that is, people's representations about the cultural meanings and rules (1972: 38). Schneider makes it very clear that in his opinion the anthropologist's sole task is the description of the 'cultural' system in that narrow sense.

This question should not be treated as an abstruse philosophical one, but as a practical problem in the construction of theories. We are not concerned here with the question, whether the description of culture as an autonomous 'level of reality' is philosophically legitimate. More modestly, the point of this discussion is to examine whether this ontological assumption is of any *heuristic advantage* in the study of cultural realities, if it makes it possible to culture certain generalities that could not be expressed otherwise. Questions of 'reduction', however, are seldom treated in that way; they are often dealt with on the basis of metaphorical, and therefore misleading arguments. Take, for instance, Geertz's statement, that 'culture ... is no more a psychological phenomenon ... than the progressive form of the verb' (1973: 13). At first sight, the analogy may seem convincing. Linguists describe abstract linguistic structures, and leave to another discipline (psycho-linguistics) the task of explaining how these structures happen to be realised by actual speakers, more precisely, what sort of mental representations are involved in producing utterances which display these structural features. In much the same way, anthropologists may want to describe cultural systems, and leave to other disciplines, notably some form of 'social' or 'cultural psychology', the task of describing how people represent them. Two aspects, however, make the analogy rather inappropriate; they relate to the achievements of the disciplines compared, on the one hand, and to their relation to psychological factors, on the other.

Let me first consider the question of actual achievements. There are simple empirical reasons why one may be justified to build a non-psychological theory of the progressive form of the verb. The grammatical regularities involved, and people's intuitions about them, are extraordinarily stable. On the other hand, cultural anthropology has not so far produced any account of any cultural phenomenon which would even approach the standards of certainty and stability which are familiar to linguists. The progressive form of the verb or the structure of nominalisation may well be adequate objects for ontological speculations; the Zande conception of witches or the American kinship system simply are not. This should lead the discipline to some measure of ontological modesty.[6]

A more important point, however, stems from the relationship between linguistic regularities described in a non-psychological way, and psychological realities. This is where Geertz's statement is rather misleading, in that it would suggest to an inattentive reader that the progressive form of the verb is an object, the properties of which are totally unrelated to cognitive processes. Even for linguists with Platonic leanings, it would be absurd to make such a claim. The particular features of the class of functions studied by syntacticians are not independent from cognitive constraints; quite the contrary. A crucial assumption of modern linguistics is the idea that the class of possible grammars for natural languages is constrained by universal (possibly innate) properties of human minds–brains.[7] Even if syntactic structures can be studied as Platonic entities, the limits to their variability are set by material (in this case biological) constraints.

This excursus into the ontology of linguistics should convey a twofold moral for anthropologists. Two conditions should be met, in order to posit an independent 'level of reality' without generating conceptual confusion:

1 positing that autonomous 'level' should make possible coherent explanatory schemes that could not be produced at a lower level;[8]
2 the theory should include a clear account of the constraints that can be imposed by the lower level, on the type of objects and processes one will find at the higher one.

Both requirements are met in the case of chemistry and physics, for example, or biology and chemistry. In the case of 'culture' and psychology, however, neither condition seems to obtain: the 'abstracted' description, in purely 'cultural' terms, does not produce explanatory schemes that could not be produced by a study of people's actual ideas, actions and discourse. This, in any case, is what the chapters in this volume try to show. Second, authors who argue for the ontological autonomy of cultural processes or realities do not seem to have any clear account of the relationship between that abstract 'cultural' level, and what is actually said and done by social actors.

This latter point is very important, because all the claims made about abstract 'cultural' objects presuppose psychological claims in at least two ways. First, descriptions of cultural phenomena are necessarily founded on data and hypotheses produced by ethnographic enquiries, which themselves are anything but psychologically neutral. Stating, for example, that the Zande believe witchcraft capacities to be inherited only from the mother is making a claim that is ultimately based on native statements and behaviour, filtered and re-interpreted by the anthropologist's intuitive notions concerning psychological processes or the links between ideas and actions. This process seems simple and unproblematic only because it is based on commonsense psychology, which precisely by virtue of being commonsense, seems self-evident or even transparent. As Holy & Stuchlik (1983: 55–80) and Sperber (1985b: ch. 1) have argued, however, the passage from observed behaviour to inferred ideas is fraught with difficulties and ambiguities. However powerful in its descriptive and predictive power, commonsense or folk-psychology should not be taken as an altogether reliable basis for ethnographic observation and inference.[9]

A second way in which 'a-psychological' anthropology presupposes psychological claims is that it purports to describe cultural realities which, to a certain extent, are acquired, memorised, modified, represented and misrepresented by the actors themselves. Even if we want to make a sharp division between 'the culture' and people's ideas, our hypotheses about the former will put constraints on the way people's cognitive capacities are conceived. To take a simple analogy, it is always possible to describe the 'laws of thought' in a logical idiom that is completely independent from psychological hypotheses. In this sense, when we say that someone's reasoning is based, for example, on *modus tollendo tollens* or another deductive schema, we are not making a direct claim about his/her mental states and processes. However, our description does entail that the cognitive processes concerned, whatever their nature and organisation, are powerful enough to perform, for example, *modus tollendo tollens* substitutions. In the same way, saying that Zande culture conveys a certain 'conception' or 'theory' of the transmission of witchcraft does entail certain claims about mental states and processes, which just cannot be ignored.

The fact that psychological realities are 'shared' by many people, more precisely, that they have important similarities in many people, does not by itself make them non-psychological, or implies an essential difference, between 'ideas', 'desires', 'inferences', etc., as described in anthropology and the corresponding objects described in psychology. It suggests, on the contrary, that cultural anthropology should comprise some hypotheses about the mechanisms whereby ideas are represented, stored and transmitted. This is the gist of Sperber's proposal, to treat anthropology as an 'epidemiology of ideas'. Pathology describes, for example, viruses and the way they affect bodies, while epidemiology describes the patterns of transmission. In much the same way, psychology describes thoughts and their production, while anthropology studies the way they spread in a population (Sperber 1985b *passim*). This is why we must examine how anthropological frameworks describe these mechanisms.

At this point, it is worth insisting on the risks involved in ignoring actual psychological processes. The main reason is that, as far as anthropological *theories* are concerned, this neglect of psychology can have momentous consequences. More often than not, it leads anthropologists to make implicit claims, the psychological plausibility of which is minimal, as we will see presently.

Cognition ignored

We now reach the third 'choice' in our disjunctive tree. It concerns the importance and the explanatory adequacy of the constraints imposed on religious phenomena by certain features of the human mind. As we will see, certain frameworks are based on the idea that such constraints are unimportant in general, or irrelevant to the kind of problems posed by religious phenomena. Obviously, the main assumption of a *cognitive* framework is to show that this negative statement is wrong, that cognitive constraints are likely to have important effects on the types of ideas, discourse and actions that constitute religious symbolism.

Religious interaction presupposes a certain level of integration in distributed representations and complementary actions. Not to put too fine a point on it, religion implies and enforces some kind of order. The main problem of a theory of religion is to explain exactly what constrains that order, what puts it in place and maintains it; and the problem is to evaluate the relative importance of *cognitive* and *social* constraints as factors of religious cohesion. There is a classical opposition in anthropology between 'Durkheimian' and 'Tylorian' (or 'Frazerian')[10] frameworks, which lay stress on social and cognitive factors respectively. The type of perspective established by Durkheim was founded on the denial of 'psychological' explanations of religion. In particular, two important premises of Durkheim's theory must be discussed here, because of their importance for current theories of religion. First, religious action and discourse are described by Durkheim as not being really about what they purport to describe, that is, extra-human objects and agencies and their relationships with human groups. Religious concepts and beliefs constitute a metaphysical representation of the social order, which they therefore contribute to enforce: religion 'is a system of ideas with which the individuals represent to themselves the society of which they are members' (1964: 225). Second, religious ideas are *constrained* by the features of social organisation. The major assumption of Durkheimian sociology of religion is that the recurrent properties of religious symbolism can be explained by recurrent features of social organisation. This may be taken to suggest, and indeed in Durkheim and many of his followers, was intended to suggest, that cognitive constraints, on the other hand, played only a minor role, or no role at all in the shaping of religious symbolism.[11] More precisely, cognitive factors are not used as explanatory principles because they are considered essentially trivial: for example, all anthropologists would accept that the storage capacity of human memory is limited, and that this makes certain possible religious configurations very unlikely. The Durkheimian stance implies that all cognitive constraints are of this trivial type.

One of the pre-theoretical intuitions on which this stance can be based is the idea that human cognition is indefinitely flexible. The precise ways in which ideas are acquired, represented, manifested and transmitted does not fundamentally change their nature of organisation. This idea of human cognition, however, is not entirely plausible. It constitutes what Bloch (1985 *passim*) calls the 'anthropological theory of cognition', and should perhaps be labelled the anthropological *non-theory* of cognition. The main assumption of the 'theory' is that people who grow up in a certain group just 'absorb' whatever cultural models are held valid in that culture, and that this process of absorption is both simple and passive. Against these assumptions, Bloch mentions empirical studies of concept acquisition, in simple domains like colour terminology or names for everyday objects. In such domains, there are complex processes of hypothesis formation and confirmation, in which the learning subject has to be described in interaction with competent speakers.[12] Surely, Bloch argues, this should apply *a fortiori* to more complex or difficult categories, for which there are neither explicit theoretical statements nor ostensive presentations of the referents.

I will return to the specific problem of concept acquisition presently. Suffice it here to say, in the wider context of cultural transmission, that some version of Bloch's argument is a necessary starting point for a cognitive study of religious ideas. Although Bloch focuses on acquisition processes, which are often neglected in anthropological frameworks, the point is in fact relevant to other domains as well. The anthropological tendency to assume that human cognition is not a constraining device for representation, that it can represent more or less any type of conceptual structure, just flies in the face of psychological facts.

In this section I have made a rather intuitive use of the notion of cognitive *constraints*, which will be characterised more precisely below. The idea, again, is directly inspired from the debates concerning the status of linguistic structures. One of the crucial assumptions of modern psycholinguistics is that the variability of actual grammars in natural languages is not infinite, that is, limited by certain properties of human minds. More precisely, the claim is that not all structures are equally *learnable*, and that some of them are not learnable at all. Cognitive functioning makes it extremely unlikely that natural languages could develop, which would incorporate these 'unlearnable' structures. In the following sections we will try to show how cultural anthropology could benefit from a rather similar usage of the notion of cognitive constraints.

Cognition invented

The implicit psychological hypotheses of anthropological models often are, to a large extent, *ad hoc* constructions. They are not based on actual data, for which they would constitute a relevant explanation. They are supposed only by the fact that they would make it possible for people to behave in the way predicted by anthropological models. This *ad hoc* psychology can lead to strange theoretical formulations, in which intrinsically psychological claims are justified by no other argument than the fact that they would be congruent with the anthropological framework put forward. 'Neo-intellectualist' models and structuralist disquisitions on 'the human mind' illustrate the dangers involved in this type of approach. Because both have been important in the development of modern anthropology, it may be of help to examine more closely in what manner their elaboration was founded on the neglect of actual psychology.

'Intellectualist' models are based on the Tylorian idea that some of the recurrent features of religious traditions can be explained by intrinsically intellectual factors, notably by the cognitive urge to explain and control natural phenomena. Against the main assumption of symbolism, intellectualist authors maintain that religious discourse should be understood literally, as an attempt to replace human experience in the wider context of cosmological order. The most recent development of this framework can be found in 'neo-intellectualist' authors like Skorupski (1976) and Horton (1982). Religious thought is described as an attempt to reach a *theoretical* understanding of the world, essentially comparable to scientific theorising (Horton 1982: 229).

The problem with neo-intellectualist interpretations is that they are true only if understood in a rather vague way, in which case they are also trivial. If expressed in a precise way, however, they fly in the face of the facts. Stating that the representations involved in religious activities *can be described as* implying or even constituting a 'theory' of some portion of the world is stating the obvious. Stating that they are sometimes *used* as 'theories' by the people concerned is equally obvious. But if we want to claim that the relevant generalities concerning religious symbolism can be captured in these intellectualist terms, that this interpretation can account for the themes, organisation and persuasive power of symbolism, then we are led to rather implausible assumptions. It is difficult to maintain, as Horton does, that traditional 'thought' consists in theories aimed at 'explanation, prediction and control' without running into serious problems of 'fit' with the ethnographic data. First and foremost, the traditional contexts where the hypothesis is supposed to apply are precisely places where people very seldom make 'theoretical' statements of that kind. This is why it is so difficult for ethnographers to reach a satisfactory, consistent picture of cultural 'models'. The only way to account for this is to assume that traditional theories are unconscious, in much the same way as syntactic rules, of which subjects are not aware although they apply them systematically. But this in turn leads to a difficult problem: if the theories are unconscious, how come people's statements are so often ambiguous or even contradictory? Against this, intellectualist theories either claim that the theory is itself inconsistent or vague (which seems to undermine the idea that it is a 'theory' in a strong sense), or that the ethnographic description is incomplete. The model therefore requires many additional assumptions, the only purpose of which is to solve the problems generated by the axioms of the framework.

Structuralism is another example of the consequences of unrestrained *ad hoc* constructions. Structuralist descriptions of cultural realities are generally based on strong assumptions about supposedly universal patterns of thinking. From a psychological viewpoint, however, such claims are generally unconvincing. If expressed in precise terms, they lead to predictions about mental processes which empirical investigation shows to be false. For instance, structuralism assumes that the most important aspect of conceptual structure is binary opposition, as well as various complex structures, like analogy, based on the combination of several binary oppositions. Psychological research, however, has never found anything of the sort in the mental representation of concepts and categories. The way human minds represent such concepts as CHAIR, CAT, GOLD or FRIENDSHIP is extremely complex, involving attribute lists, mental images, prototypical templates or scripts. Binary oppositions, however, play virtually no part in these representations.[13] In the same way, a central tenet of Lévi-Straussian analysis of myth is that these same binary oppositions are crucial to the memorisation and transmission of stories. Again, however, empirical research in this domain has uncovered many complex processes to do with the re-organisation of stories in memory and the modification of thematic content,[14] none of which have anything to do with structuralist oppositions. In so far as it is making claims about the 'human mind', structuralism seems to be pointing to realities which elude any psychological investigation. This is a crucial problem for structuralism, because its methodology is notoriously sloppy, as many critics have noted. The data that seem to 'fit' structuralist models are not especially reliable, since they have been carefully selected in the first place. In other words, structuralist theories combine the familiar empirical weaknesses of anthropological theories, with a special lack of psychological plausibility, a combination which casts doubt upon the relevance of the whole paradigm.

The point of this admittedly extreme example is to show that it is very easy, in cultural anthropology, to skip from 'as if' descriptions into hypothesised realities. Contrary to symbolist authors, who more or less *ignore* cognitive mechanisms, neo-intellectualists or structuralists simply *postulate* them. This constitutes the main difference between such models and the cognitive approach we are trying to define here, in which psychological claims are in principle based on the actual data that can support them, not on the sole premise that they are consistent with anthropological theories.

These criticisms may seem excessive or irrelevant to actual anthropological work. After all, very few anthropologists go as far as structuralists, in terms of fanciful psychological apriorism. In the same way, very few of them literally believe that religious thought conveys 'theoretical' claims about the world in Horton's strong sense, that is, claims of the same nature as those of Western science. Most anthropologists, however, share the attitude which consists in positing psychological realities for the sake of theoretical convenience. These remarks should not be understood as a 'holier than thou' attack on cultural descriptions. The essays contained in this book contain many rather fragile claims about mental processes, and this introduction is no exception. The tendency to posit *ad hoc* psychological processes, in other words to tailor cognition to anthropological needs, is perhaps a 'built-in' tendency of anthropological descriptions. As I noted above, anthropological descriptions necessarily include *intentional* ascriptions, that is, they are couched in terms of beliefs and desires ascribed to the actors. Commonsense psychology is the only idiom in which it is possible to describe observed human interaction in a way that makes sense. Precisely because it is an indispensable descriptive idiom, however, it is very difficult not to extend commonsense psychology to a domain where its relevance is far less certain, namely the production of *explanatory* hypotheses about human behaviour. This is precisely what a cognitive framework is supposed to avoid.

To sum up, 'classical' anthropological models adopt either one of two very problematic styles: one such style is based on the idea that cognitive realities and processes are entirely shaped by social or historical constraints; the other style consists in 'solving' the difficult problems of symbolism by putting forward *ad hoc*, and often implausible versions of human cognition. Cultural anthropology here relies too much on an extremely vague descriptive vocabulary that mixes description and interpretation in a rather unclear way, and relies almost exclusively on commonsense intuitions about mental processes. The monographs and theoretical essays inspired by this classical approach certainly provide invaluable insights into the workings of traditional religion. They do not, however, provide any significant answer to the questions concerning their psychological aspects.

Cognitive anthropology and the problem of symbolism

The problems of religious symbolism lie at the intersection of two established traditions in cultural anthropology. One is the 'classical' or 'mainstream' anthropological study of religion. The previous sections mentioned all the problems generated by the diverse frameworks that can be grouped in this very wide category. The other tradition, albeit a rather recent and still marginal one, is the sub-discipline of 'cognitive anthropology', which grew out of American 'ethnosemantics', sometimes called 'ethnoscience' or 'the New Ethnography'. Without anticipating too much what will be described in more detail below, I must indicate that cognitive anthropology, at least in its present state, does not seem to provide a satisfactory account of the cognitive aspects of ritual symbolism. It is worthwhile, however, examining in some detail its models and hypotheses, if only to gain a more precise understanding of the specific problems posed by religious symbolism. This investigation completes the 'strategic' overview of the previous section, focusing this time on a set of theories which, contrary to 'mainstream' cultural anthropology, do take cognitive aspects of cultural phenomena into account, and try to describe them in terms at least congruent with current cognitive research.

Knowledge representation in cognitive anthropology

The starting point of cognitive anthropology was the lack of psychological plausibility of most anthropological claims. The new discipline of sub-discipline was therefore to provide anthropological descriptions based on more solid psychological foundations. The point of this section is to give a brief survey of *modern* cognitive anthropology, and to evaluate to what extent it can contribute to a study of religious symbolism. I will not dwell on the beginnings of cognitive anthropology, which are described in detail in Atran's chapter (see below pp. 48–69). The brief description that follows is only intended as a reminder of the general issues and theories modern cognitive anthropologists inherited from their predecessors.

The main task of cognitive anthropology is to find an adequate format, or series of formats, for the description of cultural knowledge, defined, in Goodenough's terms, as 'whatever it is one has to know or believe in order to operate in a manner acceptable to [the] members [of the culture considered]' (Goodenough 1957: 32). In much the same way as linguistics studies what one has to know in order to produce grammatical sentences, the task of (early) cognitive anthropology was supposed to be a description of 'cultural competence'. As Keesing puts it (1974: 77), cultural knowledge was conceived as 'inferred ideational codes lying behind the realm of observable events'. The linguistic analogy was pervasive; cultural knowledge was conceived as similar to linguistic knowledge, and by many authors as part of it. A general assumption of cognitive anthropology was that some form of 'cultural grammar' could be built. It would be an idealised description of the unconscious or implicit rules followed by members of a culture, in the interpretation of their natural and social environment (Goodenough 1956).

Early cognitive anthropology produced stimulating analyses of many domains of linguistic and cultural knowledge, to do with biological classification, kinship terminologies, etc. By and large, however, it failed to provide a significant answer to any important anthropological problem. Its main flaw was the uncritical adoption of a simplistic framework, in which cultural knowledge was taken as formally equivalent, in many ways reducible to, linguistic knowledge. Also, the notion of cultural competence as a set of shared context-free rules proved to be virtually useless, because many representations are not shared and many rules are not even represented in any sense (D'Andrade 1987: 90). Thirdly, cognitive anthropology stuck with models inspired from structuralist linguistics at the very time when the development of generative grammars showed that such models were unsatisfactory, and that the very notion of a 'grammar' had to be reconceptualised in a much stricter way.[15] Finally, and most importantly, although cognitive anthropology defined itself as an intrinsically *psychological* project, it did not pay enough attention to actual cognitive processes, beyond those involved in lexical semantics.

Modern cognitive anthropology tried to go further and refine its descriptive and explanatory apparatus. As Dougherty-Keller puts it (1985: 7), 'the notion of a cultural grammar [gave] way to contextualized organizations of knowledge'. The main impetus for this radical change came from the extraordinary development of cognitive sciences, particularly cognitive psychology, in the 1970s. Cultural categories are conceived as embedded in complex structures which specify certain beliefs and constrain the range of possible other beliefs. The structures posited in order to describe the mental representation of cultural knowledge come in many different formats, most of which are directly inspired by parallel research in psychology and artificial intelligence. In current cognitive anthropology, the description of cultural knowledge is mainly inspired by the notions of *schemata, mental models* and *scripts.*

1 *Schemata.* There are many different definitions, and indeed understandings, of this important notion, the main function of which is to provide a format for what Miller called the 'practical' information associated with concepts, as opposed to 'lexical' information (Miller 1978). Knowing that a knife is a 'utensil used to cut materials' is part of the lexical information associated with the concept KNIFE. Knowing that most knives have a non-metallic handle, that good knives cannot be made of rubber, etc., pertains to 'practical' information. A schema is a stable structure that specifies default relations between certain concepts in a domain, and makes it possible to organise the comprehension of situations as well as expectations about them (see e.g. Miller 1978).[16]

The notion is used extensively in cognitive anthropology. A very clear illustration is Hutchins's analysis of land litigation among Trobriand islanders (1980). The description is based on accounts of litigation procedures. Hutchins's aim was to uncover the principles on which such discussion are based, that is, both the notions and the inferential rules which are tacitly admitted by all participants. The transcriptions show that it is possible to consider the various arguments as demonstrations based on abstract principles of 'schemata'. A schema typically designates a certain relation between variable ranges, for instance: 'X has rights R over L'. If all the variable slots are filled, the resulting formula is a *proposition*, that is, a formula that can be true or false (Hutchins 1980: 51). Hutchins also shows that various rules govern inferences from one proposition to another, for instance: 'If X has rights R1 over L, then X's descendants have rights R2 over L'. The demonstration is all the more impressive because the transcribed discussions seem to be governed mainly by intuition or vague conceptions of what is right or wrong. In each case, however, Hutchins shows that the inferences are based on a limited series of abstract schemata.

In a similar way, D'Andrade's study of modern American folk-concepts of the mind (1987) posits a system of inter-related propositions about the types of objects that can be 'contained' in the mind, their double description as either processes of states, the way the mind makes inferences and its relationship to both internal and external events. There are many other examples of such *propositional* theories, that is, theories in which it is assumed that some domain of cultural knowledge can be described as a set of formulae linking conceptual entities, and giving the rules for proper inferences from one proposition to another. The formulae are generated by abstract rules which specify which formulae are well formed and which are not.

2 *Mental models*. Although many cognitive domains can be satisfactorily described in schematic terms, cognitive research has shown that in some cases they are not entirely adequate as a description or prediction of actual performance. 'Anti-propositional' arguments have come from many sources.[17] The main one, as far as problems of cultural knowledge are concerned, comes from Johnson-Laird's theory of *mental models*. The starting point of the theory was the observation of people's performance in solving syllogistic problems. The typical mistakes are not adequately predicted by models which assume that people have a 'mental logic', that is, mental representation of the axioms and inferences, the rules of deduction and quantification (Johnson-Laird 1980: 23–40). According to Johnson-Laird, a more powerful description can be achieved by positing the existence of analogue models, structurally similar to the states of affairs they represent (1980: 419). There are many different kinds of mental models, from image-like 'sketches' to relational, causal or temporal models (422). For example, the representation of the relation 'there are more As than Bs' can be given by the following mapping:

A–B
A–B
A–B
A

The important point here is that important information about the relation (notably, its being non-reflexive and asymmetric) is *implicitly* given by the very structure of the model. In the same way, if a second model, corresponding to the proposition 'there are more Bs than Cs' is integrated in the above mapping, it produces the following model:

A–B–C
A–B–C
A–B
A

which makes it immediately obvious that there are more As than Cs, in other words, that 'more than' is a transitive relation. In the same way, analogical representations provide a good description of subjects' performance with spatial-relations problems, for example 'if A is to the right of B and C is to the left of A and B is to the right of C, which is at the centre?'

The relevance of this approach is even greater in more complex domains of knowledge, for which subjects build complex representations, combining analogue models with propositional elements. Mental models have been used to describe 'naive' or 'folk' theories (as opposed to expert scientific representations) of simple physical processes, like gravity or evaporation (see de Kleer 1977; Gentner & Stevens 1983; Hayes 1985). A good illustration is Gentner & Gentner's analysis of modern American representations of electricity (1983), which are based on two conflicting mental models, the 'teeming crowd' and 'flowing liquid' models.

3 *Scripts.* A third theme that inspires important research in cognitive anthropology is the notion of *scripts.* The idea originated in artificial-intelligence research, notably in Schank & Abelson's work on the 'comprehension' of simple stories by computer programs (1977). A script can be characterised as the generic representation of a routine sequence of events, for example, GOING TO THE DOCTOR. The script specifies the actions involved and their order, as well as certain causal relations between them. It is a generic representation, as opposed to a specific memory of a given event sequence, because it specifies conceptual *slots* that can be filled with particular values. The existence of such generic representations is made plausible by the fact that subjects can make inferences about such standardised actions, even when they are presented with fragmentary accounts. Another general property of scripts, to which I will return presently, is their hierarchical or nested organisation (Abelson 1981). Some of the slots in a script can be filled by sub-scripts, which themselves comprise ordered sequences of actions or events. Scripts provide a typical representation of experiential routines, the details of which are assumed

to be valid unless additional information is supplied, in much the same way as computer programs use *default values*. In Graesser's model, for instance (see Graesser, Gordon & Sawyer 1979; Nakamura *et al.* 1985), the representation of social episodes consists of a 'script pointer', on the one hand, which indicates which type of situation the episode is a token of, and a 'tag', which provides information about the particular features of the episode. This hypothesis is consistent with experimental results, showing that subjects remember the standard parts of scripted events as well as the inconsistent, surprising elements, better than elements of the situation which are neither necessary to, nor obviously contradictory with, the script.[18]

The notion of scripts provides a particularly economical model for people's memorisation of multiple instances of social routines. It also makes it possible to illuminate, to a certain extent, the complex processes concerning the constructive nature of autobiographical memory (Fitzgerald 1986: 128–32). More importantly for our problems, scripts seem to be involved in the representation of social interaction beyond everyday routines: for instance, Quinn's analysis of the concept MARRIAGE in the United States (1987) describes the subjects' representation of prototypical scripts, standard sequences that provide both a description of various elements of marriage (the actors' positions, their intentions and other mental states) and the causal links that can be established between these elements (how certain expectations of intentions can lead to specific results).

'Symbolism' as a problem

Obviously, the above survey is a compressed summary of the variety of hypotheses put forward in modern cognitive anthropology. The survey is accurate, however, in that few of these models and theories were directly applied to problems of religious ideas and behaviour. As Keesing points out in his appraisal of a particularly rich volume (Holland & Quinn 1987), the cultural models described in modern cognitive anthropology 'comprise the domain of (culturally constructed) common sense. They serve pragmatic purposes. They explain the tangible, the experiential ... the probable' (Keesing 1987c: 374). The domain of religion, on the other hand, does not seem to be considered in such models. Obviously, there are notable exceptions to this (see e.g. Frake 1964a, b; Dougherty & Fernandez 1980, 1982; Dougherty 1985; Ellen 1988) and several chapters in this volume are directly inspired by the theories mentioned above. By and large, however, it would not be unfair to say that modern cognitive anthropology, in much the same way as early 'ethnosemantics', has not dealt with the central anthropological problems of religious ritual and belief.

This is the point at which we reach the fifth choice in the list of disjunctions presented at the beginning of this introduction. The problem here is whether the domain of religious action and discourse can be considered similar, in most relevant features, to that of everyday thinking. If the representations involved in religious action and discourse are different, then the absence of satisfactory cognitive descriptions is the consequence of certain special properties and difficulties of the domain considered. This, in any case, is the starting point of most contributions to this volume, and leads us to reconsider the question of 'symbolism', a term used so far in a fairly intuitive way.

The specific problems posed by religious action and discourse can be conveniently summarised as *the problem of symbolism*. The gist of the 'problem of symbolism' is that we must provide a psychological description that would account for two seemingly opposite properties of the cultural phenomena considered. On the one hand, an obvious feature of religious, as opposed to everyday knowledge, is the remarkable *plasticity* of the ideas and beliefs concerned. The beliefs in question are often couched in metaphorical terms, or associated with vivid imagery rather than elaborate definitions. Also, they are typically related to memories of singular social episodes rather than non-contexual theoretical statements (Boyer 1990: ch. 1). Thirdly, there is often a notable uncertainty in the subjects' own attitude to the object of belief, a point to which I will return below. At the same time, however, it is obvious that there are some *constraints* imposed on the range of beliefs and ideas grouped under the category 'religious symbolism'. These characteristics are well known to any anthropologist who works on religious discourse and action, and are not especially problematic as far as ethnographic descriptions are concerned. Anthropological theories, however, seem to have some difficulty in producing frameworks in which these characteristics can be accounted for.

So the main idea behind the label 'symbolism' is simply that we are dealing with processes and representations that are different from, and more problematic than, what is usually described in everyday domains of knowledge. This simple observation may lead, however, to the two crucial misunderstandings, which have marred the anthropology of religion, and which can be called the *domain-specificity* fallacy and the *cryptological* fallacy. These must be considered in some detail, as most models described below are designed in order to avoid them.

The domain-specificity mistake consists in assimilating a distinction between *domains* (the everyday as opposed to the religious) and a distinction between varieties of *cognitive functioning*, that is, in thinking that the everyday and religious domains correspond to two particular types of cognitive mechanisms. Such distinctions are the starting point of many anthropological discussions of 'modes of thought': for instance, Hollis assumes that in religious discourse and thought, people make use of a particular (coherentist) conception of truth which is incompatible with their everyday (correspondencist) conception (Hollis 1970: 223). Another example is Southwold's distinction between two types of beliefs, used in the 'factual' and the 'religious' domains respectively (1979: 631ff.): again, the implication is that the cognitive *functioning* itself is quite different in these two domains. In this interpretation, religious and everyday thought differ not only in their typical contents but also in the very operations applied to these contents.

Claims to domain-specificity for religious 'symbolism', however, are not entirely convincing. They are invariably flawed in two symmetrical ways. First, the type of cognitive mechanisms attributed to the religious domain is more often than not of a purely *ad hoc* nature, very similar in that respect to the anthropological models described above. In the same way, they tend to label problems rather than solve them. Saying that 'religious belief' is different from 'factual belief', for instance, is not very helpful if the only characteristics of religious belief happen to be what make them different from the factual ones. Second, most distinctions of this kind are based on a simplistic vision of what constitutes the 'everyday' or non-religious side of the opposition, which lumps together people's representations about living kinds, about artefacts, about persons, their memories of social routines and scenes, most of their lexical and practical knowledge, as well as their tacit beliefs, etc. These are domains between which there are many crucial differences in terms of cognitive functioning, so that the idea of a straightforward opposition between this variety, on the one hand, and religious representations on the other, does not make much sense. It seems more reasonable, at least as a starting point, to conceive 'symbolism' as non-domain-specific, that is, as involving cognitive mechanisms that can be found in everyday thinking too, although perhaps in different configurations. Most of the chapters in this volume focus on such specific 'configurations'.

Let me now turn to the second question, that of the 'cryptological' aspects of symbolism. The very term 'symbolism' conveys an assumption which is at the origin of many anthropological and psychological frameworks, namely that the ideas involved are substitutes for other ideas. It would be difficult, in the space of this section, to try and summarise all different versions of this assumption.[19] I will focus on Turner's framework (Turner 1967, 1968) and its critique by Sperber (1975b), which will allow me to introduce some notions and distinctions which will be relevant to the rest of this introduction. Turner treats certain aspects of religious ritual and belief as 'symbolic' in the sense that they express hidden meanings: for example, the *musengu* tree is used by the Ndembu as a ritual symbol because it provides a material embodiment of the notion of FERTILITY, on which many rituals are focused. For Sperber, however, such descriptions of symbols as (sign, interpretation) pairs are problematic. To begin with, to say that the Ndembu utilise the *musengu* as a 'symbol' of fertility is to put forward an exegesis which is itself symbolic. There is no evidence that any form of symbolism can be reduced to a list of (sign, signification) pairs. In many cultures, subjects agree that a certain ritual requires the use of certain objects, while having the most varied, and sometimes incompatible justifications, for these precise choices, while in other cases they have no justification at all. Analysing cultural 'symbols' in terms of cultural exegesis, which is itself symbolic, the interpretation is bound to generate an infinite regress.[20]

Against this unsatisfactory model, Sperber contends that symbolic phenomena are the output of a special cognitive device. In this view, there is a sharp distinction between what Sperber calls the 'rational' and the 'symbolic' modes in cognitive processing. The rational mode consists in the deductive treatment of perceptual information, using representations available in memory. The symbolic mode, on the other hand, is activated whenever the input cannot be treated in the rational mode, for instance in the case of figurative utterances or of obscure religious statements. In other words, symbolic interpretation is what the mind does to information it cannot treat following the rational processes. The symbolic mode first directs the subject's attention to the violations of the constraints of rational treatment, and then triggers an 'evocation', that is, a search in memory for representations which, if added to the input, would make the rational treatment possible. This makes it possible to understand an intuitive difference between rational and symbolic processes. While the former deal with a bulk of information by using a limited set of generalisable hypotheses, 'symbolic discourse ... only retains from experience a minimum of fragments to establish a maximum of hypotheses, without caring to put them to the test' (1975b: 4).

Here I will not dwell on the details of the cognitive theory that is implied by Sperber's account of symbolism.[21] Suffice it to say that this account, however succinct, introduces two assumptions which are at the foundation of the various hypotheses presented below. The first one is that a cognitively plausible account of religious symbolism is not necessarily based on claims to domain-specificity; quite the contrary. The study of religious symbolism can be furthered only by examining the various modes of symbolic processing involved in different domains of everyday thinking. This assumption is implicit in most of the models put forward in this volume, and its consequences will be outlined in the following pages. The second assumption is that the treatment of religious symbols in people's minds consists in a search for relevant interpretations, rather than the imposition of a culturally fixed model. The most we can say about a symbolic interpretation is that, given a certain set of circumstances, the triggering item will be more likely to guide people's imagination in a certain direction than in others. This brings us back to the general question of plasticity and constraints. Sperber's account, because of its critical stance, lays stress on the first aspect, showing that most anthropological accounts of the constraints on symbolism are misguided. It remains, however, to provide an account of the cognitive constraints on symbolism.

Issues and directions

Let me now turn to a more specific description of the hypotheses and theories with which a cognitively plausible anthropological framework could try to tackle the questions outlined above. As will become clear in this section, most hypotheses are of a speculative nature. In some domains, far from providing a dogmatic account of the processes involved, the discipline is still at the state of trying to present a clear picture of the questions themselves, in order to avoid certain conceptual confusions of classical anthropology.

As I mentioned above, three problems emerge as the main organising themes in the study of the cognitive constraints on religious symbolism. The first one is *knowledge representation*, more precisely, the description of the conceptual structures which direct people's use of religious categories and their expectations concerning religious entities. The second theme is *belief fixation*. This label encompasses a series of different questions, to do with the acquisition of concepts, the processes of persuasion, the memorisation and transmission of particular items of knowledge, etc. The unifying theme here is that a proper theory of religious symbolism should have at least a minimal account of the processes whereby certain ideas and actions are made intuitively plausible to human subjects. The third theme concerns *ritual action*, and the cognitive processes involved in performing and representing these actions, as well as the cognitive constraints on the forms of ritual interaction.

On these three topics, as we saw above, the performance of classical anthropological theories is less than satisfactory. Anthropology does not have much to say about the representation of religious ideas, because it does not have a very clear theory of the representation of knowledge in general. In the same way, the questions of knowledge acquisition and belief fixation are often ignored in anthropological theories, which aim at describing cultural knowledge as such, not the processes whereby it is acquired. As for the special characteristics of ritual action and inter-action, they are often described in an intuitive and metaphorical way, which achieves its goal in terms of ethnographic vividness, but is not theoretically precise. In the following pages I will indicate in what way these questions could be reformulated, taking as a background results and hypotheses from cognitive science.

Religious categories and conceptual structures

Let me first deal with the question of conceptual structures. Religious symbolism seems to be centred on certain crucial concepts, for example, SPIRITS, ANCESTORS or WITCHCRAFT SUBSTANCE. A cognitive study should focus on the way these categories are mentally represented, on the repre-sentations and processes that make it possible to use a term in a proper way in linguistic interaction. The problems involved concern both the 'internal' and the 'external' structure of the categories: that is, (1) what holds a category together and makes it a mental structure that can encompass various objects or events or thoughts; and (2) the way different categories are related, the type of 'networks', 'theories' and other complex structures in which categories are embedded. Obviously, one cannot solve the difficult problems involved in a description of *religious* concepts, without having some precise hypotheses about the description of concepts in general. As we will see, the special difficulties encountered in the description of religious symbolism may stem from the fact that anthropo-logical descriptions are grounded in a set of vague, implicit assumptions about what sort of mental structures concepts are.

Two main approaches can be distinguished here. Each makes certain claims about religious conceptual structures, and about what makes them particularly difficult to describe in psychologically precise terms. A first approach is based on the idea that the knowledge activated is mentally represented in the form of *schemata*, as defined above. In this case, the special difficulties of symbolism arise either from incomplete ethno-graphic descriptions, of from the fact that the schemata in question are particularly complex. Another approach tries to account for the difficul-ties encountered in describing symbolic schemata by positing that they are not schematic at all; they are essentially *metaphorical* structures. In this case, the difficulties stem from the error of describing metaphorical representations in terms of literal ones. This idea has a long history in anthropological conceptions of religious symbolism, and many attempts have been make to link metaphor and symbolism (see e.g. Sapir & Crocker 1977; Fernandez 1986). In a somewhat different perspective, Lakoff's notion of *conventional metaphors* constitutes a more directly cognitive approach to metaphor. Although conventional metaphors are not 'live', poetic figures, they are not taken literally either. Their use does not entail the beliefs they seem to imply (Lakoff & Johnson 1980; Lakoff 1987; Lakoff & Kövecses 1987). An excellent illustration is the English way of talking about LUCK. Usual phrases convey the idea that luck is a fluid or substance that some people possess ('I don't have much luck'), a scarce commodity ('some people have all the luck') or a personified agency ('luck was not with me today'), etc. (Keesing 1985: 209). The corresponding beliefs, however, are clearly not there. The anthropological relevance of this approach has been emphasised by Keesing (1984, 1985, this volume pp. 93–109), on the classical case of the Melanesian and Polynesian notion of *mana*. Keesing shows that it is possible to analyse such seemingly mystical notions in terms of conventional metaphors.

Let me take a simple example, that will illustrate both the differences and the difficulties involved in the choice between schematic and metaphorical models. Among the Fang of Cameroon, many religious beliefs and behaviours focus on the notion of *bekong*, which can be roughly glossed as 'ghosts'. Ghosts are the object of a particular cult, and are generally considered responsible for many aspects of everyday social life. They established its institutional framework (codes of conduct, rules of marriage, prohibitions, etc.) and are often directly involved in its disruption by disease and misfortune. That is to say, events such as illnesses and deaths can be attributed to the ghost's anger at the living, who do not fulfil their obligations, particularly their ritual duties, in the way prescribed by the ancestors. Every living person is destined to become one of the *bekong*, who live in mysterious villages in the netherworld. The idea that people become *bekong* is linked to the fact that a person's shadow is called *kong* (plural *bekong*), and that the shadow, together with the body and the mind (located in the heart), constitutes one of the elements of a complete personality.

This last point is particularly interesting, because it shows how a simple point of ethnographic description can be based on ambiguous psychological description. The connection between ghosts and shadows could be construed, ideally, in two different ways. We could assume that we are dealing with a theoretical or schematic conceptual representation. In the schema, the Fang concept of a PERSON is construed as consisting of three distinct components (heart–mind, body, shadow). One of these, the *kong* or shadow, survives after death and becomes a member of a village of ghosts, and in that state is endowed with particular powers over the living, like the power to send misfortune. This description is roughly consistent with most native utterances, but it poses some difficult problems. For instance, it seems to imply that the mind does not survive after death. But ghosts–*bekong* are typically represented as creatures which have all the usual mental capacities of the living. They are supposed to have thoughts, feelings and even memories of their times as living people.

In order to avoid these difficulties, we could assume that the connection between ghosts and shadows is in fact metaphorical; the conventional metaphor could be paraphrased as GHOSTS ARE LIKE SHADOWS. What is conveyed by the simile is that ghosts are essentially intangible, elusive, and shadows provide the best example of an intangible or elusive reality, yet tied to personal identity. This interpretation is supported by two series of facts: first, the elusiveness and intangibility of ghosts is a recurrent theme in Fang discourse about these entities; also, while Fang people are typically confident that 'one's shadow becomes a ghost', they are rather uncertain about what happens to a mind, or about such technical details as the problem of having shadows with mental capacities. In other words, they seem to treat the central statement about the connection between shadows and ghosts in the same way as people commonly treat metaphors. They have intuitions about the point of the metaphor, but remain uncertain about the possible implications of the trope beyond that point.[22]

In order to go further than these two alternatives it may be necessary to take into account the more precise models of conceptual structure which are available in the cognitive literature. Theories of conceptual structure have undergone significant changes in the last two decades. They evolved from what is now commonly called the 'classical view', through 'prototype' theories, to a new emerging paradigm which could be called the 'theory theory'. The 'classical' theory was founded on the idea that concepts are represented as lists of singly necessary, jointly sufficient features which constitute conditions for membership in a set. To take a classical example, all objects which are (1) human beings, (2) adult, (3) male and (4) unmarried are (in principle) members of the set 'bachelors', so that the conceptual representation of the category BACHELOR could be described as consisting of the list of four features given above. Empirical research on conceptual representation, however, showed clearly that this Fregean notion of necessary and sufficient conditions was not entirely satisfactory as a psychological description. The main problem was that it made it difficult to account for prototypicality effects, that is, for the fact that membership of a category is not always, or not only, a yes/no question, as the classical view would predict: for instance, although both robins and ducks are birds, the former seem to constitute better, more 'typical' instances of the category BIRDS.[23] This led E. Rosch and her colleagues to propose a 'non-classical' or 'prototype' view of conceptual structure, following which membership of a category is a matter of graded judgement, between 0 (non-membership) and 1 (full membership). The degree to which any single instance belongs to a concept depends on its similarity to a mentally represented prototype (see Rosch 1977; Rosch & Lloyd 1978). Prototype theory, however, was itself insufficient in that it often confused identification processes, on the one hand, whereby an exemplar is identified as a member of a certain class, and conceptual structure itself, on the other (Osherson & Smith 1981). Even if prototype effects can be generated for many categories, this does not always show that the concept is itself represented as a graded structure. Indeed, such effects could be generated even for categories which are clearly represented in terms of necessary–sufficient properties, like ODD NUMBER (Armstrong, Gleitman & Gleitman 1983; Roth & Shoben 1983). The distinction between concept and identification processes makes it possible to understand that the classical approach and prototype theory, far from constituting alternative accounts of conceptual structures, are in fact focused on different aspects of those structures.[24]

The classical view and prototype theory shared a crucial defect in that both assumed that conceptual structures are founded on *similarity*, that they group together objects on the basis of resemblance. While the classical approach construed similarity in terms of shared features, prototype theory expressed it in terms of resemblance to a stored template. Similarity, however, is not sufficient as a foundation for conceptual structures. Two objects can be considered similar or dissimilar from indefinitely many viewpoints. Conceptual structures specify not only that different objects are similar, but also what sort of similarity is relevant for them and often why it is so.[25] Take the example of the concept CAR. People who have the concept CAR know that most cars are similar in certain respects; for instance, they all have engines. But this type of featural similarity does not exhaust the concept. People who have the concept CAR also know that functional features (e.g. having an engine that drives the wheels) are relevant for membership in the class CAR, whereas other features, such as colour or country of origin, are not. Acquiring the concept does not only imply storing the list of features present in all exemplars (as the classical view would predict) or the family resemblance between exemplars (as prototype theory would assume); it also implies acquiring a set of organised assumptions about the relevance of certain features, and the reasons why they are relevant.

These facts have led some psychologists to put forward a more complex description of conceptual structure. What makes it the case that someone has a concept is that they have acquired a set of relations that connect various assumptions about the objects denoted. The assumptions specify which kinds of features are pertinent. They are not simply juxtaposed; in many cases there are causal connections between the various assumptions made about a particular concept. For instance, people who have the concept CAR know that having an engine is a more critical feature than having headlights. This is because cars are designed primarily as means of transportation. In other words, having the concept means establishing some causal connections between the various assumptions one makes about the objects. 'People not only notice feature correlations, but they can deduce *reasons* for them based on their knowledge of the way the world works' (Medin & Wattenmaker 1987: 36). This is the reason why such conceptual structures are sometimes called 'micro-theories' (Murphy & Medin 1985; Medin & Wattenmaker 1987). Although the term may be misleading, for the reasons mentioned above, the basic intuition here is that concepts are intrinsically *relational* entities, which establish links, particularly causal connections, between expectations about a class of objects (see e.g Keil 1989: 267–77). Without a description of these links, we cannot understand how conceptual structures constrain people's expectations and conjectures.

This point is directly pertinent to the study of religious categories, and shows the limitations of both 'schema-based' and 'metaphor-based' accounts. From a theoretical standpoint, the terms of this debate are probably much too vague to be of any explanatory value in the description of religious symbolism. We must keep in mind that neither alternative constitutes a very precise description of cognitive processes. In fact, both theoretical frameworks are themselves based on metaphors. The idea that cultural knowledge can be described in terms of quasi-theories which people somehow store in their memories is based on an analogy between scientific or other forms of explicit theories, of which we know very little, and mental representations, of which we know even less. Explicit theories are publicly available, externally represented sets of propositions. When we say that some cultural representations constitute a theoretical schema for a certain domain, it is not really clear to what extent we want to pursue the metaphor in describing private representations: for instance, it is not clear whether we should take for granted that all features of external theories will be relevant for internal representations. As for the metaphor paradigm, it is based on a central metaphor, too. The analogy is between figures of speech, as used in oral or written communication in a natural language, and cognitive processes. Again, we have many assumptions about the way metaphors work in linguistic communication, but it is not clear to what extent they all apply to 'metaphorical cognitive structures'. In fact, the various authors who use the metaphor paradigm are often extremely vague about this central problem, and seem to find a metaphorical usage of the term 'metaphor' quite satisfactory.

In order to go beyond such descriptions, which are common in anthropological descriptions, we must therefore specify the connections established between the different assumptions which constitute the conceptual structures. This, however, may not be possible on the basis of ordinary ethnographic data. The kind of intuitive data we tend to find sufficient in the anthropological description of religious belief-systems typically under-determine the theoretical choices concerning cognitive frameworks. In order to find out what conceptual structures underlie people's usage of certain religious categories, one would need more fine-grained information, for example about the range of inferences people are likely to make about ghosts, about the extension of certain non-central properties of shadows to ghosts, etc. Data of that kind may not be within the range of ordinary anthropological fieldwork, and may require quasi-experimental methods.

Concept acquisition and belief fixation

Let me now turn to the second domain of investigation, concerning the processes whereby people are led to find plausible a set of cultural assumptions concerning supernatural entities and events. This domain is generally neglected in anthropological frameworks. This may seem an unfair contention, since a whole sub-discipline is devoted to such mechanisms, under the label 'socialisation'. However, the role given to such studies in anthropology is unsatisfactory. First, as I suggested above, it is generally assumed that socialisation processes do not impose any *constraints* on religious symbolism. When anthropologists want to account for some properties of religious symbolism, they seldom turn to the acquisition process as an explanatory variable. Second, the very notion of 'socialisation' is generally used as a vacuous concept in general anthropology. It designates a 'black box', a series of mechanisms such that they produce the observed output, without much consideration for the ways in which they produce it. Finally, the artificial distinction between the study of 'culture', on the one hand, and of its acquisition, on the other, extends to ethnographic descriptions. Very few monographs on religious symbolism make more than a passing mention of acquisition processes; conversely, very few studies of cultural acquisition deal with religious representations.[26]

Against this background, a study of religious acquisition should provide a description of the actual processes whereby subjects use the available cultural material, an informal aggregate of utterances and actions, in order to build stable conceptual structures. More precisely, the study should describe the processes of concept acquisition and belief fixation, whereby subjects gain a proper understanding of cultural categories, and establish connections between religious entities and actual experience. This suggests two important revisions of the conventional wisdom of anthropology. First, one must discard what Bloch called the 'anthropological theory of cognition' (see above), the insufficiency of which is obvious in all empirical studies of cultural acquisition. The processes involved in concept acquisition are interactive, that is, they involve the production of multiple hypotheses from the learner's part and some patterning of responses from the expert. In other words, there is no greater mistake than the idea that teaching is all there is to learning (Wentworth 1980; see also Jahoda & Lewis 1987). The study of religious symbolism would certainly benefit from a 'Vygotskian' approach, which clearly locates cognitive development in its social contexts and traces patterns of development as a function of interaction (see Vygotsky 1978, 1986; Wertsch 1985). This revision should not be too difficult, since, after all, it consists in emphasising the properly *social* aspects of cultural acquisition, which were paradoxically under-estimated in mainstream anthropological theories. A second revision, however, may require a more detailed justification. It concerns pervasive assumptions about the learning process, and the ways in which anthropology consequently describes the relationship between universal cognitive capacities, especially learning capacities, on the one hand, and variable cultural material, on the other.

It seems perfectly natural or self-evident to most anthropologists to describe religious constructions as 'culturally constructed' and 'culturally determined'. It is particularly difficult, however, to give this sort of statement a precise empirical content. Religious ideas are certainly culturally transmitted, in the trivial sense that subjects raised in different cultures will tend to build different sets of religious ideas, each closely resembling that of previous generations in their social group. This much is obvious. From this obvious point, however, cultural anthropology often proceeds to the dubious conclusion that there are no constraints imposed on the actual variation, no cognitive constraints in particular.

To see why this is misguided, one must, again, leave strictly anthropological problems aside for a while. We must consider in some detail the general assumptions, concerning learning processes, that should provide the basis for a theory of cultural acquisition. Obviously, it would be absurd to try and summarise here all the hypotheses and findings that could be relevant to anthropological theories. I will only mention one point, derived from recent experimental research in conceptual development, which may be of direct importance in our description of the constraints imposed on cultural acquisition.

In what may be called a 'classical' or 'Piagetian' understanding of conceptual development, the child is assumed to apply general learning heuristics to a variety of experienced phenomena. The developmental stages identified in Piagetian frameworks are mainly described in *formal, non-domain-specific* terms. At each stage the child is described as applying to a variety of domains certain formal intellectual procedures, which do not depend on the type of phenomena concerned (see e.g. Laurendau & Pinard 1962; and a critique in Carey 1985). Most recent research, however, tends to show that conceptual development is more complex, in the sense that it is mainly based on *domain-specific* mechanisms rather than general-purpose learning heuristics (Gelman & Baillargeon 1983; Carey 1985). The way children reason, at any stage, depends on the conceptual domain to which the intellectual operations are applied. To take a simple example, even four-year-olds seem to make instance-based inductive generalisations in a different way, whether the objects concerned are artefacts or exemplars of living kinds. They presume that certain properties, such as breathing underwater versus breathing above surface, can be induced from one exemplar of a living kind onto any other exemplar, even if the two exemplars are perceptually very different (Gelman & Markman 1986: 203–5; 1987: *passim*). This type of 'essentialist' induction leads them to think that exemplars of a living kind cannot be transformed into exemplars of another kind, even if all their external features are modified. This presumption seems entirely absent from their notions of artefacts and generalisations on artefacts.

This kind of research indicates that children's conceptual development proceeds on the basis of strong *theoretical presumptions*, concerning the type of properties and generalities to be expected in different ontological domains (Keil 1979, 1987). The presumptions concern large ontological domains such as physical objects, artefacts, living kinds, persons. They constitute 'naïve theories' of the domains in question. In that sense the process of knowledge acquisition refines, revises and extends intuitive theories of physical objects (Spelke 1990), of biological processes (Keil 1986, 1989) and of mental processes (Astington, Harris & Olson 1988; Wellmann 1990). These intuitive principles impose strong constraints on the development of adult notions concerning these domains of reality. They seem to develop *spontaneously*, independently of tuition or objective changes in the available information. For instance, children seem to shift from a 'desire-based' naïve psychology to a 'belief + desire' type of psychological explanation when they are about four. This shift is not related to any changes in the kind of explanations (explicit or not) offered in their social environment. To put it crudely, children learn much more than they are taught, because prior principles orient them towards certain types of domain-specific theories. Such naïve conceptual presumptions are connected in a complex way to later theoretical development. In some cases, such as commonsense or 'folk'-psychology, adult conceptions seem to flesh out the conceptual skeleton provided by naïve conceptions. They provide more material, more explanatory schemes, but never go against the spontaneous assumptions. In other cases, such as the acquisition of mathematics or physics, it is necessary for subjects to acquire counter-intuitive principles (such as the difference between *force* and *motion*). In such domains, even schooled adults are often uncertain about the notions which conflict with their intuitive theories.[27] In other words, the intuitive principles impose very strong constraints on the learnability of further conceptual developments.

Let me now return to religious ideas. As I pointed out above, to understand religious symbolism implies that we understand the specific combination of plasticity and constraints that seems to characterise religious ideas. Now the findings and hypotheses mentioned above make it possible at least to envisage how a study of cultural knowledge could tackle that problem. At first sight, the domains in question seem to be very far from religious knowledge. The development of intuitions about physical objects, or of expectations concerning living beings and mental processes, do not seem to have any connections with religious ideas. They constitute the intuitive basis of the commonsense understanding of everyday events. On the other hand, religious ideas seem to focus on extra-empirical realities and processes. Religious ideas, however, are invariably based on numerous and constraining assumptions concerning everyday phenomena. To return to the example mentioned above, the Fang of Cameroon have explicit notions concerning the intangibility and invisibility of ghosts. These two properties make the ghosts very different from any other kind of beings people are supposed to deal with. However, when people describe or imagine the kinds of thought processes that ghosts have about living people's behaviour, they spontaneously resort to a form of psychology that is applied intuitively to everyday interaction with other people. The ghosts are, for instance, described as being 'angry' because people have neglected them (i.e. have not performed rituals) and as wanting to remind them of their duties. Ghosts are therefore seen as having thoughts, memories and reasonings that are strictly similar in their functional properties to those of the living. This may seem obvious, and indeed it is obvious to Fang and outsiders alike, because these assumptions about psychological processes are part of our intuitive or naïve psychology, most of whose principles are implicit. To sum up, ghosts are certainly explicitly conceived as non-everyday entities, with strange properties and powers. One must remember, however, that many ideas about them are based on the projection of principles which are implicitly used in everyday contexts.

More generally, religious notions, however removed from everyday experience they may appear to be, are invariably represented by using a host of implicit assumptions derived from commonsense knowledge. This assumption seems fairly obvious, and it would not entail much of interest in the study of religion if we maintained a classical view of conceptual development, following which children apply an all-purpose inductive learning heuristic to all domains of experience. However, the data and theories summarised above seem to indicate that, on the contrary, children apply strongly constraining, domain-specific principles to experience. Moreover, it shows how the learnability of conceptual structures may depend on their compatibility with intuitive domain-specific principles. Now this makes the whole question, of the relationships between everyday knowledge and religious ideas, at once more complex and more tractable. If religious systems, like all systems of ideas, must be learnt on the basis of intuitive principles that constrain commonsense thinking, it should follow that, all else being equal, their learnability or ease of acquisition will depend on the way they integrate those intuitive principles. Fang children, for instance, have no difficulty acquiring the principles of ghost-psychology, since they are directly projected from intuitive psychology. They have more difficulties in acquiring intuitions about ghost-physics, since these are construed in explicit violation of intuitive physics.

In order to understand why certain types of religious ideas are particularly recurrent, it would therefore be necessary to examine their connection to the intuitive principles that structure certain domains of commonsense thinking. This, however, requires investigations which so far are not undertaken in the course of anthropological enquiries. Such investigations should first examine to what extent the intuitive principles uncovered by specialists of child development are cross-culturally valid. Since their emergence and changes do not seem to depend on significant changes in the child's experience, there is, of course, a strong presumption that they constitute cognitive universals (if a mechanism is not acquired from experience, it could not be acquired from cultural transmission, which is a sub-set of the child's experience). However, the precise extent to which such developments are cross-culturally similar cannot be evaluated in the absence of real experimental studies.[28]

Such an anthropological study implies a revision of the intuitive notion of 'cultural construction' on which many anthropological theories are based. Anthropology generally has no precise hypotheses to describe the processes whereby people construct stable sets of ideas and expectations out of cultural experience. The material that is available in such experience is, after all, fragmentary, often confusing or even contradictory. People, however, seem to build relatively similar conceptual structures out of the available data. This process would become less 'mysterious', and less likely to be described in quasi-magical terms, as some form of 'cultural absorption', if we assumed that intuitive commonsense principles were implicitly applied to the religious material.

The representation of ritual action

The third domain that should be tackled by a cognitive study of religious symbolism is that of ritual action. Anthropological theories of ritual and ritual action are often paradoxical. Their aim is to extract the 'meaning' of ritual acts, to uncover their association with cosmological themes, world-views or cultural models. An initiation ritual, for instance, may be described as based on, and displaying cultural premises concerning sex, gender and processes of natural growth, as well as ideas about pollution or the power of secrets. This, of course, is a necessary part of the analysis of rituals. The paradox, however, is that religious symbolism is treated as though it was communicated or transmitted, not *because of* the ritual action, but *in spite of* the fact that it is embodied in ritual action. There is nothing wrong in positing that rituals 'express' or 'manifest' certain cultural premises. The problem, however, is that this assumption does not provide us with any clue, as to what is *specific* about ritual contexts or situations, what happens in rituals and does not happen in other types of interaction.

Rituals are often intuitively contrasted with other types of social episodes, on the basis of two properties of which we may call *apartness* and *scriptedness*. As Kapferer puts it, the performance of ritual is made different by the fact that (1) it is 'marked off from or within the routine of everyday life' and (2) it specifies 'in advance of its enactment, a particular sequential ordering of acts, utterances and events, which are essential to the recognition of the ritual' (Kapferer 1983: 2).

Let me first deal with the question of 'apartness'. It is one of the central properties of ritual that it constitutes a domain of action that is intuitively perceived, by all participants, as distinct from ordinary or everyday action. This 'markedness' of ritual action is often expressed implicitly, by using a specific repertoire of words, formulae or gestures that cannot be

found in everyday usage. It can also be stated in explicit, though metaphorical terms, for example in situations in which a ritual specialist
delineates a 'ritual space' in which actions must be performed. Although
this aspect is intuitively obvious, it is not easy to understand what
cognitive mechanisms give rise to the intuition of 'apartness'. Bateson, for
instance (1972), tried to define ritual 'frames'[29] as essentially comparable
to animal or human play, that is, as contexts which provide both messages
and 'meta-messages' about the interpretation of the message. This,
however, does not take into account the obvious intuitive differences
between pretence and ritual, notably what Rappaport (1974) calls 'the
certainty of meaning' in the latter case. Rituals simply have cognitive
effects that do not arise in play situations.[30] What we must account for are
the specific properties of the ritual 'frame', that is what distinguishes such
situations from human play, on the one hand, and from animal forms of
play and ritual, on the other. This implies having a set of precise psychological hypotheses, concerning the particular cognitive processes underlying the representation of ritual actions.

This brings us back to the property of 'scriptedness', which may seem a
rather obvious or unproblematic aspect of religious ritual. After all,
rituals are generally represented, and explained to outsiders, as ordered
sequences of actions or events. Because people who perform rituals are
often acutely aware of their stereotyped sequencing, it may seem tempting
to use in this context the type of hypotheses and models developed in
cognitive anthropology for the study of everyday 'scripts'. It may therefore seem adequate to describe religious rituals as a particular variety of
scripts, made special by the kind of conceptual premises associated with
the actions performed. In this view, while everyday scripts are concerned
with human actions and the various causal links between them, religious
scripts include actions directed at supernatural entities; while the content
may be strikingly different, the formal aspects of the scripts are essentially
similar. This view, however, is not entirely satisfactory, for reasons that
have to do with the formal aspects of religious rituals, notably with (1) the
relation between goals and scripts in religious rituals and (2) the processes
underlying the identification of ritual actions. These aspects must be
described in some detail, as they introduce some crucial problems in the
cognitive description of ritual representations.

Let me first deal with the question of goals and actions. The relationship between actions and goals is probably not represented in the same
way, in ritual sequences and everyday scripts. As I pointed out above,
everyday scripts are often organised in a hierarchical way, as consisting of
sub-scripts which themselves have sub-parts, and so on. For instance, the
classical example of CONSULTING A DOCTOR may comprise identifying a

medical problem, making an appointment, seeing the doctor and getting the prescribed remedies. Now, in much the same way as the general script is linked to a general goal (e.g. getting rid of those headaches), each of the sub-scripts is linked to a sub-goal. Schank & Abelson's original study of script representation (1977) already mentioned this inter-dependency of the hierarchy of goals and sub-goals, on the one hand, and that of scripts and sub-scripts on the other. Now this important structural feature is generally absent from ritual situations. Obviously, the sequence as a whole is often linked to a general goal (e.g. turning the boys into men, in the case of a male initiation ritual), but the analogy does not extend to the lower levels. In the case of initiation rites, for instance, they are generally conceived as a 'package', as a series of actions the final result of which will be the desired transformation. In many cases, the actors who know the general goal of the whole sequence have and need no specific rationale for each of its different sub-parts. They follow the prescribed sequencing in much the same way as inexperienced cooks do with long and complex recipes, that is, trusting that the final result depends on accurate execution of the whole recipe without knowing in what way it depends on each of the prescribed actions.

To sum up, the relationship between goals and sequences makes rituals formally different from everyday scripts and other such forms of social routines. This has important consequences, notably as concerns the *identification* of ritual acts. What makes a certain sequence of actions a performance of ritual x? This question may seem odd; in fact, its apparent oddity provides a good illustration of the differences between ordinary anthropological approaches and a (hypothetical) cognitive description of symbolism. The question may seem strange because one assumes that all participants in a ritual share a certain mental description of the ritual sequence to accomplish; people act on the basis of that mental description; and if the resulting sequence is (roughly) congruent with their mental description, then they are satisfied that they have performed the ritual x. These assumptions justify the anthropological practice, following which rituals can be described either from direct observation, or from some informants' explicit statements about the prescribed actions or from any combination of those two types of information.

From a psychological perspective, however, each of these assumptions is extremely problematic. First, the existence of different perspectives on, and different representations of a single ritual cannot be ignored. A general feature of religious rituals is that they require the cooperation of different actors, supposed to occupy different social positions. An equally general feature is that these actors' representations of the ritual situation are likely to differ in significant ways. More importantly, it may be the case that ritual interaction *requires* that their representations be differ-ent.[31] Second, even if representations are similar in different types of actors, there may be significant differences in the type of memory task that is required by ritual performance. For instance, performing a Catholic mass adequately constitutes, as far as the priest is concerned, what would be described in psychology as a *recall* task. The priest must remember what actions to perform and in what order. For most of the audience, at least part of the performance is based on a (simplified) *recognition* task: being presented with the priest's ritual acts, they activate a general pattern in order to judge whether it corresponds to their mental concept of what a mass should be like. It is difficult to have any precise hypotheses about the transmission of ritual sequences, without first examining what precise tasks of recall and recognition are involved. A third problem concerns the assumption that the recognition of ritual types is unproblematic. That is to say, people are described as examining the congruence between the actual performance and a mental 'check-list' of features, and identifying ritual actions on the basis of such a congruence. Now this is an over-simplified view of the identification procedure. Performing a series of actions is a necessary, but not a sufficient condition for the proper performance of a ritual. There are always a number of background conditions which must obtain, if the ritual is to be considered effectively performed. Participants are supposed to respect certain ritual prohibitions, some of them are sup-posed to have undergone other, preparatory rituals (e.g. priests must have been ordained), etc. Now many of these conditions focus on states of affairs which, in practice, are not directly observable. It follows that the identification of a particular performance, as an exemplar of the ritual x, is a conditional and corrigible identification, as long as the relevant back-ground conditions are assumed, rather than observed to obtain. If the identification of ritual actions is thus corrigible, it would be pertinent to examine the processes whereby subjects are led to *strengthen* the assump-tion, that all relevant conditions are met.

To sum up, many anthropological models take ritual action as a context which manifests or 'expresses', in a particularly salient way, certain aspects of religious knowledge. This, however, may lead to ignor-ing the specific features on which the intuitive difference between ritual and other contexts is based. In this domain, describing religious sym-bolism in a psychologically plausible way requires that we have precise hypotheses about the representation of social episodes in general, some-thing which is still lacking in anthropological theory.[32] Moreover, des-cribing the mental representation of ritual action requires developing more sophisticated accounts of the processes whereby participants' memories are activated in the course of ritual performance.

Conclusions

In the course of this section, I examined three domains which are crucial in a description of religious symbolism: namely, the conceptual structures underlying people's ideas and expectations concerning religious entities; the acquisition processes whereby some aspects of those conceptual structures are made natural; and finally the ritualised social episodes focused on the religious entities. In these three domains, I have presented speculative arguments, which constitute the elements of different research programmes, rather than a doctrine. In the sections above, I listed a series of crucial problems in a cognitive study of religious symbolism. Now it should be obvious that none of these questions could be properly answered, on the sole basis of the type of data produced in ordinary anthropological fieldwork. The various forms of 'participant observation', intuitive hypothesis-testing and informal interview techniques favoured by anthropologists constitute an indispensable grounding for the study of religious symbolism. However, they are not designed to provide the kind of fine-grained description of mental representation that is necessary in a *cognitive* study of symbolism. This will probably require a different mode of data-gathering, in which traditional fieldwork methods are completed with more constrained experimental studies, an example of which is given by Toren's studies on conceptual development in Fiji (this volume).

Beyond the domain of religious ideas, such studies would probably yield important results in the more general domain of cultural acquisition and transmission in general. As I indicated above, there is no reason to think that the category of 'religion', whatever its characterisation in anthropological terms, corresponds to specific cognitive capacities or to a specific type of mental contents. From a cognitive viewpoint, it seems difficult to maintain that religious ideas are anything other than a motley of representations, taken from different cognitive domains. Subjects must, for instance, acquire notions concerning the *ontology* of religious entities, that is, the types of beings that are posited in a religious system. Associated with religious ontologies are specific *causal claims* about the propensities of religious entities: ancestors, gods or spirits are represented as having particular causal powers that set them apart from other kinds of beings or things. The acquisition of a set of religious ideas often implies that one represents certain people (e.g. shamans, priests, etc.) as belonging to special *social categories*, with particular capacities or destinies. Also, particular *episodes* of social interaction (notably rituals) are represented as exemplars of certain recognisable types. In all these four domains, we are dealing with cognitive processes which extend beyond religious matters. As I tried to point out in the previous pages, we cannot have a satisfactory cognitive description of religious symbolism, if we ignore the obvious continuities between such commonsense cognitive capacities and their religious usage. At the same time, however, religious symbolism deserves to be studied as such, because it constitutes a crucial domain for the study of cognitive constraints on cultural representations. Religious ideas are not limited by practical constraints. Their non-referential nature implies that their variation is only limited by (1) general cognitive constraints on the type of representations that can be acquired by human minds and (2) distributional constraints, imposed by the types of social interaction in which ideas can be acquired. In other words, religious ideas constitute a domain in which it is particularly necessary to describe the interaction between contingent cultural material handed down from past generations, on the one hand, and cognitive or inter-actional constraints imposed by human minds and the types of social groupings humans create on the other.

NOTES

1 The structure of the tree is partly inspired by Lawson & McCauley (1990: ch. 1). Their main assumption is that the interpretation versus explanation dichotomy is an important organising principle of the anthropological litera-ture on religion (1990: 12–31).

2 For a more historically oriented survey, see Morris (1987), a detailed and nearly exhaustive source for theories of religion. Evans-Pritchard (1965) presents a more fragmentary, but very perceptive account.

3 Arguments of this nature always oscillate between descriptive and normative claims, that is, between the idea that anthropology *is* a way of generating meaningful discourse about exotic cultural objects and the idea that it *ought* to be just that. See, for instance, Boon (1982), Clifford & Marcus (1986), Geertz (1983, 1988) for a recent explanation of the hermeneutic stance. The intel-lectual origins of the movement lie in various hermeneutic writings, for example Cassirer (1953[1924]) and Langer (1942). For a discussion of sym-bolism as consisting of hidden meanings, see the section, below, on 'Sym-bolism as a problem', pages 23–7.

4 Two remarks must be made about this: first, the contrast between pre-cognitive psychology and the post-cognitive, 'enlightened' era should not be taken too strictly, although the contrast is a fundamental one. Second, the fact that thought is naturalised does not imply that a straightforward reduction of thought processes to brain events provides an explanatory hypothesis. Although all thought events are brain events, their neural implementation is not necessarily the best level at which to describe their regularities. On questions of reduction and explanation in psychology, see Churchland (1981), Dennett (1978, 1987), Dretske (1981) or Fodor (1981, 1987, 1990). The rele-vance of this point for anthropology is discussed in more detail below (see also note 8).

5 As indicated above, for the sake of clarity I follow here an analytic order which does not exactly follow common distinctions between authors or schools. This is why, for instance, Durkheim appears here, in the discussion of 'collective representations', as well as in the comments on social constraints on cognition (see pp. 14–15 below). The ambiguities and difficulties of the notion of collective representations are discussed by Harris & Heelas (1979) and Jahoda (1982).

6 To put it crudely, the gist of this argument is that ontological independence is earned by hard work, as it were, not obtained by fiat. The relative autonomy of chemistry from physics, or of biology from chemistry, was earned by producing explanatory generalisations, not by virtue of an *a priori* decision in the absence of any such principles.

7 For a defence of the 'Platonic' interpretation of linguistic structures as abstract objects, see Katz (1981) or Bever (1982). The opposite, 'realist' conception of linguistic structures as idealised descriptions of the speakers' knowledge has been repeatedly defended by Chomsky; see, for example, Chomsky (1975, 1980; in particular 1985: 31ff.) or Wexler & Culicover (1980).

8 The main problem in anthropological discussions of this question is a persistent confusion between reduction and explanation. To put things in the simplest way, the fact that *all* natural phenomena are reducible to physical ones, to events happening at the level of quantum mechanics, does not entail that their *explanation* can be formulated in terms of quantum mechanics (Putnam 1983: 290ff.; Fodor 1987: 32ff.).

9 See Dennett (1978, 1987), Stich (1983 *passim*), Fodor (1987, 1990) for discussions of the relevance of folk- or commonsense psychology to cognitive science.

10 These terms should be taken as roughly defined ideal types rather than accurate historical characterisations. The opposition between 'symbolism' and 'intellectualism,' is explained in more detail in Lawson & McCauley (1990: 32–41) from a cognitive perspective, and Skorupski (1976: 1–17, 53–68) from a 'neo-intellectualist' viewpoint. The other main tenet of 'symbolist' models, namely the idea of 'hidden signification' in religious ideas and rituals, is discussed below (pp. 25–7).

11 See Lukes (1973) for a discussion of Durkheim's thought on religion and cognition. For a modern defence of an 'extreme' Durkheimian position, on both the question of collective representations and that of cognitive versus social constraints, see Douglas (1970, 1975, 1982).

12 For general surveys of theories of language acquisition, see Clark (1973) and Bowerman (1978, 1982). Carey 1982 is the most comprehensive survey of theories on semantic acquisition. Katz *et al.* (1976) focus on the acquisition of names (for objects as well as proper names); the theory is developed in more detail in Katz 1982. See also Durkin (1987) on the necessary social dimensions of language acquisition. This point is, of course, made even clearer in studies which focus on the acquisition of complex interactive routines, that is, on the way children learn to talk appropriately as well as correctly; see, for instance, Schiefflin and Ochs's introduction to their collection on language socialisation (1986).

13 There are some conceptual domains where a structuralist description may be relevant: for instance, there is an intuitively obvious structural pattern in

conceptual sets such as man–woman–child, bull–cow–calf, horse–mare–colt, etc. Such domains, however, are extremely limited and even the pattern itself is not of the classical structuralist type. Classical sources for theories of concept representation are Rosch & Lloyd (1978), Smith & Medin (1981) and Neisser (1987). See also below, pages 30–3.

14 Experimental studies on the memorisation and transmission of stories were first conducted by Bartlett (1932). See Beaugrande (1982) for a survey of the hypotheses concerning the structure of stories and the mechanisms of recall.

15 No early cognitive anthropologist would have claimed that 'cultural grammars' could generate, by recursive iteration, all culturally 'correct' or 'well-formed' ideas or behaviours, and rule out the 'culturally irrelevant' or 'improper' ones, a requirement which is now considered minimal in the definition of a grammar.

16 The notion was originally put forward by Bartlett (1932: 201ff.) and used in many different senses in various psychological frameworks. For Piaget, for instance, a schema is 'an instrument of assimilation, and hence of generalization' (Piaget & Inhelder 1977: 403). In its modern (and rather vague) sense, the notion encompasses what Minsky called 'frames', that is, stable structures linking various concepts and specifying their relations: 'when one encounters a new situation ... one selects from memory a structure called a frame. This is a remembered framework to be adapted to fit reality by changing details as necessary' (Minsky 1981: 95–6). For a more general discussion of various types of 'schemata', see Neisser (1976: 51–78).

17 Here I will ignore the important debates on mental imagery, which had virtually no effect on anthropological theory.

18 On the presence of scripts even in young children's event memories, see Mandler (1983), Nelson & Gruendel (1986). On their role in conceptual development, see Fivush (1987). Most research on scripts focuses on scenes taken from modern American daily life. See Frake (1975) for a pertinent account of the relevance of the notion of non-Western cultures.

19 Many versions of this idea of symbolism as signification are expressed in the context of the hermeneutic frameworks, described above (pp. 8–9). This is why I focus here on a very limited range of frameworks, those in this religious symbolism are explicitly described as potentially explained, not only interpreted, by this assumption.

20 That this infinite regress is more or less inevitable in such descriptions is admitted by Geertz, who calls it the 'hermeneutic circle' (1983: 69), and, of course, takes it not as a problem, but as an index of the 'interpretive' nature of cultural descriptions. Obviously, the circle is not problematic in Geertz's theory, since it does not purport to *explain* religious symbolism.

21 Some aspects of Sperber's original formulations were criticised by Toren (1984). Sperber (1980) gives a more detailed description of the relationship posited, between the memory stores and the inferential device. The mechanisms of relevance and interpretation are presented in much greater detail in Wilson & Sperber 1986.

22 This is a very common property of metaphorical statements and conceptions. The idea that INTELLECTUAL ARGUMENT IS WARFARE, to take one of Lakoff's examples, seems to have clear central implications, like 'it usually involves

people trying to win rather than lose', 'it may trigger strong emotional effects', 'you feel better if you win', etc. The possible peripheral implications, however, are less certain. Does the metaphor imply that intellectual arguments could evolve with technology, as warfare does? Could arguments be made different by the fact that people use computers? People who routinely use (and understand) the metaphor are typically uncertain about such possible inferences.

23 This can be tested in a variety of ways: for instance, the mental image people spontaneously create when prompted with the word 'bird' looks more like a robin than like a duck; or, given an identification task, people are quicker at deciding that the picture represents a bird if shown a robin than if the display shows a duck.

24 For more detailed accounts of theories of conceptual structure, see Smith & Medin (1981), Neisser (1987) and Keil (1989).

25 This point is particularly salient in cases where similarity and class membership lead to different groupings; for instance, a live frog is (externally) much more similar to a plastic frog than to a tadpole; or a coin is more similar to a chocolate chip than to a banknote. Subjects have no difficulty in conceptually grouping together dissimilar objects and ignoring irrelevant resemblance. See Murphy & Medin (1985) and Rips (1989) for experiments and general remarks on the relationship between similarity and conceptual structure.

26 There are, of course, notable exceptions. See, for instance, Keesing (1982a), a general study of Malaita (Solomon Islands) religion, which begins with the type of representations accessible to young children, and their gradual complexification. Also, consider Rabain's study of the socialisation of Wolof children (1979). Rabain provides a thorough description of the ways in which the representations concerning spirits and ancestors shape the interaction between children and their lineage. Toren's monograph (1991), some results of which are summarised in her contribution (this volume, pp. 147–63), is probably one of the very few examples of sensitive ethnographic work which comprises experimental studies on concept acquisition.

27 See McCloskey (1983) about adult subjects' failures to reason on the basis of physical principles which are not compatible with their intuitive notion of 'force plus motion', and a discussion in Kaiser, Jonides & Alexander (1986) and DiSessa (1988).

28 Jeyifous's work on Nigerian children (1985) constitutes one of the very few attempts in this direction, and confirms the hypothesis of significant cross-cultural principles. Research on biological taxonomies is another domain in which we have significant data, which point to the same conclusion (see e.g. Brown 1984; Atran 1990).

29 Note that Bateson's usage of 'frame' differs from the current meaning of the term in cognitive psychology and artificial intelligence (see note 18).

30 Anthropological comparisons between ritual and play (see e.g. Bateson 1955) are often based on an intuitive and rather simplistic description of the organisation of play and pretence behaviour in man and animals. See Krasnor & Pepler (1980) for a survey of the problems involved, and Bretherton (1984) on the specific question of the different types of pretence children engage in. On the related questions of the evolutionary aspects of play, see, for example,

Fogen (1974) and Smith (1982) among many other sources. Handelman (1979), on the other hand, tries to distinguish ritual from play, arguing that ritual actions are embedded in a specific frame which conveys the 'let us believe' meta-message rather than the 'make-believe' one. This distinction, however pertinent, is, of course, of a purely *ad hoc* nature, and therefore a starting point rather than an explanation.

31 Take, for instance, initiation rites, commonly shrouded in secrecy. The overall performance would not be possible, if the different types of participants (neophytes, initiators and outsiders) were not acting on the basis of substantially different views about the ritual (see Houseman, this volume, for a detailed demonstration). For a general discussion of this point, see Boyer (1990: 20–2).

32 Anthropological attempts in this domain are few and far between (see e.g. Agar 1974; Dougherty & Keller 1985). This is a domain where anthropological theories might well find at least some inspiration in the experimental literature of social psychology (e.g. Tversky & Hemenway 1983; Rifkin 1985).

2   Whither 'ethnoscience'?

Scott Atran

'Ethnoscience', far from portending the arrival of the anthropological millennium, may well turn out to be another and perhaps minor 'school'.
(Roger Keesing)

Culture is something I put in the same category as unicorns.
(Noam Chomsky in response to Lawrence Hirschfeld, Royaumont Conference, 1975)

Introduction

In the 1950s a new way of doing cultural anthropology emerged in the United States, variously called 'ethnoscience', 'ethnolinguistics', 'ethnosemantics', 'cognitive anthropology' and 'the New Ethnography' (Sturtevant 1964; Colby 1966). It aimed at bettering ethnographic analysis by extending the techniques of structural linguists, like those of Bloomfield (1933) and Sapir (1921), beyond the realm of phonology and grammar to the fundamental 'codes', or 'grammar', of culture. First employing rigorous elicitation procedures in the controlled questioning of native speakers, the New Ethnographers then sought formally to analyse and evaluate the recorded data for those distinctive mental features that account for human cognition of the world and drive social activity (Conklin 1962; Black 1963).

Although the native's mental categories could not be directly observed, the ethnoscientist would thus infer their existence. Implicit in the technique of using distinctive features to differentiate and assemble atoms of linguistic behaviour was a key assumption of behaviourism (the dominant Anglo-American philosophy of the time, but still close to the original empiricist tenets of Locke and Hume). These techniques would assumedly mimic the way that natives build their conception of the world: using relatively few perceptual criteria of 'similarity' and 'difference', the native supposedly associates those perceptual stimuli that 'naturally go together' into percepts; then, by an effort of abstraction, the native likewise forms the concepts that are appropriate for grouping and extending those percepts into thoughts.

True, the New Ethnographers endeavoured to distance themselves from the classical behaviourism of stimulus–response in at least two respects: the ethnographer's task would not be to predict behaviour as such but to establish culturally adequate 'rules' of behaviour, and to discover rather than prescribe the significant stimuli in the subject's universe (Frake 1964a,b). However, the premise that culture is a symbolic system modelled on phonology and phrase structure effectively prescribes what native mental structures must be. It also limits the system of 'rules' for behaviour to a non-creative typology incapable of explaining or predicting the significant, powerful and surprisingly novel forms of thought that characterise any individual or culture of our species.

If the ambition of cognitive anthropology is to understand culture as 'whatever it is one has to know or believe in order to operate in a manner acceptable to its members' (Goodenough 1957: 167), then clearly one has to know more than simple-minded codes. Of late, ethnoscientists have evinced a more nuanced appreciation of the many-faceted aspects of human cognitive capacity: 'the notion of cultural grammar is giving way to contextualized organizations of knowledge. Language is still key in the study of cognition, but the models for representation are diverse' (Dougherty 1985: 7–8). Rejection of the code, or 'semiological', model has still not gone far enough, however. Unsatisfactory, too, is the broader notion that cultures are 'symbolic systems' (Geertz 1983). It is unlikely that cultures are systems of integrated rules; nor do they appear to manifest any unified notion of symbol that includes, say, the categories of folk-biological taxonomy and the ideas myths are made of.

Intellectual antecedents

The New Ethnography originated at Yale University. At the time, Yale's anthropology department largely revolved around the Institute of Human Relations headed by George Murdock. The Institute's principal task was the Cross-Cultural Survey,[1] from which 'an integrated science of human behavior' would, it was hoped, emerge. It was also at Yale that the renowned linguist Edward Sapir finished his career in 1939. Sapir, along with Benjamin Lee Whorf, championed the notion that the structure of language – including the organisation of vocabulary, syntactic categories and metaphor – affects the way in which people perceive their world (Sapir 1921). Thus, if language does play an important role in determining a community's 'world-view', then Hopi Indians of the American Southwest purportedly would not have our intuition of time as a smooth flowing continuum with a past, present and future, since Hopi grammar does not provide a straightforward past–present–future distinction of verbal forms (Whorf 1956).

To a significant extent, the New Ethnography sought to reconcile the apparently conflicting approaches to the analysis of human society, that is, in terms of descriptive universals and in terms of culturally specific linguistic categories. It became a basic premise that cultural traits, to be significant, must not only be attributed form and function; they must also be imbued with 'meaning'. In this sense, the New Ethnography would draw on the tradition of the Columbia University anthropologist Franz Boas, for whom every culture constitutes an indissociably rich complex of customary attitudes, perceptions, techniques, values and other 'social habits' (1940: 79).

A more direct influence on the New Ethnography stemmed from two of Boas's most important, and heretical, disciples at the University of California at Berkeley, Alfred Kroeber and Robert Lowie. From Berkeley, came a 'superindividual', or 'superorganic', view of culture and an affirmation of the validity of cross-cultural, or comparative, sociology. For Kroeber, although culture 'is always first of all the product of men in groups' (1963: 8) yet it lies beyond their individual knowledge and control. The anthropologist's goal would be to discover the cultural patterns and processes that give meaning to group activity: 'a set of ideas, attitudes, and habits – "rules" if one will – evolved by men to help them in their conduct of life' (Kroeber 1963: 10). These patterns and processes would also seem to be 'organic' in a functional sense akin to that of British social anthropology (Radcliffe-Brown 1935). So, 'concentration on any one of them to the exclusion of all others is an impractible undertaking'; however, comparative 'acquaintance with adjustments in one society after another ... enlarges our notion of social potentialities as the conception of n-dimensional space enlarges the vision of the non-Euclidean geometrician' (Lowie 1920: 13). The kinship typologies proposed by Kroeber (1909) and Lowie were designed to illustrate this comparative approach.

Although the hypothesis of linguistic relativity remains controversial to the present day, it was soon apparent to the new ethnographers that many of the arguments from language to cognition were premature at best, circular at worst. For example, nobody ever took the fact that English has a class of modals for future tense rather than the simple future form of most European languages as serious evidence for the conceptual absence of a single continuous future in the minds of English speakers. But if the argument works for speakers of Hopi, why not for speakers of English? Still, ethnoscientists generally did not deny that each language expresses its own 'world-view'. They denied only that world-views are incommensurable.

World-view: codes, components, taxonomies

In defining culture as a 'code', the New Ethnography would seek to reveal the particular ways by which diverse peoples perceive their universe through a general analysis of the ways in which they speak about it (Tyler 1969: 6). Not only grammar, but myth, ritual, kinship, cooking, artefacts, diseases, living kinds, spirits, etc. would each be studied as a sub-coded domain of the larger code of culture, so that different cultural codes might then be compared: 'the primary goal of ethnoscience must be to search for some formal device or system ... the device should be such that one world view is as easily mappable onto it as another, or else it could not account for observed changes of world view' (Werner 1970: 171).

The analysis would proceed through several stages. First, the language of a given community would be variously divided into 'lexical sets' or 'series'. A lexical set would be comprised of all semantically opposed lexemes which, in a given cultural context, share at least one characteristic trait (Lounsbury 1956). The conceptualised reality designated by the lexical set was referred to as that set's cognitive 'domain' (Conklin 1962). The ideational components making up each culturally important type of thought or activity, if systematically represented in the language, would then be discovered through a rigorous 'componential analysis'.

The leading idea behind this approach was Saussure's (1974) notion of value or contrast: like phonemes, concepts attain significance by their opposition to other elements rather than by any inherent positive aspect. In the investigations of Floyd Lounsbury and Ward Goodenough, ethno-science initially centred on kinship terminology. Beginning in the early 1960s the focus turned towards the study of other hierarchically ordered systems of 'folk taxonomy': 'a taxonomic hierarchy comprises different sets of contrasting categories at successive levels, the categories at any one level being included in a category at the next higher level. Taxonomies divide phenomena into two dimensions: a horizontal one of discrimination (poodle, collie, terrier) and a vertical one of generalization (poodle, dog, animal)' (Frake 1961: 117). Generalising from Yale anthropologist Harold Conklin's (1954) ground-breaking thesis on the folk-botanical classification of the Hanuno'o of the Philippines, Charles Frake extended the analysis of hierarchical ordering of contrast sets to the diagnosis of disease among the Subanun of Mindanao. Conceived broadly as any lexical domain organised according to inclusion of reference in this way (Conklin 1962), taxonomies were soon treated as principal constituents of culture and the human mind (Frake 1962b). Ethnoscientists noted that whereas in some domains (e.g. American kinship) the contrast between the terms of any given level of a hierarchy might be plausibly conceived componentially (such that the feature definitions of the lexemes are known), in other hierarchically ordered domains (e.g. Hanuno'o plants or Subanun diseases) they could not be (Kay 1966). Nevertheless, with the advent of studies of folk-taxonomy, componential analysis often became synonymous with the attempt 'to reveal the structure of the logical calculus which is employed in the given taxonomy associated with the terms' (Wallace 1962).

The universalist pretentions of ethnoscience to study 'man the thinker' bore almost exclusively on broad cross-cultural and cross-domain principles for 'structuring' meaning in terms of contrast sets, taxonomies and codes. The substantive aspects of particular cognitive domains were considered specific to the culture in question. Thus, while a given folk-biological taxonomy might appear to structure hierarchically the local flora and fauna, and to accommodate biological species, varieties and genera, yet there would seem to be no more direct correspondence between a given folk-biological taxonomy and the Linnaean system than between any two folk-biological taxonomies.

Such was the initial position of Berkeley anthropologist Brent Berlin and his colleagues, based on their fieldwork with the Tzeltal Maya (Berlin, Breedlove & Raven 1966). The main evidence came from the level of terminal contrast, that is, the level at which terms are not further distinguished or sub-divided. At that level, one finds a biologically confusing array of terms, some of which denote species, some varieties, some genera, some even entire biological families and orders. The conclusion was that only when the specific interests of the society in question are taken into account does the apparent biological confusion of the native become culturally explicable.

In sum, by the mid-1960s it seemed (1) that any given culture could be defined by the 'world-view' encoded in its language, (2) that even world-view sub-divided into discrete cognitive domains, (3) that each domain might be separately sub-coded in the lexicon as hierarchically contrasting sets of necessary and sufficient component features and (4) that cross-cultural comparisons would reveal purely 'formal universals', such as 'contrast set', 'taxonomy' and 'code', but that substantive universals, like 'elementary family' or 'folk species', would prove much more problematical, even specious.

Problems with universals

The chief error of ethnoscience in those years was to raise questionable methodological procedures to the status of epistemological principles. Regarding the methodology itself, there was often a good deal of confusion over just which procedures might prove relevant to a given situation. Colour terms, for instance, neither obey a strict hierarchy nor do they lend themselves to componential analysis: what nameable attributes, for instance, could possibly distinguish red from orange from blue from violet, etc.? From the beginning, ethnoscientists recognised that 'in some areas of the lexicon, semantic structure may be so complex that it is impossible or unprofitable to approach it ... with Aristotelian class logic and the "same or different" pragmatic test as principal tools' (Lounsbury 1956). Not just the componential approach, but taxonomic analysis also was criticised for not treating rather obvious problems of indeterminacy (Burling 1964).

All the same, rather than call into question the psychological reality of the analytic techniques used for eliciting and evaluating information from native informants, vague notions of 'limited' or 'non-orthogonal' componential analysis, 'overlapping' or 'fuzzy' taxonomies and 'multilevel' codes were invoked.

Even Berkeley anthropologist Paul Kay's (1971) formalisation of taxonomy in terms of inclusive orders of semantic contrast only confused the psychological issues involved. As in most of the literature in anthropology and cognitive psychology, taxonomy has been conceived as 'a system by which categories are related by class inclusion' (Rosch 1978: 30). Yet, it is doubtful whether any cognitive domain fits the ethnoscientist's (or cognitive psychologist's) usual notion of taxonomy. Judgements concerning the relative inclusion of artefacts, for instance, are not strictly transitive (e.g. 'car-seat' may be considered a variety of 'seat' but not of 'furniture', although 'seat' is generally viewed as a kind of 'furniture'). Moreover, such notions of 'category' and 'taxonomy' fit neither folk-biological classification nor the Linnaean system.

In biological classification, 'category' denotes a hierarchical rank and not the taxonomic grouping, or taxon, itself. Taxa are the elements of categories. Organisms are the elements of taxa. Species, genus, family and class are Linnaean categories. As we shall see, 'generic specieme' and 'life-form' are the names of folk-biological categories. Disjoint taxa are termed higher and lower with respect to one another not because they stand in any inclusion relations, but because they are members of different categories. 'Robin', 'pike' and 'gnat' are taxonomically related to 'cat' by reason of common generic-specieme rank, that is, they belong to the same class of classes. They are not directly related by reason of inclusion of reference within some shared superordinate taxon, that is, they are not sub-classes of the same higher-order class.

Since the late 1960s, recognition of the failure of traditional ethno-linguistic techniques to capture psychologically compelling regularities in human societies has accompanied a shift in interest from cross-domain linguistic universals to domain-specific cognitive universals. Take the case of colour. Until Berlin and Kay's (1969) pioneering work on basic colour terms, the dominant view of colour naming and perception was that advanced by Whorf and Ernst Cassirer (who spent his last years at Yale) and implicitly held by Saussure and most Anglo-American empiricist philosophers (see Quine 1960). From that viewpoint, the coloured partitioning of humankind's visual universe is not based upon physiological factors, and the so-called 'natural' colour spectrum does not exist. Rather, each culture apprehends the spectral continuum, divides it into units and names these units in a wholly arbitrary manner.

To the contrary, Berlin and Kay's findings indicate that basic colour foci are perceptually invariable across cultures. Thus, for example, an object will always be called 'red' or the equivalent in another language if (1) the language has at least one colour term in addition to those for 'black' and 'white', and (2) if the object exhibits a colour very near that of focal red (a small region of the spectrum definable by a particular combination of the three dimensions of hue, saturation and brightness). Moreover, it appears that names for these foci emerge before names for all other non-focal colours, and in a set order, in all languages. Later work strongly indicated a neurobiological basis to the cross-cultural regularity in colour perception and to the other in which basic colour terms are acquired. Findings by Berlin and Kay as to the apparently domain-specific organisation of colour terms and percepts were soon heralded as providing a fundamental contribution to cognitive psychology: 'in short, far from being a domain well suited to study the effects of language on thought, the color space would seem to be a prime example of the influence of underlying perceptual–cognitive factors on the formation and reference of linguistic categories' (Heider 1972).

Meaning and reference

Eleanor Rosch sought to extend this fundamental insight to other domains of 'natural objects', including artefacts and living kinds. She conjectured that 'it is possible that children initially define a category by means of its concrete clear cases rather than in terms of abstract criterial attributes', whereas adults would continue to use prototypes 'as the basis for processing' (Rosch 1973: 142). She found that both children and adults had faster reaction times when they responded 'true' to true statements of the form 'An x is a y' when x was a central member (e.g. doll, robin) of y (toy, bird) than when x was a peripheral member (skates, chicken). Subjects also rated sentences such as 'The tree has about twenty birds perched on it' as more acceptable when a typical subordinate (robin) was substituted for the superordinate subject (bird) of the sentence, than when a peripheral subordinate (chicken) was (Rosch 1975).

Taken as a theory of meaning, prototype theory favours the notion that 'good' instances or average examples of any given concept are crucial to determining the concept's proper extension or domain of reference, that is, the set of objects that fall under the concept and to which the term(s) associated with the concept truly applies. Moreover, it is assumed that the actual extension of such prototypically based concepts is indeterminate and that membership in the set is in truth a matter of 'more or less'. Thus, whether or not a given item instantiates the concept depends on the extent to which that item perceptually resembles focal types and on the degree to which it fulfils their usual sort of function. Prototype theories of meaning also generally carry the complementary assumption that the class of defining attributes that constitutes the intension of the term(s) are not severally necessary and jointly sufficient, but constitute an 'imperfect community'. Natural classification, then, might best be considered 'poly-thetic' (see Needham 1975), rather than a 'monothetic' ordering of dis-tinctive features. This implies that the right criteria for the application of words and concepts cannot be wholly dissociated from the (partially) idiosyncratic, contingent and episodic contexts of their actual use. Hence, naturally occurring concepts are rarely formed, and naturally occurring terms seldom associated, with criteria necessary for every context of application or sufficient for all contexts.

Prototype theory's emphasis on the perceptual and cognitive, rather than purely linguistic, determinants of concept formation stimulated important psychological and anthropological investigations of the natural conditions in which terms and concepts are applied as opposed to the artificially contrived circumstances of the laboratory and the ques-tionnaire. However, the wholesale generalisation of prototype theory to 'meaning' in general has proved unfortunate. Simply reversing the sup-posed relationship between language and thought has also done little to undermine the fundamental empiricist assumption that meaning is exten-sionally based or 'world- (rather than mind-) oriented'. A corollary of this assumption is that the abstract cognitive principles that structure differ-ent domains of meaning are all basically the same: it is the perceptible structure of the world that distinguishes domains of natural objects (and events), not innately articulated domain-specific cognitive principles.

As a result, aspects of meaning have been confused with reference. In other words, the semantic features that drive the logical entailments involved in classification are confounded with the mnemonic, perceptual and other recognitory strategies involved in identification, verification and instantiation. Furthermore, interesting findings pertaining to the cognitive structure of one domain have often been trivialised by being inconsiderately applied to others. The conflation of findings for artefacts and living kinds provides an example.

It is the fact that artefacts are primarily defined by the functions they serve, rather than by any inherent perceptual properties, that allows a given item to belong to different categories of artefacts in different circumstances. That is why one and the same item can literally be an instance, say, of 'waste-paper basket' in one context and 'tabouret' in another if oriented differently (according to putative function). In other words, instances of artefacts do not have intrinsic physical natures that make those items the kind of thing they are. In short, the itemised extensions of artefact categories may be indeterminate; however, this in no way implies that the conceptual distinctions between artefacts are themselves fuzzy. The defining characters of living kinds presumably 'come from nature' and the organisms themselves, and not from any culturally parochial function that may be assigned to them. It may make sense to say that consideration of whether a given surface constitutes, say, a 'table-top' or 'seat' depends upon the context in which a function is assigned to it; but it makes no sense to say that culturally parochial notions of language and function 'lead us to consider wings as a separate part' of a bird (Rosch 1978: 29). Comprehensible, too, is the claim that we often have difficulty in deciding when an item is a 'cup', a 'bowl' or a 'mug' (Kempton 1978); but it is incomprehensible to claim that 'some breeds of "dog" (such as the retriever) are more representative of the "meaning" of dog [than a Pekinese]' (Rosch 1973: 111). Perhaps there is a lesser degree of confidence in recognising (especially for the child) that a Pekinese or Boston terrier is a dog and not another basic kind as a cat, than in recognising that a retriever or German shepherd is a dog rather than a cat. But Pekinese and Boston terriers cannot be anything but dogs.

The reason is that members of a living kind, but not an artefactual kind, are presumed to have essential underlying physical natures that operate in a causally identical manner regardless of the extent to which those members actually differ in physical appearance (Atran 1987a). The semantic properties of living kinds advert to these presumptions of underlying nature, rather than to perceptible features as such.

A universal belief in (possibly unknowable) underlying nature thus constrains the character of semantic and conceptual knowledge, in general, and of living kinds, in particular. Surely, one of the principal aims of cognitive anthropology must be the discovery of these sorts of domain-specific constraints. They are clearly necessary to any explanation of the relatively uniform acquisition of such knowledge across cultures and the relative ease with which it is acquired by the children of any given culture.

In short, it cannot simply be assumed that distinct semantic domains are structured in the same way. Until independently assessed domains can be shown similar, meaning should be assumed a motley, not a monolith. This is not to deny that anthropologists and psychologists might one day discover that different cognitive domains share interesting organisational principles; but such a discovery would constitute a significant (and surprising) scientific advance only if those principles were first detailed independently for each separate domain. This suggests a direction in ethnosemantics that is more modest and piecemeal than has generally been the case. From this standpoint, the subject of cognitive anthropology is ripe with hitherto untouched possibilities. Examples include such barely studied pan-human domains as artefacts (see Gelman 1988), person concepts (Carey 1985), space, time, causality (Spelke 1988) and propositional attitudes (e.g. every language marks a conceptual distinction between 'promise', 'know' and 'believe' – automatic distinctions whose analysis is by no means obvious even to professional philosophers).

Domain specificity

The most significant influence on the development of cognitive studies, and certainly the most revolutionary, has derived from Noam Chomsky's (1965) avowedly Cartesian conception of linguistic grammar as a highly organised cognitive domain whose principles are unique to our species and to no other cognitive domain of our species. The most far-reaching implications of Chomsky's outlook, however, have continued to elude many cognitive anthropologists and psychologists. Assuredly, ethnologists are less inclined to model culture directly on grammar, and the models of cultural representations are now diverse; although 'generative principles' and 'deep structures' may still be sought as explanations for, say, 'grammatical' versus 'ungrammatical' Ban Chiang pottery designs (Van Esterik 1985). Often, however, there remains the dubious (methodological and epistemological) presupposition that a general theory of culture, and its constituent semantic domains, is plausible and desirable.[2]

Further studies into folk-biological classification systems especially seem to support the universality of domain-specific cognitive principles and to undermine the 'world-view' approach to anthropology, psychology and linguistics. Folk-biological classification, it appears, is everywhere taxonomic, being composed of a fairly rigid hierarchy of inclusive classes of organisms, or taxons. At each level of the hierarchy the taxa, which are mutually exclusive, exhaustively partition the locally perceived flora and fauna. Lay taxonomy, it appears, is universally and primarily composed of three absolutely distinct hierarchical levels, or ranks: the levels of unique beginner, basic taxa and life-forms (see Berlin, Breedlove & Raven 1973).

The unique beginner refers to the ontological category of plants or animals. These categories constitute a primary partition of our conceptual universe that is logically and psychologically prior to all subsequent classification of living kinds. They determine a crucial part of the structure of language (as dominant semantic categories) and are intimately bound to the perceptual and conceptual organisation by which we apprehend the world – what might be characterised in Kantian terms as 'synthetic a priori . . . regions of object-giving intuitions' (Pap 1960).

The basic level is logically subordinate, but psychologically prior to the life-form level. Ideally, it is constituted as a *fundamentum relationis*, that is, an exhaustive and mutually exclusive partitioning of the local flora and fauna into well-bounded morpho-behavioural Gestalts (Hunn 1975a). For the most part, taxa at this level correspond, within predictable limits, to those species of the field-biologist that are spatially sympatric (i.e. coexisting in the same locality) and temporally non-dimensional (i.e. perceived over at most a few generations), at least for those organisms that are readily apparent, including most vertebrates and flowering plants (Mayr 1969: 37). But this basic folk kind also generally conforms to the modern conception of the genus, being immediately recognisable both ecologically and morphologically. In fact, the scientific distinction between genus and species is often irrelevant in any local area since many local genera are represented by a single species.

Informant acknowledgement of the commonsense relation of 'natural causality' that is (universally) presumed to relate the morphotype of a species to its putative underlying essence constitutes one important way of determining the basic level of any given folk-biological taxonomy. Although children – whether American (Keil 1986) or Yoruba (Jeyifous 1985) – may initially entertain little more than mere presumptions of underlying nature for basic biological kinds, from an early age people appear to build living-kind taxonomies (see Stross 1969) and to root these in presumptions of underlying essence for all and only living kinds: 'Thus, for Rofaifo [of New Guinea] species share an essence which . . . immediately renders the idea, species, intelligible in a natural (biological) sense' (Dwyer 1976: 433).

Clearly, folk beliefs about biological essences cannot be *post hoc*. They must constitute conceptually *a priori* impositions on the taxonomic ordering of perceptual stimuli into morphotypes. Otherwise, how would it be logically possible for the child to take an instance of experience (e.g. a single encounter with a new animal in a zoo) and 'instantaneously' predict its extension to an indefinitely large set of complexly related instances? A presumption of essence plausibly enables the young child rapidly to fix a morphotype in mind despite very limited encounter with exemplars. This, in turn, allows the child immediately to classify and relationally segregate an example from instances of all other taxa. The child, it seems, just perceptually 'fills in' abstract taxonomic schema that are naturally at the mind's disposal.[3]

The life-form level further assembles generic speciemes into larger exclusive groups (tree, grass, moss, quadruped, bird, fish, insect, etc.). Life-forms appear to partition plants and animals into a contrastive lexical field. This comprises a pre-theoretical *fundamentum divisionis* into positive features that are opposed along one or more perceptible dimensions (size, stem habit, mode of locomotion, skin covering, etc.) (see Brown 1977, 1979). By and large, plant life-forms do not correspond to scientific taxa, while animal life-forms approximate modern classes.

The claim for universal principles of folk-biological taxonomy is not for the universal status of particular taxa, only for taxonomic categories. The categories of generic specieme and life-form are universal; the delimitation and placement of particular taxa is not. To claim that life-forms are fundamentally pragmatic notions (Randall & Hunn 1984) is belied by obvious fact; for instance, children – be they three-year-old Americans (Dougherty 1979) or Mayans (Stross 1973) – certainly do not learn 'wood-use' when they learn 'tree' (Atran 1987c). Also, claims as to any 'universal principles' governing the sequence in which life-forms appear in the language of any given society (Brown 1984), whether or not such principles are related to societal complexity, may have little to do with taxonomic principles. A persistent empiricist bias confounds the *a priori* nature of abstract taxonomic schema with substantive patterns derived from experience. Categories as such have no historical dimension, even though particular sorts of taxa may.

In sum, linked to the cross-cultural stability of the living-kind conceptual domain, we find that the learning of ordinary living-kind terms is remarkably easy and needs no teaching. At a limit, one need only once point to an animal (even in a zoo or book) and name it to have young children immediately classify and relationally segregate it from all other taxa. The naming might, of course, be done (and in a zoo is likely to be done) with pedagogic intent ('This, children, is a sheep'); however, it may just as well occur in an utterance not at all aimed at teaching ('Let's feed this sheep') and provide the required input. Such basic human knowledge of living kinds does not depend on teaching, nor is it gradually abstracted from experience. It is spontaneously acquired in accordance with innate expectation about the organisation of the everyday biological world.

Appreciation of artefacts, too, might be governed by innate expectations: 'even preschoolers clearly believe that artifacts tend to be human made and that natural kinds are not' (Gelman 1988: 88). Although, for lack of systematic analysis, the character of these expectations is wide open to speculation, it seems that in this domain as well humans are able to categorise fragmented experiences and, with little or no 'trial and error', extend the resulting categories to an indefinitely large set of complexly related experiences. As in any other area of cognitive endeavour, it is difficult to imagine how such spontaneous learning could succeed without a powerful set of innate organising principles. It is an entirely empirical question whether or not these principles cross domains, and, if they do, which domains they cross. No *a priori* assumption in the matter is justified. The implication for research strategies is clear: in the absence of sufficient further evidence, results from a potentially autonomous cognitive domain should not be extended to other domains. We should be prepared to discover that, after all, the structure of human concepts is a motley rather than a monolith.

A more revealing indication of basic, domain-specific knowledge comes from a source that has barely been tapped: the study of cultural transmission (Atran & Sperber 1991). Some bodies of knowledge have a life of their own, only marginally affected by social change (e.g. colour classification, ordinary living-kind groupings), while other bodies of cultural knowledge (e.g. totemism, molecular biology) depend for their transmission, and hence for their very existence, on specific institutions. This suggests that culture should not be viewed as an integrated whole, relying for its transmission on undifferentiated human cognitive abilities. Rather, it seems that human cognitive resources are involved in different ways in the many more-or-less autonomous psychological sub-systems that go into the making of culture.

Culture as mental contagion

Now, if totemism, myth, religion and other symbolic activities of the mind do not constitute well-defined cognitive domains, how can the ethnoscientist aspire to study these unquestionably pervasive and striking cultural phenomena? Moreover, there obviously are connections between various domains of thought that need to be accounted for, as must the effects of material life on cultural variation in the forms of mental representations.

One promising approach is Dan Sperber's (1985a, 1990) proposal to treat culture by means of an 'epidemiology of representations'. For

Sperber, culture consists of mental representations, that is, psychological things produced by individual minds, which become 'cultural' to the extent that they are distributed among a given population. Some thoughts, like personal day-dreams, even if recounted, hardly carry beyond the individuals who have them. Representations of other things, such as fashion and rumours, spread fairly rapidly but may be rapidly transformed as they spread. Indeed, they may disappear without ever attaining a relatively widespread and constant degree of 'steady-state' distribution within the culture.

Other sorts of representations, like those associated with notions of honour or equality, may have a long-lasting and wide distribution in a given society, but not in other societies. Such representations, although culturally idiosyncratic, may proliferate among a population because of their ability to affix themselves to a large range of institutionalised hosts in the cultural ecology. Alfred Gell has suggested that social equality, for example, may be rooted in psychologically more primary representations of physical or numerical equality; but the root sense within political and social discourse has been simplified to an intrinsically dimensionless notion of 'sameness' that can be attached to virtually any cultural dimension – like a bacteria that readily adapts to practically any habitat.[4]

Some ideas diffuse 'contagiously' through any given community with little alteration over space or time because of their psychologically fixed and universal basis. From this perspective, consider Lévi-Strauss's (1963: 2) insight concerning the persistent use of animal and plant species in totemism and other forms of cultural symbolism. They are 'better to think' because all human minds are constitutionally disposed to apprehend them in pretty much the same way with minimum triggering experience from the environment. As they are so easily fixed in the mind, they conveniently serve to anchor more fluid symbolic thoughts. Basic conceptions associated with factual, everyday, commonsense domains such as focal colour perception, the taxonomic apprehension of living kinds, distinctions in propositional attitude between knowing and believing, etc., are prime candidates for these most 'catching' – hence 'cultural' – of representations. Such representations might be the product of distinct mental faculties – basic cognitive dispositions naturally selected for survival over the course of millions of years of hominid evolution.

Along with these basic dispositions, evolutionary by-products may have emerged, somewhat as the susceptibility to catch colds emerged as a by-product of the evolution of the respiratory system. Such secondary 'cognitive susceptibilities' might include various scientific aptitudes and diverse forms of symbolic activity.[5] They might initially develop in the mind within less constraining parameters than basic representations, and be transmitted through a population with greater elasticity. These higher-order representations would lend themselves to a new type of cognitive elaboration precisely because rational constraints on internal consistency and factual compatibility with other beliefs may be relaxed.

Humans thus appear to use their 'susceptibilities' to 'meta-representation', that is, the capacity to form representations of representations, so as to retain half-understood ideas. By embedding half-baked notions in ideas we can have about them, such notions can be extended into full knowledge or otherwise further conceptually articulated. In the case of science, as in that of a child's acquisition of ordinary knowledge, this disposition to form higher-order representations – to play with the idea of an idea – allows the construction of conceptual stages towards a full understanding. In the case of symbolism, this ability 'also creates, however, the possibility for conceptual mysteries, which no amount of processing could ever clarify, to invade human minds' (Sperber 1985a: 84).

The elaboration of such higher-order cognitions, then, differs greatly for symbolism, including mythico-religious thought, and science. Ultimately, symbolic and scientific treatments of higher-order speculations about the empirical world tend to be diametrically opposed. Symbolism often aims to draw people ever deeper into unfathomable mysteries by pointedly outraging everyday experience. These outrages are rarely indiscriminate (indiscriminate outrages seldom become part of the cultural repertory). Rather, by contradicting common sense at the most salient junctures of customary empirical knowledge, symbolic analogies provide rich conduit metaphors for linking together diverse phenomena that would otherwise be lost to an uncompromisingly rational mental processor. However, the goal of symbolism, unlike science, is not to resolve phenomenal paradoxes or increasingly to restrict the scope of interesting conceptual puzzles. Instead, cultural symbolism aims at eternal truth. This is sustained by faith in the authority of those charged with the task of continually re-interpreting the truth and fitting it to new circumstances.

Consider the following: people doubtlessly have a basic cognitive disposition to compare animals to themselves. For children in our own society, experimental evidence clearly suggests 'a central role for knowledge of humans and human activities in organizing the child's knowledge of animal properties' (Carey 1985: 114). Taxonomically, this basic human disposition is reflected in the unmistakable cross-cultural tendency to under-differentiate invertebrates, that is, to consider them as phenomenally 'residual' or left over from the primary concern with the 'man-like' creatures of blood and bone, especially mammals (see Brown 1979).

Yet it seems that humans everywhere ordinarily make a fundamental ontological distinction between being human and being anything else, even an animal: 'In regarding people as a separate, unique category, the Rangi [of Tanzania] are in accordance with the vast majority of people the world over'; and modern naturalists, too, 'feel unconsciously the same demarcation as do the Rangi and other peoples' (Kesby 1979: 44; cf. Keil 1979). Also, 'the young child restricts the extension of the word "animal" to exclude people and will vehemently deny that people are animals' (Carey 1985: 138), although 'all of the general animal properties a child knows about are seen in terms of human activity' (139).[6]

Now, one characteristic of both science and mythico-religious symbolism is the endeavour to unify phenomenally diverse sorts of experience, including the integration of fundamental ontological domains that manifest *prima facie* differences. Animistic magic and mythical anthropomorphisations, especially with respect to animals, would 'naturally' seem to constitute a core element of the symbolic repertory of many, if not most or all, traditional societies; although actual practice and interpretation vary greatly. Using people as a model, the unknowns of other domains can be variously associated and managed; but the analogy can work both ways, so that even the unknown in people might be vicariously handled by external agencies (after all, magic also aims at human objects and myths also seek to account for human habits).

The moral: fundamental, plausibly innately grounded, commonsense dispositions to think about the everyday world in certain cross-culturally recognisable ways are necessary, if not sufficient, for any scientific or symbolic elaborations of that world. The tree of knowledge, it appears, has a solid trunk of basic commonsense dispositions that branches into two largely independent developments of cognitive susceptibilities: towards the relatively unfettered growth of symbolism, on the one hand; towards well-pruned scientific graftings, on the other. At least from this vantage, then: 'It is therefore better, instead of contrasting magic and science, to compare them as two parallel modes of acquiring knowledge' (Lévi-Strauss 1966: 13). This is not to deny that symbolism and science can feed off each other; only they do so in fairly distinct ways. Symbolism, it seems, may imprudently use just about anything to its advantage; but science must carefully pick and choose the elements about which it can speculate in order properly to eliminate unknowns.

Complex categories

The acquisition of all cultural knowledge depends upon its mode of transmission. For complex cultural categories, like 'equality', 'honour' or 'wisdom', what is transmitted depends crucially on how it is passed along.[7] But the acquisition of first-order forms of knowledge does not seem much influenced by the sequence in which it is communicated. Taxonomic knowledge of living kinds, for instance, is roughly comparable across similar physical environments regardless of whether it is 'ideologically formless' in one society or has a 'high rhetorical profile' in another. Thus, the Hanuno'o possess detailed basic botanical knowledge that they take every occasion to demonstrate and pontificate upon (Conklin 1954); but the Zafimaniry of Madagascar, whose tropical environment and swidden technology are rather similar to that of the Hanuno'o, appear to pass on their equally detailed basic botanical knowledge quite informally and with little or no commentary (Bloch 1988).

This is not to deny that Hanuno'o eloquence on general botanical matters, like specialised Zafimaniry concern with wood, relies on complex modes of transmission governing social 'wisdom'. Nor is it to suggest that such complex notions as 'wisdom' – which comprise the traditional bread and butter of anthropologists – can be studied exclusively with the techniques typically employed by cognitive psychologists. It does suggest, however, that cognitive study is pertinent to the more traditional approaches associated with participant observation. Consider the following: in this volume, Keller and Lehman argue that the semantic representations associated with concepts that presuppose 'culture-specific cosmological assumptions' are 'complex'; that is, they cannot be treated like focal colour categories or other 'basic' concepts. Take the metaphysical notion *hkano* in traditional West Futunan (Vanuatu, Polynesia) cosmology, which the authors translate as MATERIAL ESSENCE. Supposedly, it can be defined only with respect to an 'elaborate' and 'formal theory' that 'constructs a particular domain', namely, things that have MATERIAL ESSENCES: 'MATERIAL ESSENCE is the obvious, basic component of culturally significant, perceptible, typically (in a "default" sense) living kinds of things such as pigs, coconuts and people but also including speech, song, canoes and playing cards' (pp. 74–92).

In so far as *hkano* is complex, it also functions with other 'causally related' concepts, like EFFICACIOUS IMAGE, as 'theorems' in a 'larger encyclopedic theory of the the world':

EFFICACIOUS IMAGE is something that shares recognised perceptible attributes with the typical representation of a culturally significant thing having a MATERIAL ESSENCE. The shared perceptible attributes creating a link between a *hkano* and its *ata* indicate an intrinsic sympathetic connection between the MATERIAL ESSENCE and its EFFICACIOUS IMAGE. By virtue of this connection, magical performances involving the EFFICACIOUS IMAGE can produce effects in the thing itself ... Significantly, but not exclusively, EFFICACIOUS IMAGES are recognised in rock formations. (this volume, p. 81)

In this sense, *hkano* differs significantly from the notion of 'essence' that is universally presumed to underlie the nature of all and only living kinds: 'Although this theory employs universal elements, it is a culturally particular construction in which selected universal, and possibly also purely parochial, elements are combined' (p. 85).

Accordingly, the 'domain' that *hkano* spans – like others of cultural interest – cannot be given *a priori*: 'the case exemplified may be the principles of life or resemblance and its significance ... A domain need not be universally defined in any obvious way; the one in question is unlike "animal", "plant" or colour in this sense' (p. 89). Note, however, that the 'typical' or 'default' sense of *hkano* refers to living things, and that 'MATERIAL ESSENCE' in the abstract is coupled with a theory of the typical member of some targeted class of 'living things' (including animated canoe hulls and tree trunks). Indeed, there is every indication that *hkano* actually constitutes a second-order symbolic derivation of the universal common sense presumption of 'underlying nature' for living kinds. In fact, the 'theory' in which *hkano* is embedded closely resembles the medieval 'Doctrine of Signatures' with its hermeneutical notion of 'essence'; but the 'Doctrine of Signatures' hardly comes to a 'theory', and the hermeneutical connections between 'essence' and 'appearance' are no more causally related than are *hkano* and *ata*.

In the Doctrine of Signatures, Foucault (1970: 30) rightly implies that symbolic resemblance has no logical or causal consistency. No strict meaning is attached, because 'it refers back to another similitude, which then, in turn, refers to others'. Like the symbolic connections between mythic elements, no fixed semantic representation can be assigned: 'the [semantic] level we imagine we have singled out will elude our grasp and automatically resume its place in a system involving a multiplicity of levels' (Lévi-Strauss 1969a: 341–2). Indeed, Keller and Lehman concede that 'the features themselves of the two categories bear no necessary or predictable relation to one another save for the fact that they must not be the same' (this volume, p. 85).

The second-order derivations of universal presumptions of underlying nature may thus take symbolic forms, as among the islanders of West Futuna, the followers of Paracelsus or Christian theologians of the 'soul'; but they can also undergo a logically consistent and empirically consequent elaboration, as in the Aristotelian theory of psyche or Linnaean natural history (Atran 1986). As second-order elaborations of those first-order cognitions restricted to the domain of living kinds, they may cross into other domains. Plausibly, one might speculate that the domains adjacent to that of living kinds on the 'ontological tree' of ordinary language (see Keil 1979) will tend to be those most often or readily crossed: for instance, humans on the one side and perhaps non-living natural substances on the other. This would accord with the apparent facts (see note 2) that children assign socially selected morphotypes to races and come to think of non-living substances in terms of natural kinds only after they develop notions about the underlying natures of living kinds. Historically, too, the Aristotelian concept of psyche, or physical essence, was explicitly modelled on the prior biological concept, just as Linnaean (and Lockean) discussions of physical 'real essences' were grounded in reflections on organic kinds.

Obviously, the more children are required, and people try, to come to grips with the world, the more they will attempt to integrate their knowledge of it. Still, no necessary or inevitable pattern of domain crossing appears in second-order elaborations of basic cognitive dispositions; to be sure, essences can be further extended to artefacts and even events, although most probably in intermittent fashion. Cross-culturally, all that can be discerned is susceptibility and likelihood. Yet the message for 'traditional' anthropology is plain: to begin to understand how the complex conceptual repertory of a particular society emerges implies first of all a psychological grasp of what may be likely or unlikely to emerge in any culture.

Conclusion

The claim so far is that some abilities, concepts and beliefs are easily acquired, without the help of instruction (formal or informal) aimed at 'socialisation' or 'acculturation', and on the basis of ordinary interactions with others and the environment.[8] What makes this acquisition easy is an innate readiness that takes different forms for different domains, or, in other terms, a set of domain-specific cerebral dispositions.[9] The existence of such dispositions is, of course, neither more nor less mysterious than that of any adaptive aspect of the species' genetic endowment.

For each culture, then, innate cognitive dispositions determine a core of spontaneously learnable representations that are highly similar across cultures. Cultures develop – with greater diversity – beyond this core. They include systems of representations that are not spontaneously learnable. On the contrary, these systems require deliberate and often long and difficult learning, which may greatly benefit from adequate teaching. With this distinction between core and periphery in mind, consider again the contrast between two types of such systems of representations, science and religion, to see how they depart from the cultural core, while nevertheless remaining rooted in it.

Core concepts and beliefs are easily acquired and tend to be adequate for ordinary dealings with the social and natural environment. Yet they are restricted to some cognitive domains and are rather rigid. Other, harder to learn representations may be less limited in their domain of application and less rigid. They involve different cognitive abilities, in particular the typically human ability of forming representations of representations. This meta-representational ability allows people to retain information they only partly understand and to work on it in order to understand it better. Such processing of half-understood information over time is typical of deliberate efforts to learn counter-intuitive ideas, and is found in both science and religion.

A major difference between spontaneous and non-spontaneous, or sophisticated, learning is that only in the former case are the individual's newly acquired thoughts directly about the objects of the new knowledge: for example, about physical properties or animals. As for sophisticated learning, the individual's newly acquired thoughts are initially about the knowledge itself: for example, about notions and ideas in physics or in biology. Only if and when these notions and ideas become fully assimilated does the knowledge cease to be non- or even counter-intuitive and become direct knowledge of, say, physical or biological facts. The passage from representation of knowledge to assimilation of knowledge is often difficult, as in the sciences. Sometimes it is not even possible, so that some forms of knowledge, such as religious ideas, remain forever meta-representational.

This metaphorical talk about a core of spontaneously learnable knowledge and a periphery of further knowledge that requires deliberate learning and teaching not only suggests that the one is more stable and central than the other; it also indicates that they are functionally related: the very existence of the periphery is made possible by the core. Sophisticated knowledge elaborates or challenges commonsense knowledge but never develops in society or the individual without reference to basic commonsense knowledge. This implies that the study of spontaneous learning, of obvious interest in itself, is also a prerequisite to enhanced understanding of deliberate and sophisticated learning and of the role teaching plays in the processes of acquiring complex cultural categories.

It is becoming increasingly clear that the really innovative work in cognitive anthropology is more closely allied to cognitive psychology than to linguistics *per se*. Lexical analysis remains the initial means for accessing information about the various cognitive domains that form the mental landscape of a given culture; but it is only one approach to concept formation and diffusion, and an indirect one at that. Often conceptual categories are unnamed or denoted in a roundabout way and, in the case of symbolism, only loosely associated in (at least partially) non-inferential structures that cannot be fixed or coded.

Cognitive anthropology and psychology differ primarily, but not necessarily, in method and emphasis. Both disciplines rely on native intuitions to elaborate theories. Testing, though, usually proceeds by way of contrived experiment in the one case and in 'seeing what the next culture does' in the other. For the anthropologist, laboratory-type experiments are frequently impractical in the field. In the main, only relatively straightforward linguistic exercises lend themselves to ready use by anthropological fieldworkers; for these exercises depend on more-or-less sophisticated questioning of informants rather than on precise measurements of reaction times and the like. Also, the anthropologist is usually concerned more with material and intellectual problems relating to the transmission, diffusion or lack of diffusion of ideas in a culture, whereas the psychologist is more narrowly preoccupied with the internal organisation of ideas *tout court*.

Plainly, if ethnoscience is to produce significant and surprising discoveries about cultural thinking and the social activities such thinking motivates, it can no longer afford to subscribe to what Saussure called the 'semiological' approach to social psychology. For that programme wrongly assumes that language is but the most important of those coded systems of a society 'comparable to ... symbolic rites, polite formulas, military signals, etc.' (1974: 16; cf. Leach 1976: 10). Nor does the inclusion of cultural phenomena into cognitive science seem consistent with Geertz's (1983) neo-Boasian view of culture as a socially established 'symbol system' rooted in the individual.

Whatever the interpretative value of viewing culture as a mental and behavioural totality, the possibility of a principled account of culture based on systematically integrated analytic categories seems remote. In some cultures kinship and art develop together, in others art and cooking, but there is likely to be no general theory that explains why this should be so: culture for the anthropologist, like consciousness for the psychologist, may well lack genuine ontological distinction and so forfeit any claim to being a true object of scientific theory. The proper task of ethnoscience, it seems, is to learn from and instruct cognitive psychology: to understand how it is that human beings, whose contacts with the world are so fragmented, limited and individual, are nevertheless able to acquire such rich, systematic and extensive forms of knowledge and belief; and by so understanding, to inform how it happens that humankind is wont to vary them into the multifarious expressions of human cultures.

This view of 'the New Ethnography' as an adjunct to cognitive psychology may well result – and may have already resulted – in its reduction to a 'minor school' of anthropology; but, if so, there need not be cause to lament its passing from the exclusive ranks of professional anthropology.

To the contrary, as with linguistics before, this could betoken its rite of passage to intellectual maturity.

NOTES

1 Initiated in 1937, the Survey represented an attempt to 'build up a complete file of geographical, social, and cultural information, extracted in full from sources and classified by subject, on ... human societies, historical and contemporary as well as primitive' (Murdock 1949: vii).

2 A preliminary issue to any possible formal comparison of language and society is whether or not cultures have finite structures like grammars. Even posing the issue, however, implies that the units and rules of culture or society are specifiable in principle. There is ample cause for scepticism on this score. Ever since people began writing about language, they have agreed on fundamentals such as the subject–predicate structure of sentences. There is also wide agreement on how to validate grammatical intuitions. But no such accord exists with respect to culture. Nor is an enduring consensus likely, unless social scientists also happen to be those who (in neo-Hegelian fashion) have the power to impose their interpretation of culture on people by force or conviction. The units and rules of society are probably as 'open' and unbound as the unforeseen contingencies of history suggest.

3 Analysis of lexical composition or contrast sets is less revealing of basic-level classification and apt to induce error. Thus, although most basic-level terms are monolexemic and most terms below the basic level are polylexemic, sometimes this is not so. 'Oak' and 'white oak' seem to fit the bill, but 'poodle' is certainly subordinate to 'dog' for ordinary American speakers, and 'Tasmanian wolf' and 'wolf' are plainly distinct basic-level terms for educated Australian speakers.

Confusion of the basic level with the level of 'terminal contrast' proves equally misleading, and is largely responsible for the persistent misjudgement that 'folk-species' do not generally correspond to biological species (Conklin 1962; Berlin, Breedlove & Raven 1966; Rosch 1975; Brown 1984). Taxa below the generic-specieme level, that is, the level of the folk-specific and folk-varietal, are culturally idiosyncratic in a way that generic speciemes and life-forms are not. Generally, only the most socially useful generic speciemes are further divided into specifics and varietals on the basis of a very few culturally salient perceptual traits (Berlin 1976). It is quite plausible that such secondary cultural categories are also psychologically subordinate to the basic concept of generic specieme and require additional cognitive processing, as appears to be the case for adults (Hunn 1975a) as well as young children (Stross 1973; Waxman 1985). The level of terminal contrast, though, is a purely ethnolinguistic artifice that indiscriminately mixes unigeneric life-forms (e.g. cactus), monospecific generic speciemes (e.g. redwood), monovarietal specifics (red maple) and folk-varietals as such (spotted white oak). This is because contrast hierarchies, as opposed to true taxonomies, do not consider the logical, psychological and biological implications of rank.

4 Gell's suggestions were made during discussions at the King's College Research Centre Conference on 'The Representation of Complex Cultural Categories', Cambridge University, 22–4 March 1988.

5 Both mathematics and language involve an ability to think creatively with discrete infinites by means of finite rules. We invent new numbers, like new words, and combine them through a few systematic operations into strings of virtually any length (see Chomsky 1988: 167, 181–5). Unlike language, however, mathematics does not spontaneously arise in every social context, but seems to require a richer and more sustained sequence of experience and instruction in order to flourish.

6 Thus, given a property that a pre-schooler believes true of humans then the child will project it to other animals according to the perceived overall similarity of those animals to humans (e.g. more to dogs than to bees), whereas ten-year-olds and adults will be more likely to generalise a property from any animal to any other. Note, however, that even young children will project human properties to atypical animals and refrain from generalising those properties to mechanical monkeys, puppets or dolls even though such artefacts more closely resemble humans in external appearance than do the atypical animals (see Gelman, Spelke & Meck 1983; Keil 1986).

7 This section draws largely from my response to arguments presented at the King's College Research Centre Conference on 'The Representation of Complex Cultural Categories', Cambridge University, 22–4 March 1988.

8 This section stems from Atran and Sperber (1991).

9 There is now an increasing body of recent literature in neuropsychology that refers to 'category-specific' impairments in brain-damaged patients. There are, it appears, impairments affecting the naming and recognition of animate objects only (Warrington and McCarthy 1983), 'vegetables' (including fruits) only (Hart, Berndt & Caramazza 1985) and animals and 'vegetables' only (Sartori & Job 1988). Although Sartori & Job fail to distinguish vegetables (and fruits) from plant kinds as such, they argue for a category-specific impairment for the naming and recognition of living things: 'the ability to identify objects and other non-living elements is ... better preserved' (1988: 129).

When tested with verbal material, the patient's knowledge about the structure of ordinary animal taxonomy proves 'quite accurate'. Moreover, 'when completing drawings the patient knows he has to add parts of the superordinate category'; but he has difficulty processing basic animal kinds: 'he adds fins to fishes, wings to birds and horns to certain mammals, but he has great problems in distinguishing e.g. the horn of a rhinocerus from the antlers of a deer' or in discriminating real from unreal creatures. Also, 'accuracy for vegetables was poor although somewhat better than for animals' (130). The 'somewhat better', however, may owe to the fact that vegetables, unlike animal and plant kinds as such, also generally involve functional attributes. Still, the impairment does seem restricted to only living things without regard to typicality; that is, the patient's performance on typical versus atypical items was 'not significant ... which is the opposite direction of what would be predicted' (130) if living-kind categories were prototypically based.

Part II

The structure of religious categories

All contributions in this section deal with the question of conceptual structure. Religious ideas are organised by concepts which carry certain tacit assumptions and constrain the range of inferences and conjectures subjects can make about religious entities and processes. The problem is to describe the mental structures which make it possible for subjects to use religious categories. The diversity of models presented here is a reflection of the variety of approaches in current linguistic and psychological theories of conceptual representation. Keller and Lehman argue for a 'theory-based' understanding of religious categories. Their argument starts with the observation that such concepts are intuitively more 'complex' than most everyday categories. This complexity can be explained by the fact that religious categories are constrained by underlying theories, rather than by external similarities. They then examine the relevance of this hypothesis on Polynesian categories of 'magical' connections. Keesing argues for the relevance of 'conventional metaphors' to the description of symbolism. He argues that cultural symbolism is typically organised around focal metaphors, and draw both their 'evocative' power and their vagueness from metaphorical structures found in everyday language. In both Bloch's and Boyer's contributions, a third approach is presented, which examines the connections between intuitive, universal knowledge of natural entities and processes, on the one hand, and cultural elaborations, on the other. On the basis of Malagasy data, Bloch's chapter shows how intuitive notions of natural kinds are both and partially suspended in religious symbolism. Boyer's contribution tries to generalise this point by showing that some aspects of religious symbolism (here the assumptions concerning religious capacities) are both crucial to their transmission and naturally entertained by human subjects. All contributions in this section argue against the widespread assumption, that all important aspects of religious representations are necessarily culturally transmitted.

3 Computational complexity in the cognitive modelling of cosmological ideas

J. D. Keller and F. K. Lehman (U Chit Hlaing)

We will focus here on cognitive anthropology's contribution to the study of the representation of complex cultural categories. We will take two metaphysical concepts from Keller's field research in Oceania, which, by intuitive standards, are complex. Using these concepts, we will explore the issues of complexity identified above. The research site is the Polynesian outlier, West Futuna, Vanuatu. The targeted concepts are ones that traditional cognitive anthropology would ordinarily have shelved for attention only after more 'basic' conceptual distinctions had been adequately specified.

We will proceed in a manner at many points at odds with traditional cognitive anthropology, although often in line with directions already being taken in contemporary research by some scholars in that field and in cognitive science generally. We proceed in the direction, however, of the sub-discipline's expressed goals of developing a theory of meaning equally applicable to all languages and all cultural contexts. In the concluding section, we will explicate some of these revisions to standard cognitive anthropology and their implications for cognition and theories of concept definition more generally.

Computational complexity

Pinpointing the topic of discussion itself, that is, complexity, is no simple task. Reflections on the literature suggest that complexity might be handled in at least four ways. We discuss this diversity below and take the position that conceptual complexity has to refer to three facets of concept definition: internal representation, conceptual embedding and, derivatively, polysemy. We will specifically exclude issues related to word usage from treatment in this chapter apart from some preliminary discussion.

We will take as background to our work a radically intensional point of view about cognition, knowledge and meaning quite similar to that put forward, as the non-objectivist position, by Lakoff (1987). We do not find it necessary to discuss or characterise that view here, but it is necessary to state the caveats, provisos and exceptions to their notion of non-objectivism that we hold to be essential. First, a concept, especially in the sense of Johnson's (1987: ch. 6 – especially 153ff.) reworking of Kant, is something more abstract than either a set of concrete, substantive features as necessary and sufficient surface conditions for category membership, or a Lakovian family of connections among sense and schemata having the same name, term or label. Rather, it is a theory (by no means necessarily propositional in character, but formally delineable), and the various schemata are generated as theorems in that theory. That some schemata may be prototypical seems obvious and unnecessary to comment upon further here. It is, none the less, premature to reject the classical notion of categories being characterised by necessary and sufficient membership conditions on the basis of the inappropriateness of observable surface 'features' for these conditions in general or on the basis of what we are able to define, early on in this chapter, as the instantiation problem (see note 7, below). It is not necessary to assume that conditions constituting a set of abstract features are anything other than some domain knowledge structure or structures; in particular, the features of lexico-semantic category or concept definition are not at all necessary semantic primes.[1]

First and foremost, complexity has to refer to internal representation of the semantic features constituting a concept. Specifically, if a particular concept definition requires more formal mechanisms in its representation than does some other concept, then the former is more complex than the latter. In elaborating this claim we cannot be exhaustive, for no comprehensive theory of the formal constraints on semantic definitions is available; but a simple example or two should suffice to show what we mean. However we define the concept labelled in English 'red' as a prime given by a unique physiological human response to light or as a set with a defining focus (Lehman 1985), a dual-focused GRUE category is more complex than RED by the criterion given above. A dual-focused GRUE category, that is, a colour category the best examples of which include both FOCAL BLUE and FOCAL GREEN, is defined by the union of two conceptual units comparable to the single focus of English RED. Dual-focused GRUE categories have been documented repeatedly in the literature (Dougherty 1977; Burgess, Kempton & MacLaury 1985). Dual-focused GRUE is more complex than RED by virtue of the greater formal complexity in specifying its internal representation. Again, to stay within a given language, take the concepts labelled by 'parent' and 'cousin' for any dialect of American English. Again, regardless of how we ultimately define the concept labelled by 'parent' (as a prime or as a construed definition),[2] this concept is simpler than that labelled 'cousin' because the latter entails the former. The concept labelled 'cousin' involves the semantic elements 'parent of' and its inverse, 'child of', in a specification of 'parent's parent's child's child'. The concept labelled 'cousin' is therefore more complex than that labelled 'parent' (Lehman & Witz 1974; Witz & Lehman 1979). It is this aspect of complexity that is focused upon by traditional cognitive anthropologists, and which might in retrospect be applied to the classic work of scholars such as Lounsbury (1956) and Goodenough (1956, 1965a).

Secondly, if a concept A is part of a domain or body of knowledge that itself is complex, that is, involves constructed premises about the structure of the world upon which the concept definitions rest, then concept A, by virtue of its embedded position in the theory of the domain, may be held to be complex. In Fillmore's (1975) terms, if the scene in which a concept fits is complex, then the concept may be properly held to be complex. In Keesing's terms (1982), if semantic information presupposes culture-specific cosmological assumptions, then the semantic representations are complex.

We develop our position starting from often-explored ground. Malinowski, in fact, argued that no concept is without a foundation of 'devices and rules' ([1935]1978 vol. II: 13). In addressing problems of translation closely related to our present problems of word meaning, he further points out that translation in the correct sense must refer, therefore, not merely to different linguistic uses but often to different cultural realities behind the words ([1935] 1978 vol. II: 14). If by 'cultural realities' Malinowski here is referring to culturally particular theories of the world, then despite his adoption of the equation of meaning with use, a position that we reject for well-known reasons, he can be taken as arguing, like us, for a view of complexity that includes internal representations and conceptual embedding. For example, basic colour categories such as RED and GRUE are defined by perceptual primes and are part of a perceptually given domain called 'colour' in English. While colour concepts may be imported into other bodies of knowledge, they are defined with respect to universally given sensations which are not based upon constructed premises.

Other concepts, however, may be embedded in elaborate formal theories constructing particular domains. A re-analysis of an example from the literature should illustrate our point. Spradley (1972) sets himself the task of analysing basic conceptual distinctions that urban nomads make to distinguish among 'flops'. While Spradley anticipates a taxonomic structure, and therefore presents his results as though such a structure were appropriate to the data, we argue that the material can be more adequately analysed as an open class of things or places usable for 'flopping', where class membership depends upon the theory of the domain of that activity itself. Spradley never formally characterises this theory, but his ethnography suggests that the basic premises include the existence of places, the need for a place in which to sleep that meets basic requirements of size, shape and seclusion as given by the concept of sleeping and the human body and the life-style of urban nomads. This re-analysis presupposes a theory about all kinds of places (Jackendoff 1985, for the notion 'place') within which those good for flopping may be found. Such premises combine universal and culturally particular assumptions about the world in the construction of a culturally salient theory of 'flopping'. The theory of flopping imposes a partial order on the whole set of all kinds of places according to their respective goodness of flopping. Conceptual distinctions such as those between something labelled 'paid flop' and something called 'a weed patch' are more complex than basic distinctions such as RED and GRUE in the domain of colours. The labels 'paid flop' and 'weed patch' stand for sets of places the members of which share, respectively, some features in common and are maximally good for flopping. These conceptual distinctions arise from the larger theory of flopping. The premises constituting this theory are not represented in the embedded, or constructed, concepts individually, yet those embedded concepts are structurally derived from that larger theory.[3]

Concepts defined with respect to constructed theories of particular domains are more complex than those defined independently of such orienting premises. The semantic features of embedded concepts need to arise as theorems (computations, that is) in a domain theory. We suspect that it is primarily this phenomenon of conceptual embedding that gives rise to the intuitive notion that metaphysical concepts are more complex than concrete concepts, for metaphysical concepts are typically embedded in larger theories; say, for example, of some aspect of cosmology. It is failure to attend to conceptual embedding in the case of culturally constructed domains that has frequently prevented cognitive anthropologists from producing adequate accounts of complex cultural distinctions. With respect to conceptual complexity, the degree of complexity will be defined as a partial function of the depth of embedding, for embedding may be recursive, requiring the successive speculation of the formal theories for multiple domains in order to clarify fully some given concept, as the re-analysis of Spradley's 'flops' suggests.

Thirdly, if a concept B is polysemously related, through a word or other sign that typically stands for it, to other concepts, then that concept B, by virtue of its connections to others, may be held to be complex. Witherspoon's (1977) analysis of the Navajo concepts represented by the word *shima* provides an apt illustration.[4] Among the concepts represented by this word are MOTHER BY BIRTH, THE EARTH or EARTH WOMAN, the SHEEP HERD, the CORN FIELD and the MOUNTAIN SOIL BUNDLE (1977: 91). Each of these concepts may be considered complex by virtue of its relation to the others. That these relations exist is made evident in part by the sharing of a common phonological image and in part by the Navajo theory of life. In fact, complexity resulting from polysemy is basically due to conceptual embedding already discussed above and adds the element of shared sound images to this. Specifying the nature of polysemous relations requires elaborating the premises upon which these conceptual distinctions and their inter-relations rest. Polysemic complexity is seen to lie in the way concepts map to phonological strings in the lexicon. Polysemy is a relation among words sharing a significant partial sense across arbitrarily distinct lexical domains, thus defying taxonomic treatment in most cases at least. We take the position that polysemy generally, and crucially, involves abstract generalisation rather than being limited to metaphorical extension of usage (Lakoff & Johnson 1980).

The same point can be made with regard to metaphor more generally. Let us begin by agreeing to include metonymy with metaphor. The *Oxford English Dictionary* admits that it is almost impossible to keep them neatly apart, and in any case, metonymy (part-for-whole substitution) is only a special case of metaphor (the class of substitution figures generally). In the second place, it is useful to divide the notion of metaphor into at least two varieties. On the one hand, we have a term that starts out having a particular concrete domain of application and then, surely by some sort of relational analogy, gets figuratively applied to some other domain. This is no doubt a metaphorical extension; but it often happens (see Johnson 1987: 50, following Sweetser) that in the course of time the term is taken to mean basically the abstract structural relation that motivated the extension to start with, so that now it would be wrong to claim anything other than that both applications are, alike, instances of that abstract idea as such, even if, as is also frequently the case, the more concrete application of the original pair may continue to be the default/prototype one. A good example is to be found in the obvious re-analysis of the time-is-money metaphor of Lakoff (1987). We think that continuing to use the word metaphor for this is somewhat confusing. It tends to give one the impression that somehow the historical origin of a range of uses of a word outwards from a particular domain of application can never be surmounted. It seems, rather, as its historical end-point, to become abstract generalisation.

On the other hand, there is the notion of metaphor according to which it is a form of symbolical usage (Lehman 1978). That is, a figure is employed in such a way that the properties motivating the extended usage are not finitely accountable: indeed, the more imaginable connections there are the better the figurative usage is. Now, whatever may turn out to be the relationship between the two senses of the word metaphor, it seems to us that it is to be the second only that the classical distinction between literal and figurative meaning ought to apply.

Finally, much discussed in the literature is the problem of *word usage*. If a linguistic sign referring to a particular concept C is used as a tool for expression in some context(s) in a sense other than some prototypical sense of concept C, then this linguistic sign, it has been argued, represents a complex conceptual unit definable by a prototype and rules for its extension (Coleman & Kay 1981; Kronenfeld, Armstrong & Wilmoth 1985). We will take the position that this phenomenon is not so much an issue of concept complexity itself as an issue of word usage applicable to more or less all words. This is the problem of mapping concepts to experience through the application of their linguistic signs. It is this mapping process that is complex here, contributing, no doubt, to what some have sensed as cultural complexity. For instance, let the default value of 'drinkable liquid' be WATER; then the problem arises of how it is that in this society to offer someone 'a drink' has a first reading of offering something alcoholic.

The issue of mapping introduces two separate problems. One is the instantiation problem, that is, whether or not something is, for example, a chair if the raised flange at the back of the seat is too trivial in height to be worth noticing or trying to lean back against very usefully. The second is the problem of saliency of categorisation, that is, whether it is as functionally, socially or perceptually consequential that something meets the conditions for being in some category C as that it meets those of category C'. This itself has two aspects as well: whether something makes as good a table as it does a chair; and the relative social, cosmic importance of one category as against another – possibly, a case such as that where the fact that something is, in a devout Christian community, a good example of a cross outweighs its also meeting the criteria for a post-and-beam architectural support. These aspects of mapping are interesting in themselves but have nothing at all to do with the nature of concept definition, except that word usage may indirectly affect concept definition through the acquisition process, in which one's extensional applications may affect the process of abstracting intensional definitions. These are aspects of the application of conceptual distinctions to the world. The notion of classical categories for meaning can be presented without supposing that in some objectivist sense the world is really or unproblematically and decidedly cut up into these as real, natural kinds.[5]

We define conceptual complexity, then, as primarily having to do with two kinds of things:

1 the formal specification of internal semantic representations:
2 conceptual embedding, with polysemy as a derivative which may compound either of the primary forms of complexity.

Any or all of these facets of complexity may be involved in any particular instance. In fact, it is likely that the two primary forms of complexity are often (though not necessarily) correlated, that is, that formal complexity tends to increase as conceptual embedding becomes increasingly complex, and vice versa.

Two complex cosmological categories: *hkano* and *ata*

The two concepts targeted for study here are MATERIAL ESSENCE and EFFICACIOUS IMAGE (Dougherty 1983). These concepts are central to the traditional cosmology of the islanders of West Futuna, Vanuatu. They are called *hkano* (MATERIAL ESSENCE) and *ata* (EFFICACIOUS IMAGE).[6] Save for one brief excerpt (Capell 1958), no discussion of these concepts appears in the literature on West Futuna prior to Keller's work, though the labels and similar concepts frequently appear in other Pacific ethnographies. As far as Keller knows, there are no other West Futunan words that refer exactly to these conceptual distinctions.

MATERIAL ESSENCE and EFFICACIOUS IMAGE each require three levels of representation. Each of the three 'senses', if you will, of either of these concepts is referred to by the same label, creating a polysemy by proper inclusion. We will, however, assume throughout that there does not exist any necessary one-to-one relation between labels and the concepts that they are used to name (see note 4).

Inverting the usual approach of cognitive anthropologists who focus on labels and their use in context, we will begin with a radically intensional account of these concepts. MATERIAL ESSENCE and EFFICACIOUS IMAGE are central contrasting concepts in traditional West Futunan cosmology. MATERIAL ESSENCE is the obvious, basic component of cultural significant, perceptible, typically (in a 'default' sense) living kinds of things such as pigs, coconuts and people but also including speech, song, canoes and playing cards. MATERIAL ESSENCE is the basic substance and form of something that either is human or stands in a special relationship to human beings. The *hkano* of a human being or a pig is the human or animal body; that of a tree, its trunk; that of a coconut is the edible flesh. The *hkano* of a root-crop plant is its edible root or corm; that of any fruit, its edible portion. And the *hkano* of an outrigger canoe is its main hull as opposed to its outrigger.

EFFACIOUS IMAGE is something that shares recognised perceptible attributes with the typical representation of a culturally significant thing having a MATERIAL ESSENCE. The shared perceptible attributes creating a link between a *hkano* and its *ata* indicate an intrinsic sympathetic connection between the MATERIAL ESSENCE and its EFFICACIOUS IMAGE. By virtue of this connection, magical performances involving the EFFICACIOUS IMAGE can produce effects in the thing itself. As Codrington (1891) says of Melanesia in general, these objects are used as 'vehicles to convey' power (1891: 119–20). Significantly, but not exclusively, EFFICACIOUS IMAGES are recognised in rock formations. The EFFICACIOUS IMAGES present in rock formations on the island of Futuna are fixed, having been given by the supernatural at the time of creation. In like manner, the highly potent *navela* were given by Nobu to the people of neighbouring Eromanga (Humphreys [1926] 1978: 171). In addition, a shadow, the chorus of a song as opposed to its verses or the outrigger of a canoe as against its main hull are among the other significant EFFICACIOUS IMAGES.

MATERIAL ESSENCE and EFFICACIOUS IMAGE are concepts simply presupposed by the people of West Futuna. They are not the subject of argumentation, but are, rather, fundamental concepts used in everyday conversation concerning the nature of events.

The aspect of West Futunan cosmology in which these concepts are embedded includes the following premises:

1 There exist material things.
2 One class of these material things are 'living' in some culturally particular sense, and/or importantly connected with (human) life. This includes human beings themselves, culturally significant animals and plants, and canoes, the third of which categories are identified with humanity through the tree spirit that originally inhabited the trunk from which the canoe hull is carved and which animates the hull. Canoe hulls are designed and ornamented to reflect this animacy. Speech, song and playing cards are likewise included in this class by virtue of their connection to the supernatural, to human beings and to the discovery and creation of order. Speech and song are exclusively a human or supernatural product. These phenomena are inherently powerful. It is through speech and song that society's history is represented, decisions are articulated, chiefly edicts are handed down, and values preserved. Cards fall into this class possibly by virtue of an association with divination. Alternatively still again, the fact that the face cards represent human images may have been a factor. In any case, cards, like songs, canoes and so on, seem to be, or to represent, what is efficacious with regard to human affairs, which appears to be the essence of 'living'.
3 A second class of material things are non-living.

4 There exist immaterial things. These include spirits, or souls (*ata*) of human beings now living and ghosts (*atua*) of those who are dead. There are also spirits that have never inhabited a human body that are associated with non-living things and magical forces based upon contagious and sympathetic connections. (See Codrington 1891 for a related discussion, especially pp. 119–20.)

5 Material things may resemble one another.

6 Resemblance in material things may be indicative of an immaterial connection between them that is either spiritual, as evidenced through descent (i.e., within a given domain), or magical, as evidenced in the relation between a living and a non-living thing (across distinct domains).

7 A resemblance between a rock and a living thing may be indicative of a magical connection between the two such that the health, physical robustness and productivity of the living thing can be optimised by a knowledgeable person working upon the EFFICACIOUS IMAGE. This is the most powerful and traditionally the most typical instance of the pairing of MATERIAL ESSENCE and EFFICACIOUS IMAGE, and it forms the focus of traditional increase rites (Capell 1958)

Examples of the perceived similarities which constitute pairing of a MATERIAL ESSENCE and EFFICACIOUS IMAGE include a rock that emits a noise like the grunting of a pig and is recognised as the *ata* of the pig, or a rock with three equidistant depressions resembling those on the inner shell of a coconut, therefore the *ata* of the latter. Humphreys ([1926]1978), citing Gunn (1914), comments with regard to West Futuna: 'of belief in spirits, ghosts, or a superior being or beings, no accounts have been given, of magic almost nothing has been written, although magical stones in the shape of breadfruit are mentioned' (Gunn 1914: 221, in Humphreys [1926] 1978: 116).

In terms of the formal mechanisms required for the specification of the two concepts, MATERIAL ESSENCE and EFFICACIOUS IMAGE, the lexico-semantic features are whatever abstract notions constitute what it means to be MATERIAL ESSENCE or EFFICACIOUS IMAGE. Such features must arise from the larger theory of cosmology as constructed by the people of West Futuna. Here we draw on the distinction between encyclopedic and semantic knowledge (Sperber 1975a, 1985a), or cultural and linguistic knowledge (Keesing 1974), which will be relevant again as we pursue the issue of conceptual embedding. We take encyclopedic knowledge to be, minimally, the theory of a particular domain, technically, a particular knowledge structure (K-structure).[7] The definitions of concepts that arise within this domain theory must be minimally specifiable in some finite way. Therefore, the minimum lexico-semantic 'feature' definition of a category has to be formed from material arising in and from encyclopedic domain theories, yet not directly incorporating the encyclopedic know-ledge itself in the concept definitions.[8]

In addition, there is an hierarchical polysemy that surfaces as soon as one attempts to specify the internal representation of these categories. MATERIAL ESSENCE is specified in the abstract on the basis of a theory of the nature of culturally significant 'living' things. By the very nature of this theory, MATERIAL ESSENCE must be represented at two additional levels. At a second level, MATERIAL ESSENCE in the abstract is coupled with a theory of the typical member of some targeted class of 'living' things. This theory of the typical member of some 'species' is not a template against which examples in the world are judged, but rather a set of default characteristics of the class. Some particular feature, or cluster of features, from among the default values is designated the MATERIAL ESSENCE of that 'species': the trunk of a tree, the edible meat of a fruit, the flesh of a pig, the body of a person, the hull of a canoe. At a third level, a token of the MATERIAL ESSENCE of some particular individual member of the targeted class is represented: the particular trunk of a particular tree, for example. The label *hkano* is used for each of these concepts. We might designate the most general representation $hkano_0$, the MATERIAL ESSENCE of some par-ticular 'species' as $hkano_1$ and the representation of a particular token as $hkano_2$ (see Jackendoff 1985 for our use of the type/token distinction).

The specification of EFFICACIOUS IMAGE is, if anything, even more complex. It is abstractly defined as a distinguished and significant way in which some object in some class, C (possibly the whole category C), bears a resemblance to (something in) another class, C', that has a MATERIAL ESSENCE. The pairing of an EFFICACIOUS IMAGE and a MATERIAL ESSENCE for culturally significant entities constitutes an inherently dualistic theory of existence. This is not a mind/body dualism, nor yet a body/soul dualism, but rather a MATERIAL-ESSENCE/EFFICACIOUS-IMAGE dualism. The EFFICA-CIOUS IMAGE of a given 'species' involves some single trait from among the default traits.[9] This trait has to be something other than that which constitutes the MATERIAL ESSENCE of the 'species'. A pig's grunt, the three depressions resembling those at the base of the coconut shell, the shadow of a human being, the outrigger pontoon of a canoe which resembles in overall shape the hull proper. For some 'species', notably for human beings, there are several EFFICACIOUS IMAGES, each defined with some characteristic other than that which constitutes the MATERIAL ESSENCE. In every case, the default feature or features indicative of an EFFICACIOUS IMAGE are not called *ata* (EFFICACIOUS IMAGE) when instantiated in the targeted 'living' thing itself, but only when instantiated in a member of some other domain such as rocks, shadows or pontoons. The concept

EFFICACIOUS IMAGE is inherently relational, cross-referencing categories of diverse domains: foods and rocks, human beings and rocks, or human beings and shadows, hulls and pontoons. The pairing of *hkano* and *ata* presupposes that life has a dual nature. This dualism exists in the magical relation betwen a MATERIAL ESSENCE and its EFFICACIOUS IMAGE.

Three levels of representation are also involved for EFFICACIOUS IMAGE: Ata_0 labels the general theory of significant likenesses and implied magical connections; Ata_1 labels the coupling of this theory with some particular 'species' and the resulting selection of particular characteristics of that 'species' as indicative of an EFFICACIOUS IMAGE; Ata_2 is the token representation of the EFFICACIOUS IMAGE in some particular object.

By now it is surely obvious that specifying the internal representation of these concepts is formally complex; but, in addition, it should be clear that these concepts are complex in our second sense as well. For, in specifying their internal representations we cannot get away from articulating the larger theories in which these concepts are embedded. Discovering their meaning is emphatically not a process of simply pointing to the world, but is rather a matter of being provided with an elaborately constructed world-view within which these concepts arise, and become meaningful.

MATERIAL ESSENCE and EFFICACIOUS IMAGE are complex by virtue of their embedding in a theory of a domain. Their definitions must arise as theorems of this domain. Some elements of such a theory are given in the premises above. Basically, according to the people of West Futuna when speaking with respect to their traditional cosmology, material things are governed by metaphysical forces that can only be controlled by an intelligent being, typically a human being with the proper knowledge and means of expression through speech and a song that have been handed down ultimately from the supernatural. Such a knowledgeable individual may direct magic to ensure the health, great size and/or abundance of things with a MATERIAL ESSENCE by acting upon the appropriate EFFICACIOUS IMAGE. One ensures the abundance, great size and health of island pigs by acting upon a rock that makes a pig-like sound when struck. When people fail to perform the necessary rituals associated with the *ata* of culturally significant things, these things decline in health, size and number. The *ata* are typically quite particular things which have been present from the time of creation either as an original gift from the supernatural, in the case of rocks, or as an inalienable part of a larger whole, in the case of shadows, choruses and canoe outriggers. Experts today know of their existence from having learned from previous generations.

These concepts, then, labelled *hkano* and *ata*, are theorems with respect to some larger, encyclopedic theory of the world. Although this theory employs universal elements, it is a culturally particular construction in which selected universal, and possibly also purely parochial, elements are combined. What is the domain to which *hkano* and *ata* belong? Possibly, the theory of the principles of life is the most basic metaphysical theory in which these concepts arise, yet as we have seen, their complete specification entails other domains as well. Whatever the most basic theory is, *hkano* and *ata* are defined with respect to one another within this domain, but not by anything as simple as direct binary contrast. Identical features with opposite binary values are certainly not centrally involved here. Nor, to speak in terms of traditional cognitive anthropology, is there a larger contrast set for which proper analysis would yield such a paradigmatic relation between these two concepts. Rather, these concepts are paired exclusively with one another and are 'causally' related within a theory of the fundamental principles held to govern life. Their constitutive features at the most abstract level may or may not all be orthogonal to one another. The lexico-semantic features for *hkano* and *ata* are derived by shared access to theories of the typical characteristics of particular 'species', but the features themselves of the two categories bear no necessary or predictable relation to one another save for the fact that they must not be the same. *Hkano* and *ata* share a cross-referencing of domains that is integral to their conceptual representation, but this cross-referencing is considerably more complex than any mechanism of binary contrast can specify.

MATERIAL ESSENCE and EFFICACIOUS IMAGE are clearly not related by polysemy at an immediate, or superficial, level to other concepts, although, as we have shown, there is a hierarchical polysemy constituting the conceptual representation. Indeed, these concepts, while central to traditional cosmology, do not appear to be easily subject to further direct polysemous elaboration. In fact, there appears to be a constraint against just this sort of conceptual complexity with respect to *hkano* and *ata*, as evidenced by the following observations.

Christianity was introduced to the island of West Futuna late in the nineteenth century. The Reverend William Gunn, who came to Futuna at the turn of the century and remained on the island for more than a decade, worked during that time to translate biblical stories and many hymns into the native language. Gunn encountered difficulty in translating the Christian concepts BODY and SOUL and ultimately settled on the traditional words *ata* and *hkano*, respectively. The reason behind this particular choice seems to have been the obvious perception that the concepts labelled by these words were central to traditional cosmology and, Gunn thought, contained elements of the Christian concepts. Perceiving the symbolic importance of MATERIAL ESSENCES to the traditional cosmology, Gunn, it seems, hoped to retain the connotations of centrality and significance from the traditional notion MATERIAL ESSENCE and yet replace the denotation with the concept SOUL. *Ata* then, by contrast, became BODY, the less important element of life by Christian standards and, Gunn believed, the less important aspect of the traditional cosmology as well (Capell 1958: 35). This translation, while it retains the central traditional labels, completely alters their definitions and imports them into an entirely different domain and theory, those of Christianity. In fact, part of what is wrong is precisely that Gunn imagined the two to form a superficial binary contrast set.

From what is reconstructable historically it appears that *hkano* and *ata* in the Christian context were rapidly modified in linguistic form by the islanders themselves in order to avoid polysemic complexity. The process was a relatively simply one linguistically. Concepts like BODY and SOUL fall into a paradigm of inalienable things, which should properly be marked as possessed with a third-person-inalienable morphological form. These concepts, like body parts and things that envelop the human body, always occur in West Futunan with a possessive pronoun from one of the inalienable-pronoun paradigms. In the case of BODY and SOUL the appropriate third-person form is *tano*. Therefore, in the Christian context *hkano* and *ata* always occurred as *tano-hkano* and *tano-ata*. The definite article in West Futunan is *ta*. A re-analysis of these forms as *ta-nohkano* and *ta-noata* (one's SOUL/BODY) followed quickly, differentiating the Christian terms from the traditional West Futunan words *hkano* and *ata* (Dougherty 1983). In fact, these two Christian usages today amount simply to near homonymy with respect to the traditional terminology. The Christian concepts are now marked as possessed by a different possessive pronoun, from the paradigm for alienable relationships of possession. 'His soul' or 'spirit' is *tiona nohkano* and 'his corporeal body' is *tiona moata*. The traditional concepts occur inalienably possessed, as *tano hkano* and *tano ata*. While some confusion does occur over the similarity between the two indigenous concepts and their labels and the introduced concepts of Christianity and their labels, the relevant domains of knowledge are kept remarkably distinct and the linguistic change described above is one process in the maintenance of that distinction.

'Extensions' and theoretical principles

One of the more difficult problems that this analysis raises is the specification of the class of 'living' things to which the concepts *hkano* and *ata* apply. *Hkano*, for example, occurs in expressions such as the following:

tano hkano iai 'what is its essential idea?' or *jikai ta hkano iai* 'there is no coherence in it' (more colloquially, perhaps, 'it makes no sense') with regard to speech or human action, which, of course, have *hkano*. It also refers to verses of a song as opposed to the refrain, to the voice as opposed to its echo or to the moral or point of a story as against its surface episodes. *Hkano* can be used to express THE MEAT OF SOMETHING, meaning its ESSENCE. A few other examples are *hkanonea*, literally MATERIAL ESSENCE THING, meaning 'naked human body' (viz., an embodiment of *hkano*); *hkano* 'taste', derived possibly from something like the ESSENCE OF A PROTOTYPICAL THING THAT HAS A *hkano* (i.e. edible meat and fruit).

Ata is used to refer to SHADOW, REFLECTION and IMAGE IN A PHOTO-GRAPH, although other terms may be used to refer to these things as well. It also refers to the sound of speech as against its meaning, the episodes of a story as opposed to its moral, the refrain of a song as against its verses. A model or a miniature version of something may be referred to as *ata*, for example a doll. The outrigger of a canoe is the *ata* of the main hull.

This surface complexity is best handled, we argue, by a coherent West Futunan theory of the principles of life. This requires further analysis of the internal representation of both MATERIAL ESSENCE and EFFICACIOUS IMAGE, and it requires a fuller analysis of the domain theories relevant to these concepts. Without this fuller analysis at hand yet, we still would argue that the class of culturally significant 'living' things to which the distinction between MATERIAL ESSENCE and EFFICACIOUS IMAGE applies includes human beings and their primary food sources. It also includes canoes because of their derivation from tree trunks, which embody living spirits. (Incidentally, coconuts also have a human origin, growing originally from the buried head of an ancestor.) The class includes, further, speech and song because of the unique association of these phenomena with human beings and the inherent power attributed to speech and song in the construction and maintenance of order. Possible reasons for the inclusion of playing cards in this class are discussed above. Anything referred to as *hkano* always has, as a concept, its *ata*. The MATERIAL ESSENCE is the direct form of something; the EFFICACIOUS IMAGE is an indirect way of accessing the true essence of something, primarily in the context of increase rites, but also in the abstract realm of linguistic meaning: for example, the episodes of a story are an image or reflection of its basic moral, what makes it possible, indirectly, to get at that moral or point; or, in the metaphorical language of chiefs, *ta furifesao*, utterances indirectly suggest a meaning; the former are the *ata* of the latter, which are the *hkano* of a chief's speech. The basic West Futunan theory of life governs the more prototypical cases of culturally significant things and their magic rocks. We do not find a prototype being extended here, but rather an abstract theory of entities and their inter-relations. Class membership, for those entities for which *hkano* and *ata* are relevant, is fixed by the theory of culturally significant 'living' things. Outside this class, extension is altogether inappropriate. A house, for instance, has no *hkano* and *ata*. Nor is there any context in which such an extension would be appropriate. While we are aware of Malinowski's caution regarding the risk of hypothetisation through lumping together homonymously symbolised concepts, our claims rest upon careful ethnography through which homonymy is distinguishable from true generalisation. However, though we argue that such an abstract theory is in principle specifiable, the problem of actually specifying this domain theory adequately remains with us.

It has been suggested (Boyer, this volume) that this larger domain of culturally significant living things is a sort of 'pseudo-natural kind', that is an extension of universal assumptions about the essence of natural kinds, roughly, classes of things linked by the (biological?) processes of self-production, to the realm of cosmology and religion. Relevantly to such a claim, ethnoscientific investigation for West Futuna reveals a basic taxonomy of living things in the universalist sense (Dougherty 1983). Yet, while extension may well be the issue here, reference to assumed essence and typical properties fails to provide an account of the principled basis for such an extension. It is towards the construction of just such an account that our research, reported here, is directed. When we consider extension from a domain of natural kinds, we must look for clear evidence that the relations among classes in the domain of such an extension has the structure of a proper taxonomy rather than that of a network of inter-class cross-references. More precisely still, unless the otherwise rather vague notion of 'extension' is clarified, any such claim is largely unassessable. For instance, taking 'extension' as plausibly some kind of map from a kind of structure (that, say, of a taxonomy) to another structure, is that map structure-preserving (in which case alone it will necessarily follow that the domain of the map is itself a taxonomy); is it a homomorphism, an isomorphism, or perhaps something as loose as a category-theoretic morphism? In the latter case, particularly, the domain of the map (of the 'extension') need not be understood as itself some sort of natural kind.

Conclusions

The approach developed above requires profound revisions to standard views and assumptions of traditional anthropology:

1 A domain is not a collection of objects, possibly closed under the operation of binary-feature contrast. It is to be accounted for, rather,

under a much richer conceptual theory, as a domain theory or knowledge structure within encyclopedic knowledge more generally. Any domain of interest, in the case exemplified maybe the principles of life or resemblance and its significance, need not be given *a priori*. A domain need not be universally defined in any obvious way; the one in question is unlike ANIMAL, PLANT or COLOUR in this sense. We have found it necessary in analysing concept definitions to start with an intensional description of the domain(s) governing them. Unlike domains such as colour, where anthropologists and informants can immediately play the language/ concept game together, the body of knowledge relevant to *hkano* and *ata* had to be discovered through long and tedious hours of questioning by the anthropologists. The islanders set the rules for the game and it was up to the anthropologists to discover them. Possibly, comparative study would allow some sort of universalist analysis, but we cannot assume this as our starting point.

The common focus of traditional cognitive anthropology on contrast sets, which, it was argued, were empirically given, such as kinds of BEER (Hage 1972) or FLOPS (Spradley 1972), prevented elaborations of these studies in the direction of clarifying the culturally significant domain theories in which the contrast sets were embedded.

2 The number of domain-constituent output categories may be quite small. In the case analysed above, the number may be just six, that is, those conceptual distinctions labelled by *hkano* and *ata*. In fact, these may be the only basic categories generated in the domain. The relations between these concepts are not simple contrast as given by opposite values of binary features in a matrix whose dimensions are nothing but such features (usually orthogonal to one another), but rather a form of effective relations (a generalisation of the idea of 'cause and effect' to such cases: see especially Weathers n.d.) given by the theory of the domain.

3 Concepts such as these may arise as theorems of a domain and be taken on faith rather than empirically motivated.

4 The formal mechanisms required for stating concept definitions here are far more complex than a simple listing of features. Minimally, hierarchical polysemy is required for concept definition in this case, but other formal mechanisms will certainly be required for specifying fully the intensional definitions and relevant domain theories.

5 The approach developed here argues for more complex and intersecting knowledge structures (domains) in the universe of cognitive constructions

and computations, rather than neat, isolated, mutually exclusive taxonomies. Intersection amongst knowledge structures, however, is no argument against some form of the modularity hypothesis with regard to cognition, an issue we are not going to pursue here, however, save for pointing out that the idea of a distinction between knowledge structures and lexico-semantic representation is understood by us as being motivated by the need for a modular language faculty to access, and be accessed by, the wider range of cognitive systems (see Chomsky 1985).

Some more general implications of this research are summarised below:

1 A priority in the study of conceptual organisation must be the development of a formal theory of the constraints on concept definition.
2 All concepts, with the exception of those defined exclusively in terms of primes, must be analysed with respect to the theory of knowledge within which they are embedded.
3 These two facets of concept definition, formal specification and conceptual embedding, subsume a theory of concept complexity.

NOTES

A large part of this essay was previously published in *Cognitive Science*, 15 (March 1991).

1 What goes along with the view we propound here, though we are not going to pursue it or assert categorically that it is a necessary conclusion, is that the appropriate version of set theory to apply in all this is not the Zemielo–Fraenkel axiomatics, to which alone Lakoff refers in his arguments, but rather a Gödel–Bemays–von Neumann axiomatics that includes crucially the distinction between Sets and Proper Classes (see Lehman 1985 for references and argument). It ought to be clear to a careful reader of Lakoff that his arguments against the objectivist use of set theory in category definition and in a technical theory of knowledge and meaning do not go through if Proper Classes, taken as Sets paired with, let us say, intensional specifications, are distinguished and not embeddable in one another. Subsequent notes will further specify the nature of our version of non-objectivist theory.
2 PARENT may be defined as a prime structure of a terminological system (Read 1984) or as a constructed definition in Primary Genealogical Space from which the particular relationship categories and the terms labelling them are projected as a category-theoretic mapping (Lehman & Witz 1974; Witz & Lehman 1979). The two representations are provably compatible just in case the features normally characterising componential definitions of terms are allowed to arise as theorems, or natural computations, in a genealogical algebra of lines and compositions of lines, rather than being given arbitrarily, by brute force.
3 Our example from kinship further illustrates conceptual embedding. If the algebra of Primary Genealogical Space is allowed to underlie the algebraic structure (e.g. Read 1984) of a culturally particular category-and-terminological system, it is clear that the whole apparatus of the algebra of Primary Genealogical Space and the mapping rules collapsing this universal space into a

more compact and culturally particular one cannot plausibly be supposed to be directly contained in the lexical specification of each, or any, particular kinship term. We have, rather, a proper domain of concepts (e.g. a Read algebra for a given kinship system) that arises as a category-theoretic morphism out of a quite different and more universal, hence comprehensive, algebra, that of Primary Genealogical Space.

4 We take the position that a natural lexicon must be ordered conceptually, with the concepts mapped to particular phonological strings, rather than as a listing of phonological forms, which leads to the idea of polysemous entries comprising a discretely branching taxonomic tree in the sense of Katz & Fodor (1963).

5 This has the important advantage of allowing for a comprehensive (and non-Fregean) idea of quantification. Lehman has demonstrated this elsewhere (1985); and also that the members of such categories are entirely conceptual entities, so that, in particular, the apparent fuzziness of the notion of membership comes from an instantiation problem. This entails that fuzziness has to do with whether any object of sense, any perceptual thing, any item of experience (or even of the imagination, in the colloquial sense – as when one has a weird dream and attempts to describe or characterise something in it) is taken as plausibly meeting or not meeting the conditions of some schema/theorem or some concept theory. It may not be clear whether or not there exist reasons to take an entity, in this special sense of entity, as meeting those conditions of membership (not at all necessarily the same thing as just a check-list of perceptual features). For example, one simply may not know whether a certain mutilated carcass is or is not the body of a dog; is it a dead dog or not? Or it may be undecidable whether the membership of an entity that technically meets such conditions of membership is really worth considering as salient when its membership in some competing category is far more important, relevant, interesting or the like. This, of course, nicely disposes of the supposed fuzziness or membership gradience of the category of lies in English (Coleman & Kay 1981), the problems which cannot be overcome by Lakoff's (1987) treatment or that of the references there cited. None of the foregoing needs to be taken as supposing that the phenomena of fuzziness/gradience necessarily implicate graded category membership. It is only necessary to remember that categories in the mind can be classical in the membership sense without its being required, as on the objectivist view, that they correspond to objective natural kinds, especially in the sense of discrete taxonomies of such natural kinds. It is at this point that the remarks (in note 1 above) about Sets and Proper Classes has its application.

6 These lexical items (etyma, more properly) are widespread throughout Polynesia (e.g. Biggs 1975). Meanings associated with them in other Polynesian languages are often related to their senses on West Futuna, and yet the particular lexico-semantic conceptual structure discussed in the present chapter is nowhere exactly replicated as far as Keller has been able to discover. Capell (1958) records these distinctions for West Futuna and Keller's work builds on this earlier record. Guiart (1961) translates *ata* as 'the spirit of a dead man' for the Niwa. In addition, the concept labelled *ata* in Tikopia, as discussed by Firth (1967), is very similar to the named concept in West Futuna.

7 Such a theory could be either grander, or more particular, than Johnson's (1987) metaphors but quite possibly could subsume them.

Encyclopedic knowledge may encompass many, and quite possibly all, domain theories for two reasons. First, it seems likely that for any given culture certain axioms may be common to more-or-less every domain/K-structure. These premises constitute less than an holistic, or global, structure for a culture but may be sufficient to account for the ubiquity of certain theorems and category relations across K-structures. Secondly, domain theories, K-structures in their minimal specification, may intersect, so that embedded concepts in one domain may call up the theories of other domains. In any case, the distinction between encyclopedic and lexico-semantic knowledge is motivated by an explicit theory of the organisation of the natural lexicon and the way it necessarily interfaces with the rest of our cognitive capacities.

8 For reasons Lehman (1985) has gone into elsewhere concerning the infinite regress problems and parsimony problems connected unavoidably with collapsing the distinction between encyclopedic knowledge and lexico-semantic representations, and in spite of Johnson's (1987: 187ff.) arguments linking what he calls background to meaning indissolubly, it seems necessary to maintain this distinction. We need a finitary version of lexico-semantic meaning as an account of the linguistic/lexical coding of understanding. This is consistent with the programme of embedding linguistic knowledge within a broader theory of cognition and is important for that part of the programme that is intended to overcome the not uncommon tendency to extension of linguistic semantics to cover all of cognition.

9 We have to allow for at least the possibility that these may include traits filled in by redundancy rules from the larger encyclopedic base. While it is true that all coconuts, or at least all well-formed and mature ones, have three depressions at the base of the inner shell, it seems counter-intuitive to suppose that this particular identifiable feature of the stereotypical coconut (stereotypical in the sense of Wierzbicka 1985) has to be a part of the minimal lexico-semantic definition of COCONUT.

4 'Earth' and 'path' as complex categories: semantics and symbolism in Kwaio culture

Roger Keesing

In the last decade, sporadic attempts have been made to bridge the gulf between cognitive anthropology and various modes of symbolic/interpretative anthropology.[1] It is no surprise that these efforts have achieved only limited success, given the seemingly irreconcilable differences between the philosophical/epistemological premises of scholars on each side of the divide. On one side, cognitive anthropologists mainly share with other cognitive researchers assumptions that approximations to truth regarding the organisation and processing of knowledge (in our society or in others) can be achieved by applying inductive and experimental methods: by collecting and rigorously analysing data. On the other side, symbolists take anthropology's task to be mainly interpretative, more akin to literary criticism than physics; and they regard the empiricism and scientism of cognitive anthropology as inappropriate to the study of humans and their cultural traditions.

The divide, with its historical origins in nineteenth-century continental social thought, remains wide. However, some productive discourse has been taking place across the chasm, as cognitive science becomes less narrow and in some respects, less confidently messianic; some artificial-intelligence researchers and linguists now look to phenomenology for insights.

Anthropological attempts to apply recent developments in cognition and semantics to complex and symbolically salient cultural categories, going beyond the older preoccupations of cognitive anthropology with folk classification, invite further dialogue, in both directions. Here, I will suggest that recent developments in the study of categorisation (especially the work of Lakoff on conventional metaphor and prototypy) give anthropologists the means to make more systematic and theoretically grounded sense of 'symbolic' meanings. I take as texts the semantics and symbolic ramifications of two categories in Kwaio, an Oceanic Austronesian language spoken on Malaita, Solomon Islands.

The Kwaio-speaking people living in the mountains above the east central coast of Malaita are an anachronism in the contemporary Pacific.

Fiercely traditionalist, they preserve many elements of their pre-colonial way of life. Resisting Christian evangelism, they continue to sacrifice pigs to ancestral spirits, and to follow the complex rules of pollution and purity the ancestors impose. Resisting capitalist penetration, they continue to give mortuary feasts using strung shell valuables, and cultivate subsistence crops in mountain swiddens. Resisting incorporation into the post-colonial state as they resisted incorporation into the colonial state, they defy the government over issues of taxation and law.

Cognitive models and Kwaio culture

In my first Kwaio fieldwork twenty-five years ago, I attempted to apply currently prevailing methods and models of cognitive anthropology, seeking to go beyond ethnographic semantics in the direction pioneered by Goodenough on Truk (1951) and explored by Frake among the Subanun (1962): to analyse the implicit 'rules' underlying Kwaio social organisation on the model of a 'cultural grammar' (see Keesing 1982b and 1987a for retrospective assessments of this project). According to the canons of the ethnographic semantics ('ethnoscience') of the time, one could begin with no *a priori* assumptions about the categories that would be culturally salient in another people's conceptual world. We were to find out what the 'things' in a people's world were through the lexical labels of their language.

In describing Kwaio social structure, I adopted a set of Kwaio labels for the ethnographic categories I distinguished. This procedure, according to the canons of the time, validated an ethnographer's claim that the units of analysis were culturally salient, not imposed on the data. For the territories centred around focal shrines that were the estates of descent-based groups, I used the term *fanua*, 'place, territory'. For these descent-based groups, I used the term *tau* (which in other contexts referred to men's houses); for the settlements scattered through a group's territory, I used the term *ifi* (which in other contexts referred to dwelling houses). In learning and speaking Kwaio, I was aware of the rich polysemy of these and other categories;[2] but the paradigm in which I was operating impelled me to attach labels to particular 'things' as if this labelling were invariant and simple.

The semantics of *fanua* in Kwaio will serve to illustrate. This is an old Austronesian word (Proto-Austronesian *banu*[w]a) for 'land'; cognate forms are widespread in Oceanic languages. In Kwaio, *fanua* can perhaps most simply be glossed as 'home place': but what constitutes the relevant home place is contextually determined. It often is used in the sense I assigned to it in my descriptions, to describe the estate of a descent-based group, made up of a patchwork of separately named land tracts clustered around the group's original or focal shrine. *Fanua aga* is 'their territory', *fanua i 'Ai'eda* is 'the 'Ai'eda territory'; but it is sometimes used to refer to a person's settlement (what I had chosen to label as *ifi* 'house' in my ethnographic accounts). It can be used to refer to a more inclusive, as well as less inclusive, 'home place'. Kwaio speakers away from Malaita regularly use *fanua ada* 'our home place' to refer to their Kwaio homeland. Sometimes *fanua naa ta'a kwao* 'the home place(s) of the white people' is used to refer to Europe, the Americas, Australia and New Zealand.

In the 1960s, the limitations of ethnographic semantics, as developed through the early analyses of folk taxonomies and componential analyses of kinship terminologies, constrained interpretative possibility in the tradition in which I was working.[3] At the same time, Victor Turner was exploring the rich multivocality of ritual symbols among the Ndembu – the multiple levels of meaning of *mudyi*, the 'milk tree', in representing breast milk, purity, matriliny (Turner 1967); but these universes of discourse were poles apart. Twenty-five years after my first Kwaio research, interpreting the semantic structures of categories richly laden with cultural symbolism lies not far beyond our grasp.

New developments in prototype semantics

In a series of important experiments and papers, Eleanor Rosch proposed that categorisation operates not in terms of Aristotelian necessary and sufficient conditions for category membership, but through a logic of prototypy. The prototypic exemplars of categories were demonstrably more cognitively salient, more easily and quickly learned, than atypical members. In recent work, Rosch has moved away from a position that the way categorisation is learned or used in experimental contexts adequately represents the cognitive structure of the categories. As Lakoff (1987) observes, 'prototype effects' are by-products of category structures. Exploration of the complex internal structure of categories, as cognitive representations, is still in its early stages; but impressive progress has been made.

Lakoff (1987) proposes that human categorisation is based on what he calls 'idealized cognitive models' (ICMs). Complex semantic categories are built through the combination of several ICMs, producing what he calls 'cluster models'. In explicating the nature of cluster models, Lakoff (1987: 74–6, 79–84) examines the category 'mother' in English. He argues that it is impossible to give a classical Aristotelian definition of 'mother' that 'will give clear, necessary, and sufficient conditions' for inclusion in the category and 'will fit all the cases and apply equally to all of them'

(p. 74). Lakoff proposes that a series of idealised cognitive models, what he calls 'base models', intersect to 'form a cluster model'. These include:

The *birth* model: the person who gives birth is the mother.

The *genetic* model: the female who contributes the genetic material is the mother.

The *nurturance* model: the female adult who nurtures and raises a child is the mother of that child.

The *marital* model: the wife of the father is the mother.

The *genealogical* model: the closest female ancestor is the mother.

These base models themselves may be based on further ICMs, as the category 'adoptive mother' illustrates. This category of a special kind of mother rests on an idealised cognitive model of adoption (in terms of which adoption of a child by a gay couple, or a lesbian couple, must be defined by categorical extension: in the latter case, are there two adoptive mothers or is there one female father?). The fact that an adoptive mother has a legal status as female co-guardian, and is (often) represented on a fictionalised birth certificate as if she were the genetrix, in contrast to a foster mother (whose status in a 'fosterage ICM' is based on the nurturance model, but may similarly be established in law), suggests that Lakoff's list of base models is incomplete.

Of course, as Lakoff observes, the possible divergence between these models has increased with modern scientific developments, such as genetic engineering and *in vitro* fertilisation. But as he points out (1987: 76), even the concept 'real mother' is ambiguous in terms of these models, as witness:

'I was adopted and I don't know who my real mother is.'

'I am not a nurturant person, so I don't think I could ever be a real mother to any child.'

I have elsewhere noted that any native English speaker understands without difficulty a sentence that builds directly on these ambiguities: 'My real mother wasn't a real mother to me.'

All this leaves aside such further modern possibilities as:

'I had a genetic mother who contributed the egg that was planted in the womb of my real mother, who gave birth to me and raised me.'

Lakoff (1987: 76) observes that 'we get compound expressions like stepmother, surrogate mother, adoptive mother, foster mother, biological mother, donor mother, etc ... Such compounds ... do not represent simple sub-categories, that is, kinds of ordinary mothers. Rather, they describe cases where there is a lack of convergence of the various models.'

Lakoff goes on to note how a complex categorical structure may be constructed through metonym and metaphor as well as the convergence of base models. He shows how the category working mother represents not simply someone who is a mother who happens to be working, but is defined in contrast to a stereotype of a housewife–mother, which is itself constructed in terms of the nurturance model of motherhood. 'Consider an unwed mother who gives up her child for adoption and then goes out and gets a job. She is still a mother, by virtue of the birth model, and she is working – but she is not a working mother!' (1987: 80).

Although Lakoff here treats metaphoric extensions of categories only in passing with reference to mothers, his own work (with Mark Johnson and Zoltan Kövecses) on conventional metaphor shows how ICMs open metaphoric connections. Den mothers are not a kind of mother, but are like them in terms of the nurturance model. Nor is a Mother Superior a kind of mother; but she is mother-like in terms of both nurturance and authority. Necessity is the mother of invention in terms of the birth model, but only by drawing a metaphoric connection between birth and causality. Metaphor also generates derived verbal forms: to mother someone is to act like a (nurturant) mother. Lakoff describes as radial structures categories such as 'mother' in which extensions from the central case are based on conventionalised variations from it that 'cannot be predicted from general rules' (1987: 84).

I might note in passing that many of the anthropological debates about 'kinship terminology' evaporate if we apply these semantic models. It is not, as Scheffler and Lounsbury would have it, that 'classificatory kin terms' as semantic categories are internally structured by mechanical genealogical extension from a focal kin type, and that the association of a behavioural role with a kin term is only contingent, a matter of connotation. Nor is it, as Schneider and many of his students have imagined, that kinship categories are defined non-genealogically, just because some people are included in the category even though they are not genealogically related, or are genealogically related in the 'wrong' way. The prototypic *tama*, in Fijian – to use Hocart's classic example – is ego's genealogical father, but also mother's husband, guardian, senior member of ego's household, member of ego's descent group, etc. Non-prototypical *tama* may share with the prototypical *tama* a set of genealogical features; but their classification as *tama* may be based on relative age, descent-group membership or behavioural role. That is, at least in a particular context, a Fijian may be someone else's *tama* by virtue of some but not all elements of prototypical *tama*-ness, including non-genealogical elements. To define *tama* as something like 'domiciled male of father's sub-clan hamlet' (in the style of Leach with Trobriand kinship) would fail utterly to capture the complex internal structure of the category, whereby a person's *tama* differ in their kind and degree of *tama*-ness (including a clear markedness relationship, where if you ask a Fijian who his *tama* is he can only appropriately give you the name of his 'real' father). I believe that most of the anthropological arguments about 'genealogy' and 'category' are by-products of deeply flawed semantic theories that can now be discarded.

Lakoff goes on (1987: 91–107) to illustrate the power of his analysis of radial categories (like 'mother' in English) with an interpretation of two grammaticalised classifier systems, those of Dyirbal (an Australian Aboriginal language studied by Dixon and Schmidt) and Japanese. For Japanese, he focuses on *hon*, used for long thin objects and – by extension and metaphor – for telephone calls, television programmes, long baseball hits and pitches and letters. The use of the Japanese classifier *hon* for actions involving a trajectory – pitches or balls hit a long way – is particularly interesting, in that it involves what Lakoff calls one 'image schema' – a (long, thin) trajectory – being conventionally depicted as a transform of another – the image of a prototypical long, thin object. Lakoff notes (1987: 105–6) that a corresponding 'image-schema transformation' equating a physical shape or spatial orientation to a trajectory motivates uses of 'up' ('stand up' and 'shoot up') in English. He further examines the image-schema transformation that connects 'The man ran into the woods' with 'The road ran into the woods'. Such image-schema transformations seem to be basic in human categorisation. Lakoff argues, drawing on the work of his philosopher–collaborator Mark Johnson (1987), that the spatial imagery on which categorisation – and metaphor – depend is deeply grounded in bodily experience, hence in an important sense 'natural'.

Some semantic categories build directly on a kind of flip-flopping between image schemas. Lakoff illustrates with 'window' in English, which is used both for an aperture in a wall (as in 'cut a window') and for the transparent covering for such an aperture ('break the window').

The spatial imagery represented by such concepts as a (prototypical) long, thin object or a linear trajectory reflects Gestalt, relational patterns grounded in perceptual experience. An image-schema transformation requires that one relational pattern be viewed as a transform of another. Conventional metaphors posit 'a relationship between the idealized cognitive models of ... two domains', entailing 'an experientially based mapping from an ICM in one domain to an ICM in another domain' (Lakoff 1987: 417). This is one basis for polysemy. Here Lakoff draws on the work of Claudia Brugman (1981) on prepositions in English to show how 'lexical items are natural categories of senses' (Lakoff 1987: 418) depending on a relational, imagery-based logic. Brugman asks what cognitive gymnastics connect the senses of 'over' in such phrases as:

talk over the fence;
talk over the problem;
talk over the telephone.

She identifies some eighty senses of 'over' in everyday English, and shows how they are connected to one another through image-based transformations.

It is important to make explicit the relationship of 'image schemas', and the transformations that connect them, to metonymy and metaphor. Lakoff sees metonymy and metaphor (as characterised in semiotic theory) as requiring analysis and explication. Consider the following (very partial list of) modes of metonymic connection:

1 a part is used to represent a whole;
2 an exterior surface is used to characterise what lies underneath;
3 the starting point of a process is used to characterise the whole process;
4 the goal of a sequence of action is used to characterise the sequence.

Lakoff would see each of these as requiring a different image-schema transformation. Metaphor requires that a relational pattern in one domain be likened to a relational pattern in another (e.g. time is space, ideas are buildings, life is a journey). Image-schema transformations, in Lakoff's terms, are required to conceptualise a pattern in one domain so that it corresponds to a domain in another. To understand 'around five o'clock', we must perform two conceptual operations, and connect them: conceptualise spatial proximity as though it were a circle around a point; and conceptualise a point in time as though it were a point in space.

Natural categorisation, metaphor and models of mind

These new approaches to categorisation have important implications for anthropological conceptions of *la pensée sauvage*. Lévi-Strauss and those who followed him in structuralist interpretations of primitive classification, ritual symbolism and mythologiques took as their paradigm of thought and perception – and cultural bricolage – the binary logic of the phoneme, as analysed in Jakobsonian linguistics. Language provided the model of mind, and the phoneme – defined in terms of binary oppositions – provided the model for language.

Recent developments in linguistics, in syntax as well as semantics, suggest that Jakobsonian phonemics provides a very limited model for language, and a very distorted paradigm of *la pensée humaine*. The logic that emerges in semantic studies is an experientially grounded Gestalt logic of relationships and patterns. The logic of metaphor depends on relational-image transformations quite different from the formulaic transformations and mediations explored by Lévi-Strauss. The connection between long thin objects and trajectories, or a man running through the woods and a road running through the woods, is not a matter of oppositions and mediators, but of Gestalt imagery and pattern recognition. Lévi-Strauss himself reflected, at the very end of *Mythologiques* (1969b), on the paradoxes with which his own project had confronted him: the patterning of music defied representation in terms of a logic of dyadic opposition. But so, too, does the human ability to recognise faces, or read handwriting – as artificial-intelligence researchers have long since discovered.

It is the ability to perceive relational patterns, the Gestalt logic of the mind deeply grounded in bodily experience, that gives metaphor such a pervasive power in *la pensée humaine*. This logic of pattern and metaphor is pervasive and dominant in language. It operates not only in semantics, but is turning out to lie at the very heart of syntax as well. The concept of causation, as represented in grammatical systems, will serve to illustrate. The prototypic conception of causality – in language after language – is intentional physical manipulation of an object by a human agent. Yet the grammaticalisation of causal relationships in causative constructions characteristically extends this prototype by metaphoric/analogic connections, to a range of relationships not involving physical manipulation. Similarly, transitive constructions build on a prototypical relationship between an agent, a physical act, and a physical object: 'John hit the ball'; but they extend them metaphorically, as in 'John felt the cold'. This latter illustrates how such fundamental syntactic categories as nouns and verbs are constructed around prototypes: 'feel' is a prototypic verb in 'John felt the texture', and 'ball' is a prototypic noun. Feeling the cold requires a metaphoric leap for both verb and noun. As Lakoff (1987: 290) observes, 'although grammatical categories as a whole cannot be given strict classical definitions in semantic terms, their central subcategories can be defined in just that way. The remaining members of . . . each grammatical category [are] motivated by their relationships to the central members.' Linguists are studying the operation of metaphor and a logic of prototypy in grammar diachronically as well as synchronically. In the process being called 'grammaticalisation', lexical forms progressively become grammatical elements – verbal auxiliaries, tense and aspect markers, classifiers, complementisers; and webs of metaphoric connection link grammatical senses to the lexical ones from which they have developed.

What ever happened to the phoneme? Phonemes have not vanished from linguistics, but they can no longer be taken as revealing the central architecture of language. Phonemic systems represent a kind of infrastructure on which the central structures of language are constructed. (Indeed, there is some evidence that the structure of phonemes as categories depends on prototypy and Gestalt logic as well as binary opposition, although that would take us far afield.)

It is not that binary oppositions do not operate in thought and perception; but it would seem that a binary logic operates, in language and more generally in cognition, at a kind of infrastructural level and a kind of superstructural level: it is what lies in between what Lévi-Straussian structuralism misrepresents and distorts. Neural systems, like all information systems, operate with a binary logic at a kind of substrate level. An analogy may clarify. If it were not possible to represent spatial patterns binarily, then television transmission would be impossible. Musical patterns are represented digitally as well (or digital recordings and compact discs and audiotapes would be impossible). But the ability to distinguish Andrew Peacock from John Howard and Bob Hawke on television depends on perceiving Gestalt relational patterns. Pattern recognition has proved one of the most difficult areas of artificial-intelligence research precisely because binarily based algorithms inadequately and weakly simulate the power of *la pensée humaine* to cognise patterns.

Dyadic oppositions operate at a superstructural level as well: I would not question that eastern Indonesian peoples are preoccupied with cosmological dualisms. But a Jakobsonian model of phonemes, a logic of oppositions, fails utterly to capture the relational patterns of metaphor and analogy that allow eastern Indonesian peoples to use the semantic categories and grammatical systems of their languages – as well as to recognise one another.

Let me go back to questions of semantics. Can mappings of complex semantic relationships of the sort Lakoff has assayed illuminate the symbolically laden categories an anthropologist encounters among peoples such as the Kwaio? In examining one semantic category in Kwaio corresponding fairly closely to categories familiar from European languages and one category more 'exotic' in terms of our own, I will suggest that these new developments in semantic theory give us more powerful analytical instruments than those of early cognitive anthropology.

Wado: the polysemy of earth

The Kwaio word *wado* can, as a first approximation, be glossed as 'earth, soil, land, ground'. Some of its senses can be gleaned from these usages:

wado 'soil'
> *wadoburu* 'black, sticky soil variant'
> *wadolago* 'sticky soil variety, good for taro, not yams'
> *wado-la* 'covered with dirt, muddy'

wado 'land'
> *me'e wado* 'a (named) tract of land'
> *wado a-gu* 'the land over which I hold (joint) title'

wado 'the earth' (an introduced usage, mainly employed by Kwaio

Christians – the only ones who have had any exposure to English and the usages of 'earth'); this then leads to

fanua lo'oo[4] *i wado* 'the earth which is our home'

lo'ooi wado 'on earth (not in heaven)'

i wado 'on the ground' (*i* is a locative particle)

to'oru i wado 'sit on the ground, sit down'

takwe-a mai[5] *i wado* 'dig from the ground'

  ai ngai[6] *i wado* 'the one which is below' (vs. *ai ngai i langi* 'the one which is above' – this opposition is also used to contrast 'something unimportant'/'something important'

  eta mai i wado 'originate from the earth', used to express autochthonous origins of the Kwaio and their customs

wado-na 'his homeland, his place of origin'

We have in these usages a core or central cluster of senses and a radial structure in which metaphoric and metonymic connections extend outwards. The core structure of the category is based – as with *terre* in French and, less directly, 'earth' in English – on the relationship between soil, as the stuff of the earth, and the territory it covers, as the surface to which human lives are anchored. Semiotically, the two senses are bound in a relationship of metonymy in which substance and surface are transforms of one another.[7] Note the conceptual parallel between these connected senses and the senses of 'window' and 'door' for both aperture and object that fits into it. We have here what Lakoff (1987: 418) calls a 'natural category of senses'; but, of course, there is more to it than that: for cultivators, whether tribal or peasant, the soil/land is the medium of life. This metonymic linkage of soil as substance and land as territory is experientially deep and salient for much of the world's – the earth's – population. The soil from which humans derive their livelihood covers the land to which they are bound by history, by rights and obligations.[8]

If we begin to trace out the linkages from these central senses of *wado*, we find them radiating in several ways. One linkage connects the soil to the depths beneath, by a kind of metonymic spatial extension. To dig something from *wado* is to remove it from the soil, as a substance, but also to bring something hidden to the surface, from the below to the above (compare the metaphoric senses of 'unearth' in English).

The spatial relationship between lowering oneself to the ground or putting something on the ground and sitting on the ground is obvious enough (although the Brugman/Lakoff analysis of the semantics of 'over' (Lakoff 1987: 418–40) serves to remind us that what is intuitively obvious may be conceptually complex). In Kwaio, this spatial relationship is mapped through an image-schema transformation onto one of relative height, using the contrast *i langi* 'up above' versus *i wado* 'down below'. A garden, or settlement, or sago grove can be distinguished from another as 'one above' or 'one below'. I have heard two men named Ba'efaka distinguished as *Ba'efaka i langi*, the one who lives in the mountains, and *Ba'efaka i wado*, the one who lives in the lowlands. This 'above'/'below' contrast is, by a further metaphoric extension of this relative spatial sense, used to contrast something as important ('up above') with something unimportant.

In a recent paper (Keesing 1987b), I have discussed the way Kwaio refer to their customs and way of life as having *eta mai i wado* 'originated from the earth'. For most Kwaio, this apparently serves to account for, and legitimise, autochthonous origins and ultimate claims to their homeland without advancing any precise mythic claims about the past. As I have illustrated, folk philosophers sometimes make more of it than that, giving a kind of rhetorical substance to usually metaphorical talk.

The symbolic continuity between humans and the earth is reflected as well in the (relatively infrequent) Kwaio usage in which a possessive suffix indicating inalienable possession is attached to *wado*. *Wado-gu* is my homeland; my ultimate place of attachment (as opposed to *wado a-gu*, using the construction marking alienable possession, which is land to which I – and usually others – hold title).[9]

The conceptual complex in which 'soil' and 'land' are bound together in relation to ultimate origins and attachment has something of that 'primordial' character Needham (1964) and Douglas (1970) sought to capture in writing of 'natural symbols'. To explore what 'primordial' or 'natural' might reasonably mean here would take us into issues only peripheral to my argument. The symbolic construction of the earth as female, linking the fecundity of the soil to the fecundity of motherhood, seems deeply grounded (if the expression can be pardoned) in human primary experience. Both the relatively contentless references to the origins of humans and their way of life in the earth to which Kwaio are given and the occasional elaborations on this theme by folk philosophers ('We sprouted from *wado* like leaves; *wado* is like our mother ... ') build on this primordial symbolism.

The question of primordiality, in the generation of key symbols, raises an issue of considerable anthropological importance in relation to the nature of conventional metaphor (we need not go off on a discursion into Freudian or Jungian depth psychology). Lakoff, in correspondence, has suggested that no such primordiality need be implied here: only the conventional metaphoric proposition that PEOPLE ARE PLANTS. But where do conventional metaphoric schemas such as this come from? Lakoff & Johnson (1980; Johnson 1987) can be read as implying that the world-view of a people lives in and through their language, and that schemes of conventional metaphor rise relatively directly out of the experiences of embodiment. In a recent paper, Quinn (1987) suggests that the metaphoric universes proposed in a language reflect and are motivated by underlying cultural/cosmological beliefs to a much more important extent than Lakoff and Johnson have explicitly acknowledged. That is, culturally constructed universes of meaning crucially intervene between experience and conventional metaphor. I shall not pursue this issue further here, but it is important to note that lively debate is going on with regard to the nature of conventional metaphors, and hence the way they are expressed in semantic systems.

On what grounds are we to take the linked senses of *wado* as 'soil' and 'land' as constituting the conceptual core of the category, and other senses – such as that in which *i wado* is paired with *i langi* as down/lower/ unimportant versus up/higher/important – as derived from them?[10] Two mutually reinforcing answers emerge; mutually reinforcing in that I believe they will lead to the same answer. One approach would trace the internal geometry of categories. If sense A is connected to sense B in terms of one conceptual transformation, and sense B is connected to sense C in terms of a different conceptual transformation, and sense C and sense A have no direct connection, we can take B to be the primary sense, and A and C the derived ones. A second approach would appeal to universal grammatical principles, hierarchies of syntactic salience, markedness, etc. In terms of such comparative grammatical theory, we would not expect a form marked with a derivational affix (e.g. *wado-la* 'muddy', as contrasted with *wado* in root form) or a usage that fits only into a clausal periphery (as with the locative phrase *i wado*) to be conceptually primary (though no doubt every language incorporates some exceptions to these general principles through peculiarities of its history).

Although the semantics of *wado* shows some special cultural twists, the category is generally transparent to speakers of European languages, because the connections drawn are familiar from these languages and because they have the aura of primordiality on which I have touched. Note, however, that in analysing a complex cultural concept of this kind following the guidelines set out by Lakoff, even in such a sketchy way, we close considerably the gap between 'symbolic interpretation' and 'semantic analysis' that faced us in the 1960s – the gulf between Turner's Ndembu milk tree, with its rich panoply of symbolic reference, and componential analysis.

Componential analysis was not the only method of semantic description assayed in the early 'ethnographic semantics', but it will serve to make a further point. As I observed some fifteen years ago (Keesing 1972), the possibility of analysing semantic fields in terms of distinctive features whose intersection defined the necessary and sufficient conditions for membership in one category or another – as with the genealogical senses of kin terms, to which componential analysis was applied – depended on a kind of conjuring trick. The trick was to establish a particular contextual frame within which a set of lexical forms contrasted; holding this context constant, one could define formally the semantic contrasts between the forms.

To specify formally the spectrum of meaning of a kin term as it moves through different contextual frames is another matter. Consider English 'father' – simple enough in its genealogical sense. In its non-genealogical senses ('He was a father to me', 'Our other Father will take confession', 'Don't father me!', 'Our Father Who art ... '), we are often hard pressed to analyse the meanings, how they are related, or what contextual information enables us to understand them. What defines 'fatherness' in these senses is not a common feature or a common behavioural role but a relational pattern of which each sense is a transform (Keesing 1972: 19).

The new developments in semantics, seeking to explicate the 'relational patterns' of which different senses are transforms, of necessity address precisely the qualities that – through metaphor, metonymy and image-schema transformations – provide the bases for cultural elaborations of symbolism in ritual and myth. Moreover, by seeking to uncover the grounding of these conceptualisations in primary experience, Lakoff's analyses bring us to the same analytical problematic as Turner's theory of symbolic multivocality. The multivocal symbols used in ritual 'work' because they connect abstract, social meanings – motherhood, matriliny – to primary 'gut' experience – birth, breast milk, nurturance.

We can now turn to the semantics of a Kwaio category that, at least in some of its structures and ramifications, is less familiar and transparent to us.

The semantics of 'path'

Kwaio *tala* 'path', like *fanua*, represents an ancient Austronesian form.[11] In rugged, rainforest covered mountains, paths must be cut from dense growth, connecting tiny settlements, and linking them to gardens. Most often, *tala* simply refers to a path. It enters into constructions such as

>*talako'uta*
>*talanialafa*
>*talabono* 'men's latrine' (somewhat euphemistic terms, lit. 'short path', 'chief's path', 'blocked path')
>*maa-na tala* 'mouth of path' (where it enters the clearing)
>*tala gari* 'detour' (lit. 'circling path', – that is, one that goes around a flooded stream or other obstacle)

By a fairly direct extension, we get:

tala i asi 'by sea'

tala i langi 'by land' ('path up above')

Here, a particular sea route is likened to a path; and going by canoe, as contrasted with walking, is characterised as travelling by a sea path as opposed to an inland path.

By a metaphoric extension, based on the ease or difficulty of walking on a particular path, we get:

talawada'u 'easy' (of a task)

A more productive direction of semantic extension rests on an image-schema transformation whereby a path is equated with the track – that is, footprint – of a person walking on it. *Tala* by itself can be used to refer to a person's track. To refer to a person's footprint, as an identifying mark, *tala* is more commonly used in compounds, or with the possessive pronoun marking inalienable possession:

talafuri-na 'footprint; mark or residue where something has been'

tala-gu[12] 'my footprint, track'

Note that although 'path' has no such semantic association in English, 'track' does: it can designate a physical path or the marks left by a human or animal that has followed a path-like trajectory and, metaphorically at least, incised itself upon the ground.

In some contexts, in Kwaio, *tala-* with the inalienable possessive construction is the path a person is to take, the way that is to be followed, a person's trajectory. Thus:

tala-na wela 'the discharge that precedes a neonate's passage through the birth canal' (lit. 'path of the child')

Metaphorically, this opens up an important direction for semantic extension – one explored in many languages, and hence representing a further 'naturalness' cognitively and experientially. In this metaphoric image-schema transformation, the life-cycle is depicted as a path a person travels (based on a schema of LIFE AS A JOURNEY, in the language of Lakoff & Johnson 1980). We have, then, expressions such as:

tala'osi'a 'grow to maturity without being seriously ill, disfigured by injury, etc.' (lit. 'uninterrupted path')

More strikingly, we get a grammaticalised extension where *tala-gu* is the path of my life. Here the form occurs as the second element in a verbal compound:

suga tala-gu 'pay the way for me' (by having made a major contribution to my father's bridewealth)

taunga'i tala-na 'bring someone to maturity by working on their behalf' (lit. 'work the way for'); and, by further metaphoric extension, 'bring an event to fruition through one's work' *beri tala-na mae-na* 'bring death to him through one's stealing' (lit. 'steal the path of his death')

By further extension, 'things' can be conceptualised as having paths or trajectories:

ngai i tala-na 'it's separate, it's different' (lit. 'it's by itself', that is, on its own path)

Finally, Kwaio grammaticalises another extension of the metaphor of one's life as a path, to create the equivalent of reflexives: 'on his own path' is 'by himself'; 'our path' is 'ourselves'. Thus,

ta-ku age-a i tala-gu 'I'll do it myself' (lit. 'do it along my (own) path')

'agolo leka tala-dauru 'Let's (the two of us) go ourselves' (lit. 'go along our (own) path')

Fa'afeloa ka lolofe' enia mola mae fana tala-na 'Fa'afeloa connected the killing to himself' (that is, implicated himself, in this case falsely) (The last part is literally 'for-it his-path'; compare English 'he brought it on himself')

We have, in this Kwaio conceptualisation of paths – paths through jungles, paths through life, trajectories of being – a set of semantic connections that does not resonate as directly with our own as those of 'earth'. If the connections are in part unfamiliar, however, they are scarcely exotic, at least given the ways anthropologists have sometimes characterised the worlds of meaning culturally constructed by non-Western peoples. 'Path' metaphors are extensively developed in many of the world's languages, notably Austronesian languages, in ways congruent with – although inevitably different from – those elaborated in Kwaio.

Interpreting cultural categorisation

I would not want to over-interpret the linguistic data by asserting that the grammaticalisation of 'selfness' with *tala-na* has any implications for the Kwaio 'concept of self'. I have warned recently (in Keesing 1985, 1987b and 1990) of the dangers of ethnographers taking conventional metaphors too literally, in languages they speak less than perfectly, and creating non-existent cosmological designs. I fear that some recent anthropological writings on the cultural construction of 'person' or 'self' rest precariously on thin linguistic data, massively over-interpreted (see Keesing 1990). None the less, we find in the semantics of *tala*, as elsewhere in the stuff of Kwaio language, abundant evidence of pervasive schemas of conventional metaphor such as those Lakoff and his collaborators have identified in English, and strong evidence of radial semantic structures formally akin to those they have explored.

Moreover, although the worlds established by conventional metaphor cannot necessarily and uncritically be taken to represent cosmological beliefs of a theological kind, they are worlds in which speakers of a language are inextricably situated. For the Kwaio, last year is *farisi (ngai) lofo'u* 'year (it's) down there', and next year is *farisi (ngai) lolo'o mai* 'year (it's) coming from up there'. We need not suppose that Kwaio explicitly conceive of years marching past the speaker (or, as other Kwaio schemas of conventional metaphor might imply, of the speaker marching into the future and leaving years behind). Kwaio cannot conceptualise, cannot speak, except in and through such conventional metaphors; nor can we. Indeed, although recently such linguistics as Lakoff and Givón have occasionally written in a Whorfian vein that seems to imply great cultural variation, what strikes me in the recent work is how culturally unique constructions are fashioned out of systems of conventional metaphor and image-schema transformation that vary much less from language to language than they conceivably might. Lakoff observes of English (1987: 440) that 'there are certain very natural relationships among image-schemas, and these motivate polysemy, not just in one or two cases, but in case after case throughout the lexicon. Natural image-schema transformations play a central role in forming radial categories of senses.' The evidence from non-Western languages, although still sketchily analysed, suggests to me that many of these 'natural relationships' will turn out to operate in most or all of the world's languages. The Kwaio conceptual world strikes me as very much like our own in its structures and logics of categorisation and the naturalness of the relationships on which polysemy is based. To analyse Dyirbal or Japanese classifiers or Kwaio or English prepositions – not to mention lexical categories such as 'earth' or 'path' – we will not, I think, need to construct a separate theory or method or logic. Each cognised and experienced world will, I expect, turn out to be a complex transform of every other: a recognisably human world. If further exploration confirms that the metaphoric universes proposed in non-Western languages are seldom as 'exotic' as anthropological discourse might lead us to expect, and that 'natural relationships' logically structure polysemy – even though the 'uniqueness' of particular cultural elaborations cannot be questioned – the new developments will bear directly on recent debates about rationality and relativism that have engaged philosophers and anthropologists (see e.g. Hollis & Lukes 1982).

The symbolism of acts and objects central in Kwaio ritual (of which I have written in Keesing 1982a) builds on metaphoric equivalences and image-schema transformations formally similar to those that structure the polysemy of complex cultural categories. In Kwaio magic and ritual, stability is symbolised through acts of planting and implanting, and through enduring, stable objects (such as leaves that, when smoked, resist decay for many decades). Such symbolism relies on image-schema transformations and the invariance of relational patterns across domains: the stuff of metaphor and polysemy.

The semantics of the common Kwaio verb *ori* 'return' will illustrate the connection between the structure of a semantic category and patterns of magico-ritual symbolism. Used as a transitive verb, with a suffixed clitic pronoun, *ori-a* is 'turn back, send away'. A whole complex of Kwaio ritual and magic (these, in Kwaio, are inseparably connected) aims at preventing or curing illnesses caused by alien, malevolent spirits, through physical acts representing expulsion or banishment. A community *ori-a* the alien spirit(s) by dramatising a sending away of unwanted forces. Symbolic analysis of this *ori-nga* ('sending away') ritual and semantic analysis of the verb *ori* (which in other senses is used to characterise descent, incest and such mental processes as remembering and harbouring a grievance) are parallel and closely connected enterprises.

Two more examples will clarify the way the same conceptual equivalences motivate both magico-ritual acts (as 'symbolic' representations of desired states or processes) and the polysemy of semantic categories. I magically suppress a potential event or state of affairs by performing an act of pressing down an object; to *bibi-a* something is to press it down physically, or to suppress it magically.

Mamu is, in its physical senses, the irresistible attraction of scent. The *mamu* of flowers attracts insects; *mamu* is also the bait one throws in the water to chum fish – to draw them to the fisherman. By attracting them (you *fa'a-mamu-a* 'mamu-ise' the fish).[13] *Mamu* is also the complex of wealth-attraction magic central in Kwaio ritual (Keesing 1982a), which uses the irresistible attraction of scent as a powerful symbol. Thus aromatic shrubs are used magically to symbolise the irresistible attraction of valuables to a forthcoming mortuary feast. In the ritual sequences leading up to the feast, an aromatic shrub is chewed and spat – on puddings, on pigs, on chests and also into the ocean, to attract fish-that-will-attract-shell money. The feast-givers *fa'a-mamu-a* their potential guests and the valuables they will bring.

Once metaphor and image-schema transformation are rendered problematic, in terms of a semantic theory that does not spuriously hold contextual frames constant, semantic analysis becomes symbolic analysis, and vice versa. 'Semantic anthropology', a misleading label for one brand of interpretative anthropology when it was first coined, might yet become an apt term for a joint exploration on both sides of an old divide.

NOTES

1 I am grateful to George Lakoff and Naomi Quinn for helpful comments on the original version. Jim Fox, Ranajit Guha, Jimmy Wiener, Gehan Wijeyeward-ene and Sarah Williams made helpful comments on a version of the paper presented in the Department of Anthropology, Research School of Pacific Studies, the Australian National University.

2 A similar rich polysemy in the labelling of social groups and categories was intuitively familiar from the semantics of English 'family' and anthropologi-cally familiar from Evans-Pritchard's analysis of *cieng* in Nuer (Evans-Pritchard 1940: 136).

3 More complex semantic analyses had by then been assayed by linguistic philosophers examining Western languages; and the puzzles of 'family resem-blance' had been set out in the later writings of Wittgenstein.

4 *Lo'oo* is a demonstrative, 'this (here)'.

5 *Mai* here is the common Oceanic directional 'hither'.

6 *Ngai* is here an 'it' pronoun serving as a relativiser to embed a locative clause.

7 Lakoff illustrates a somewhat similar but less symbolically and emotionally laden polysemy with 'window', as referring both to an aperture in a wall and a glass covering of the aperture.

8 Not surprisingly, the soil/land conceptual complex, like of *fanua* in Kwaio, spans a hierarchy of senses: 'English soil', etc.

9 Rather more commonly, for 'my homeland, my ultimate place of attachment' Kwaio use *furi-gu*. (*Furi a-gu*, using the alienable possessive construction, is 'my bed'.)

10 This question was raised by my colleague Jim Fox, in comparing semantic structures of Kwaio and Roti, in eastern Indonesia.

11 Various reconstructions of the initial consonant have been advanced for proto-Austronesian; **jalan* 'road, path' is an approximation.

12 The *-gu* possessive pronoun is 'my'; *-na* is 'his/her/its'.

13 *Fa'a-* here is the Kwaio reflex of the common Oceanic causative prefix.

5 Domain-specificity, living kinds and symbolism

Maurice Bloch

This chapter is highly speculative. It explores the possibility that some recent work in developmental cognitive psychology might help us to understand aspects of what has often been called ritual symbolism. In particular, it is concerned with the old question of the prominence in many religious practices of living kinds, both as objects and concepts.

In a number of recent articles S. Atran (1987a) and D. Sperber (1985a) have been making increasingly strong claims for the existence of a specific cognitive domain concerning 'living kinds'. In this they have been following recent suggestions made by Fodor (1983) which make the case for the existence of numerous such distinct cognitive domains. They have accompanied their claim for the existence of a specific cognitive domain for living kinds with suggestions concerning the significance the existence of such a domain might have for anthropology. For the purpose of this short chapter only, I shall assume that Atran and Sperber are right without further discussion, none the less, and in some ways, I shall want to go further than they do. I shall also be using their hypothesis to illuminate an area of concern which is not theirs.

Atran (1990, and this volume) argues that in all cultures cognition about living kinds is governed by different rules than cognition about other kinds and that in all cultures the rules governing the cognition of living kinds are the same. Such an observation leads to the suggestion that there is an innate predisposition among all humans for constituting a 'living-kinds domain'. Such a predisposition to a particular form of cognitive development relevant to a limited area of human cognition would be similar to the much more certainly hypothesised innate predisposition for learning grammar or face recognition. According to Atran and Sperber, the child is pre-programmed, 'hard-wired' to use the common jargon, to learn particularly fast and in particular ways about living kinds and their implications. As a result, living kinds are not only learnt about in a different way, the very concepts of living kinds are different from, for example, categorical concepts of artefacts. For Atran the core of this difference lies in the fact that categorical concepts of living kinds presume an underlying nature while categorical concepts of artefacts are defined by functions.

Atran's evidence is circumstantial but suggestive. First of all, he turns to the extensive work done by such ethnoscientists as Berlin, Breedlove & Raven (1973) concerning the classification of plants and animals. This suggests striking regularities in the organisation of folk taxonomies of living kinds. In particular, these authors draw attention to what Berlin and his associates have called the generic level, a level which corresponds roughly to our 'species' level and which seems to be the basis of plant and animal classification in all cultures (but see Mandler & Bauer 1989). This basic character derives from the fact that other superordinate or subordinate levels are, according to these authors, always much less elaborated than the generic level and also always depend on it. For Berlin, Breedlove & Raven the generic level corresponds to what other cognitive psychologists have called the basic level.

The other type of evidence Atran turns to comes from the related work by psychologists such as Eleanor Rosch (1978) concerning prototypes and especially the work concerning bird classification, which in many ways established prototype theory. Atran seems to be arguing that prototypically organised concepts are characteristic of categorical concepts of living kinds but may not exist beyond this domain.

Finally, Sperber and Atran turn to independent evidence which seems to suggest that subjects, especially children, treat living kinds in a unique and distinctive way. Atran thus argues that once the child has understood that an animal, even an animal she has never seen such as a tiger, is indeed a representative of a living kind, she will make a number of very strong assumptions which she would not make for a representative of a non-living kind. For example, the child will presume that even when the animal has lost all its empirical characteristics (stripes, legs, etc.) the thing will still remain for the child *essentially* a tiger.

Subsequent research by psychologists such as Mandler & Bauer (1989) and Carey (1978, cited in Smith, Sera & Gattuso 1988) seems to give some backing to Atran and Sperber's theories, since it shows that very young children seem to distinguish between animate and inanimate objects so early that it seems inconceivable that distinction could be learnt through interaction with the environment.[1] On the basis of this admittedly fragmentary evidence I feel justified to take, for purposes of presentation, Atran's and Sperber's highly tentative argument as though it were proved. None the less, even here, this argument sems to require serious qualifications.

Following Berlin, Breedlove & Raven, Atran argues that one of the distinguishing characteristics of cognition concerning living kinds, at least as far as 'the ordinary understanding of the everyday world' is concerned (Atran 1987a: 28), is the certainty with which species are linked to superordinate and subordinate categories. This degree of certainty contrasts with the unsure and changing way concepts concerning artefacts are linked to other levels of classification.

In making this last point, Atran has to face some familiar objections. For example when discussing the categorical concept indicated by the word 'tomatoes', psychologists such as Rey (1983: 248) noted how tomatoes are ambiguously classed, sometimes as vegetables, sometimes as fruits. This, according to Atran, is irrelevant to theories concerning the cognition of natural kinds because such words as 'fruit' and 'vegetable' indicate concepts concerned with artefacts which are therefore *functionally* conceptualised in contrast to natural kinds.

The difficulty raised by a case such as 'tomatoes' may, however, be quite significant. Even though one may accept Atran's argument and one may have removed from one's mind any suspicion that we are simply dealing with a tautology, the apparent ambiguity of 'tomatoes' is much more suggestive to the anthropologist than might appear from Atran's dismissal. Atran says of such cases:

In general, when living kinds enter the space of concern with human function and use, such as eating, gardening (weeds and flowers), farming (beasts of burden), entertainment (pets, circus and fair animals), they cease to be of taxonomic importance ... For items that pertain to the conceptual space of human function and use, then, there may well be 'unclear cases' of category affiliation, but this has no relevance to folk biological classification. (1987a: 43)

Such reasoning may be acceptable as a way of dealing with a specific theoretical difficulty, but it also highlights two quite different but related issues of fundamental importance.

First there is a practical side to this matter. One cannot but be struck by how important, literally vital, these 'awkward' conceptual bridges between living kinds and artefacts are for the survival of human beings, who, after all, rely on the transformation of living kinds into artefacts for their food and much more. It seems, therefore, unreasonable to make these 'passages' a minor issue of theory since they certainly cannot be a minor issue for people living in anything but the most artificial conditions.

Secondly, these cognitive 'bridges' between natural kinds and artefacts themselves reveal what must be a central cognitive process if we accept Atran's theory and the existence of specific cognitive domains. The fact that such things as tomatoes can be both living kinds and artefacts draws attention to an aspect of things which Atran seems to have forgotten. Atran's evidence for the differentiation of living kinds from other concepts comes presumably from adults or at the very least children who have learnt to speak. However, the manifestation of innate domain potentialities, leading to a specific cognitive mechanism for the formation of concepts of living kinds, seems to develop very early on. Subsequent to the formation of these very early concepts much development will follow. This subsequent development may mean that early concepts may be reformed to change character and perhaps to lose the prototype characteristics so typical of natural kinds concepts (Keil & Batterman 1984). Secondly, and probably closely related to the *characteristic-to-definition* shift, is the fact of greater systematic integration of knowledge which must occur during later stages of cognitive development (see Fentriss 1984). What this must surely mean is that although we may accept that there are specific distinct innate propensities for the cognition of different domains in the young child, a significant part of cognitive development must be the *linking* up of such domains, whether we believe that such linking up affects or does not affect the specificity of domains.

The linking up of domains seems to be a relatively unexplored area. However, it is fascinating that such a crucial coordination as that between the domain of artefacts and of living kinds, should imply both a reorganisation of general cognitive-patterns process and at the same time the cognition of an essential practical process. The possibility of such a correlation between cognition, cognitive development and the dialectics of life is thought-provoking enough for the anthropologist, but here I want to discuss yet a further related fact.

It would appear that much religious ritual symbolism is also concerned with these coordinations and passages between living kinds and artefacts, thereby somehow replicating what one may presume are fundamental sequences of cognitive development concerned with the essential processes of human life.

In recognising this parallel between symbolism, the fundamental processes of human interaction with the environment and the development of cognition it is not possible to posit a causal connection. However, in noting the cognitive trajectory of the symbolism and seeing what this trajectory might mean in terms of associations within domains and crossings over between domains, we might get a further insight into the mental processes operated by certain symbolic systems and even some intuition into the evocative power of this symbolism.

In this chapter I want to look briefly at an example of such a symbolic system which is central to the representations of a particular group of people. This will illustrate how symbolism so often seems to focus on the cognitive and practical significance of the transformation of living kinds into artefacts, the 'awkward' cases of Atran's theory.

The Zafimaniry

The Zafimaniry are a group of shifting cultivators living in Madagascar who rely mainly on maize, beans and taro.[2] They number approximately 20,000. They live in a narrow band of mountain forest at an altitude of approximately 1,400 metres. Like all Malagasy people, a central theme of their culture is a concern with the impermanence of living human beings. The most commonly quoted Zafimaniry proverb is: *ny tany tsy miova fa nyolombelona no moiva*.[3] This is best translated as 'While the land[4] does not change (or transform), the living people[5] change.' This proverb, and many others which are almost identical, reflect a constant awareness of the fragility and impermanence of human life in a world which is not concerned with their problems and which therefore affects them randomly; but such a saying also suggests a solution: the attaching of human beings to the permanent land by means of the mediation of permanent materials, in their case especially hard wood of which the houses should ideally be made.

The Zafimaniry conform surprisingly well to what Lévi-Strauss has called 'house-based societies' not only because certain houses are central religious focuses but also because the symbolism of houses is, as he predicted, closely linked with the supreme valuation of the unity of a married pair.

Zafimaniry sexual unions are extremely unstable but little by little some of these unions are proved to be successful by their fertility and they then become established. This long, uncertain and gradual process is marked by a complex series of rituals, among which the building and blessing of the house, the setting up of the central post and the hearth by the couple are particularly important. Like the marriage, the building of the house is a gradual process which is marked by the 'hardening' of the house. This occurs when flimsy impermanent materials, such as woven bamboos and mats are replaced by massive decorated wooden planks, which are called the 'bones' of the house. Again like the marriage, the growth and hardening of the house continues long after the death of the original couple as children, grandchildren, etc. continue to add to the structure and replace rotten wood. By then the house has become a 'holy house' (*trano masina*) which is a source of blessing for the descendants. What has happened is that the house has changed for the descendants from a structure sheltering the original couple to the original couple in a new, more mature form. The holy houses are, for the Zafimaniry, their ancestors made permanent. This is especially so for the central posts and hearth of the house. These are respectively the man and the woman of the original couple. When the descendants seek blessing from their ancestors they address the post and the hearth as though they were the ancestors of the group themselves. Again, when certain offerings to the ancestors are made these things receive the offerings by being given honey or rum and occasionally the blood of cattle.

What has therefore happened is that with the passage of time people become replaced by artefacts. It is the most impermanent aspect of people, their attraction to each other which becomes one of the most permanent Zafimaniry artefacts: the totally wooden house. In order fully to understand this transformation, however, it is important to turn not only to Zafimaniry ideas concerning houses, but also to their ideas concerning the wood and the trees of which the houses are made.

The Zafimaniry use the same word for both TREE and WOOD, *hazo*, thereby perpetrating the same 'muddle' which Atran noted for TOMATO, since in doing this they are merging a natural kind with an artefact. In one way this linguistic fact might be taken simply to indicate that the great divide stressed by Atran is ignored by Zafimaniry in their language and this might therefore throw doubt on the distinction between artefact and natural kind at least for adult Zafimaniry. However, this would be misleading, as the Zafimaniry are very aware of the distinction between natural kinds and artefacts and in this case the fact that a natural kind can become an artefact is continually discussed. Similarly, the ritual symbolism of the Zafimaniry also suggests an awareness of the paradox of living kinds becoming artefacts and, if anything, the symbolism emphasises the passage from one kind of thing to another. Zafimaniry never tire of pointing out that great trees start as soft pliable little plants 'like grass', but that these soft little plants end up as gigantic, hard, straight things which, in the form of wood, can last almost for ever.

The importance of trees for the Zafimaniry is very great. This is both because of the fact that they totally depend on wood and also because of the prominence of trees/wood as a topic of discourse. I have already noted how Zafimaniry houses are made of wood. Nearly all their implements also are made of wood. In the past, and to a certain extent still now, their clothes were made of wood because they were woven from bark fibre. Their medicines are exclusively powdered mixtures of different woods. Very importantly, it is wood and the burning of wood which makes the fields on which they grow their crops as a result of the clearing and fertilising of the land by fire. Finally, and probably most crucial of all, they warm themselves continually with woodfires. Without these continual fires life would be impossible in such a cold and wet country, and equally importantly it would be impossible to preserve crops. This is because in order to store maize, which is their main staple, they hang it from the rafters of the house so that the fire will dry it and cover it with a black shiny coating of soot which protects the cobs from being eaten by little weevils. The Zafimaniry are well aware of their symbiosis with wood and the forest to the extent that they say that people are not Zafimaniry, even though their ancestors were Zafimaniry, when they live in villages where, as a result of over-swiddening, the forest has disappeared.

The Zafimaniry call a set of very strong woods 'ancestor woods'. Then they distinguish amongst these by means of sibling terminology which marks differential seniority, so that the strongest wood of all, *nato* is the 'older sibling' of the second strongest, *amboneka*. Above all, what distinguishes ancestor woods is that they have something which is called *teza*. The importance of the concept of *teza* in Zafimaniry thought is central. One of the meanings of the word, which is Malagasy wide, is at the root of the verb which means 'to last a long time'. (Interestingly, but not surprisingly, Malagasy has several verbs which correspond to the English verb 'to last'.) The same word can also be used to mean human bones. In some contexts it can be used for ancestors. However, the typical meaning of the word, that is the one which Zafimaniry will give as a definition when asked about the word out of any particular context, refers to the core of ancestor trees (or wood).

These very hard woods develop, as they grow older, a clearly demarcated darker impacted core. This is called *teza*. This core is totally absent in young trees of these species but develops little by little so that in old trees it represents the majority of the tree. This is the hardest and most resistant part of the tree and the Zafimaniry will often point out with satisfaction that after the burning of a swidden the *teza* of those trees remains unburnt.

In Zafimaniry ideas about wood and about its straightness and *teza*, their central concepts about the body are involved, but they are displaced, so to speak, away from the human body to that of trees. One side of the association can be understood as a parallel. The growth of ancestor trees with *teza*, which can mean BONE and/or ANCESTOR, is like the growth of humans, starting soft, supple, wet and without hard straight bones; but with time the hard straight *teza* becomes defined and increases: ultimately, it will take over. This is like the hardening and straightening of bones which will ultimately mark elderhood and ancestorhood. However, trees achieve the process better than humans and are seen to do so. Unlike human bone, the bone of trees (*teza*) continues to grow, increase and harden progressively on a very long time scale, so that ultimately it practically takes over. Human *teza*, on the other hand, although it starts off all right, soon goes into reverse with old age and death, as human beings patently do. Trees can thus materially fulfil the ideal of what should happen to humans. They pass from fluid transformative things to things which are very hard, very permanent (very *teza*) and which can therefore form an almost permanent bond with the land and thereby share in its stasis, as the proverb quoted earlier in this chapter seems to demand.

Secondly, and probably because of the very fact that trees achieve materially the ideal of development which humans fail to achieve in their bodies, wood is made to gradually *replace* humans. This happens when the unstable marriage of young living people so hardens and stabilises that it becomes a hardening house, made of wood obtained from trees with *teza*, with its central post and hearth which are the source of blessing for descendants and which *are* the 'ancestors'.

Discussion

The brief outline of Zafimaniry symbolism given above none the less covers the most salient aspects of the system. The system is based on a set of transference from humans, to trees, to wood, to houses. The fragile relationship of two opposite-sex humans matures and hardens in a way that the Zafimaniry see as part and parcel of the maturing of the body of the pair. A process which is believed to involve both the proportional growth of bones as against flesh, as well as the hardening and straightening of these bones. This first transference which consists of passing from the stabilisation of the relation of the two partners to the maturing of their bodies is to the Zafimaniry fairly straightforward, since both processes are seen as merely two manifestations of the same general process of maturation which, for the Zafimaniry, links inseparably growth and reproduction.

The next passage, however, is more complex. The relationship of the body to trees can at first be seen as metaphorical. As the body grows, so do the trees; as the body becomes more rigid and straight, so do the trees; finally, as the bones in the body become defined and strong, so does the *teza* inside the trees. However, it is, I believe, quite wrong to see such a relationship simply as a kind of 'ritual metaphor' (Fernandez 1977). This is because all theories of metaphor imply a fixed relationship between vehicle and principal, while what is characteristic of symbolism, especially when it is linked to ritual, is that the relationship is a continually evolving one. What is characteristic of this case, and others like it, is that what starts out as a metaphorical parallel ends up as a substitution. The substitution occurs when the wood in the house comes to represent, or rather to *be* the original couple. This is a process which is only completed after the death of both members of the original couple, and when their house, 'hardened' through the contribution of planks and carvings from the descendants, becomes the couple and is addressed as such in, for example, ancestral evocations.

This passage from impermanent humans to permanent artefact, however, reveals on closer examination to be itself made up of several analytically distinguishable elements. First of all there is the jump from person to tree. One aspect of this jump seems to me to depend on the recognition of the fundamental unity of trees and humans deriving from the fact that both are living kinds. This underlying unity is seen above all in the common fact of growth and of maturation, which is one of the more salient characteristics of living kinds. Thus, the very general, and if we are to believe Atran and others, the very primitive concept of living kinds gives the basis for what still remains a fairly complicated and unexplored cognitive operation, involving the transformation of a metaphor into a substitution. This first element of the passage is, however, only a first stage in a further transformation where the living tree is transformed into an artefact: wood. This process is, as the Zafimaniry themselves continually stress, long drawn out. It involves the cutting of the tree, the drying and seasoning of the wood, the cutting of the trunk into manageable pieces, the making of planks which will become the 'bones' of the house, ultimately perhaps the decorating of these 'bones' with carvings.

Now this second process involves precisely what Atran had seen as the 'muddle' between a living kind: trees (in Zafimaniry *hazo*) and an artefact: wood (in Zafimaniry *hazo*). Alternatively, we could say it involves the crucial process of transformation between living kinds and artefacts on which life depends. I would suggest that there is a little truth in both formulations. What underlies the full process is the fact that the symbolic seems to play with the cognitive dissonance between living kinds and artefacts as well as the unity between humans and trees, on the one hand, and, on the other hand, the unity, linguistic and practical, of trees and wood. In fact, it would appear as if this passage in the wider symbolic task of transference from humans to holy houses was, at this point, 'de-intellectualised', and handed over to the empirical world, where the barrier between living kinds can be crossed by means of a number of techniques, the most obvious and necessary of which is killing and which in this case is the transforming of trees into planks.

The passage from people to trees was possible in the mind because it is premised on the unity of the domain of living kinds. On the other hand, the unity and specificity of the domain makes the necessary passage from living kind to artefact difficult if it occurs purely in the mind. It therefore, requires for its operation the use of material symbols which themselves can make the jump. Of course, this is not to say that the process of transformation from living kinds to artefact cannot be cognised. That would be ridiculous. But perhaps the kind of effortless slippage from one living kind to another, such as the passage from humans to trees, is not so easy or symbolically satisfactory if it involves passing from one domain to another, because it then follows conceptual connections of a more secondary character, established at a later stage of cognitive development characterised by definitions rather than characteristics. This lack of ease in demonstration of a proposition which, like all symbolical ritual propositions is a-logical and largely evocative, may explain why it requires external help in the form of material symbols at critical moments where the mind seems to recognise boundaries.

Speculating so far from one largely anecdotal case might seem barely legitimate, but in fact this case is far from an isolated instance. Much religious symbolism seems concerned with the transformation of parallels into substitutions, of living kinds into artefacts and sometimes back again. Thus African sacrifice provides us with another example. There, the sacrificial animal is at first a metaphorical parallel with the person for whom the sacrifice is being carried out, and this parallel depends on the fact that humans and cattle are living kinds. Then, as the ritual proceeds, the parallel is turned into a substitution (Evans-Pritchard 1965: ch. 10). Finally, the cattle which has substituted for the person for whom the sacrifice is being carried out, is transformed through killing, butchering and cooking into an artefact: meat.

The parallel between African sacrifice and Zafimaniry wood and tree symbolism is not accidental and can easily be repeated all over the world. The reason is that all religious symbolism is about the dialectics of life, growth, decline, reproduction, eating and excreting and about the re-representation of these processes in more or less paradoxical forms. But having said this, the cognitive processes underpinning these re-representations still remain to be explored.

NOTES

1 Although Atran talks of the evidence for the specificity for a domain for living kinds in general, the evidence he adduces, as well as the subsequent work, actually only relates to animals and not plants.
2 Research among the Zafimaniry was first carried out in 1971 thanks to a grant from the Economic and Social Science Research Council and in 1988–9 thanks to a grant from the Spencer Foundation.
3 The proverb occurs in a number of variants but the meaning is constant. The version mentioned here is the simplest one.
4 The Malagasy word *tany* has a very similar range of meanings to the English word 'land'.
5 The normal Malagasy word for 'people', *olonbelona*, literally means 'living people' but I have kept the rather pedantic form in full as it seems to me the most revealing. R. Dubois, partly rightly and partly wrongly, makes a great song and dance about this point (Dubois 1978).

6   Pseudo-natural kinds

Pascal Boyer

The starting point of this chapter consists of two simple, seemingly trivial observations. The first one is that, in any particular culture, there are definite limits to the range of beliefs people entertain about religious agencies and events. The existence of such limits accounts for the relative convergence of people's beliefs and statements about such matters. The second observation is that explicit tuition can only account for part of this convergence. This is especially striking in contexts of oral religious tradition, in which explicit tuition is often minimal. In order to 'go beyond the information given', specific heuristics must therefore be activated. Here I will try to describe some such heuristics, which consist in applying to religious matters implicit assumptions which govern the representation of non-religious domains of reality. I will try to describe certain cognitive processes of belief formation and fixation, and examine to what extent they make it possible to account for some recurrent features of religious symbolism.

Social categories and identification

Let me turn to an ethnographic example, which will illustrate the difficulties of the question.[1] Among the Fang of Cameroon, some people are said to possess an internal organ called *evur*, which allows them to display particular talent in various undertakings outside the domain of everyday activities. People with great oratory skills or a particular ability in business, people whose plantations are especially successful, are commonly said to be *beyem*, that is, having an *evur*. Many cases of illness or misfortune are caused by the state of the patient's *evur*. The notion is crucial in the domain of magic and witchcraft. Only *beyem*, that is, people with *evur*, can engage in witchcraft, which consists in leaving one's body at night and wandering in the forest and the villages, 'throwing' diseases at the sleeping victims. On the other hand, only *beyem* can fight against witchcraft and cure the victims of witchcraft-induced illness or misfortune. *Beyem* are capable, in certain circumstances, of launching invisible 'attacks' against other people, either non-*beyem* or persons whose *evur* is weaker than theirs. Such attacks bring about misfortune, illness or even the death of the victim. There are very few examples of successful people who are not, in one way or another, suspected to have committed such witchcraft murders, in order to steal others' goods or talents.

Various social categories are linked with the possession of *evur*. There is, for instance, a category of specialised story-tellers, called *mbommvet*, who sing long historical and mythical epics, accompanying themselves on the instrument called *mvet* (Boyer 1986 *passim*). A Fang *mbommvet* can be defined as someone who plays the instrument and knows the repertoire of epic tales. These are the two criteria invariably cited by Fang speakers. However, many people who fulfil such criteria are not considered *mbommvet* at all. This concerns not only young inexperienced story-tellers, but also musicians coming from distant clans. Moreover, it sometimes happens that some person formerly said to be a *mbommvet* is not considered to be one anymore. There is therefore a not insignificant number of people who apparently meet the requirements for membership of the category MBOMMVET, yet are not considered members of that category. The same can be said of other ritual positions among the Fang. Traditional healers, for instance, are generally called *ngengang*. For Fang speakers, *ngengang* typically perform specific healing rituals, during which they communicate with ancestors/ghosts (*bekong*) and 'return' to the world of the living with specific recipes for treatment. Again, there is a certain degree of uncertainty whether a given healer is or is not a *ngengang*. Some people who perform the rituals and commonly prescribe medicines are still not considered *ngengang*.

The reason for this uncertainty lies in the conceptual structure in which these categories are embedded. *Ngengang*, *mbommvet* and other such terms are, in fact, subordinates of a larger category, that of *beyem* ('people who see'). *Beyem* are supposed to be different from other people in that they have the unobservable property called *evur*, sometimes described as an invisible organ in their body. Some people have *evur* and others do not. Since being a *beyem* is not an observable, 'surface' property, it is forever impossible to be certain whether a given person is or is not a *beyem*. What is certain is that the person either is or else is not a *beyem*; there is no medium position. The uncertainty about healers, as well as the discussions about story-tellers, are a direct consequence of this question of *evur*. Story-tellers who are said not to be *mbommvet* are, in fact, suspected not to be *beyem*, not to have what it makes it possible for story-tellers to acquire secret knowledge from the ancestors. In the same way, when someone performs the healing rituals yet is not considered a *ngengang*, it is because he/she is not considered a *beyem*. It is admitted that such people may know successful remedies. For all their knowledge, however, if they are not *beyem*, that is, if they do not have *evur*, then they are not *ngengang*.

To sum up, the link between certain activities and membership of a social category is not a direct one. Performing certain typical rituals does not entail membership of the category. Activities are an index of membership only in so far as the person is seen as having another, unobservable quality, namely *evur*. Furthermore, people who, for some reason, are not considered to be members of the category any more, are not supposed to have lost the quality in question. It is generally assumed that they never had it, that they had been mistaken for genuine members of the category.

Both properties are very common in social positions linked to religious performance. Another illustration can be found in Fabrega & Silver's study of shamanism in Zinacantan (1973). Shamans (*h'iloletik*) are characterised by their specific medical powers. They are the only ones who can actually receive messages from the gods. They have access to the world of the gods, which ordinary people do not have. There are women *h'iloletik*, but they only perform private curing ceremonies, although they are still considered of 'higher' status than other women (Fabrega & Silver 1973: 204ff.). The process of becoming a shaman is particularly interesting here. As Fabrega & Silver suggest (1973: 35), it consists of a process of *recognition* rather than election, and the process is 'gradual, informal and covert'. In this case, as in most societies with shamanism, the fact that someone is a shaman is a process of gradual discovery of one's powers and of recognition of these powers by the surrounding community. Subjects typically have strange dreams, in which they are ordered by the ancestors to become shamans, or they have epilepsy fits, which are taken as an obvious sign of uncontrolled possession by the gods or ancestral spirits. They then learn from other shamans, to which they sometimes add original recipes directly inspired by the gods. They first perform rituals to cure close relatives and other people in their villages. Then the rumour spreads and the reluctant practitioner is forced to admit that he is a shaman. He marks this by taking part, *qua* shaman, in one of the public ceremonies, with the symbols of his office (Fabrega & Silver 1973: 31ff.).

This informal process is not the only path to recognition, however. There are formal ceremonies of 'election', during which a new shaman is supposed to receive official recognition of his 'powers'. The ceremony is called *tsva'an sba h'ilol*, 'to stand up as a shaman'. The new shaman and an older specialist visit all the shrines and sacred springs of the surrounding villages, asking the god to collaborate with the new healer. This ritual is, in fact, an enlarged version of the public curing ceremonies. A striking feature of Zinacantan shamanism is that this formal recognition, which supposedly identifies the person as a shaman with the gods' blessing, in fact triggers more doubt about the shaman's abilities than the informal process. Fabrega & Silver observe that 'most [shamans] do not undertake a debut ceremony, and many view one as a sign of incompetence, feeling that the new [shaman] who performs it has not undergone an authentic vision and is not *p'ih* (intelligent and spiritually outstanding)' (1973: 34). The premise here is that the new shaman needs the intervention of an older one because he is not competent enough; he has not received efficacious prayers and formulae in his dreams.

The idea is congruent with the widespread notion that shamans are not all equally efficient: 'some *h'iloletik* are authentic and competent, having received their powers from the ancestral spirits. Others are spurious and have no abilities; they practice only to get chickens, meals and liquor by cheating their patients' (Fabrega & Silver 1973: 41). These are not considered 'real' shamans (*ibid.*, 148). Doubts about the shaman's real abilities are typically voiced when the shaman becomes too drunk during the offerings, or insists on using alcoholic beverages to the exclusion of other offerings (*ibid.*). Zinacaneteco representations about what makes the difference between shamans and non-shamans are rather vague, although there is a definite intuition that a person either is or else is not a *h'ilol*, and that this is some form of predestination. The diseases that afflict the shaman-to-be are conceived as a consequence of unobservable properties, that make him a *h'ilol*. The doubts concerning the healer's abilities are typically expressed in terms of doubts concerning his identity as a shaman. In this framework, there is no such thing as an unskilled shaman, but there may be imposters who perform rituals, yet are not shamans at all.

To sum up, we are dealing here with social categories explicitly linked to religious performance. In the local characterisations of these categories, we typically find two types of representations. On the one hand, people who are members of these categories are sometimes construed as having a special 'knowledge' that is reserved to specialists. Also, members of these categories are recognised by the fact that they typically perform certain religious activities. However, in the representations concerning the categories, all these features are insufficient. Knowledge itself is invariably conceived as insufficient. Religious specialists are not just taught, they have to undergo complex initiation rites which go beyond the mere transmission of information.[2] More surprisingly, perhaps, the activities themselves are also conceived as neither necessary nor sufficient. Obviously, the idea that traditional positions are classified in terms of activities contains some truth, in that occupations are the idiom in which ideas about positions are usually expressed. The activities, however, cannot constitute the mental *definition* of the positions, since they provide neither necessary nor sufficient conditions for membership of the category. In most cases of traditional positions, activities are only *part* of what is required for membership. In order to belong to the category, one has to be seen as having 'something more' that marks the 'true' or 'real' holders of such positions. This 'something more' is usually not defined. When asked what a *mbommvet* is, Fang people almost always answer that it is someone who plays the *mvet*. When reminded that so-and-so plays the *mvet* and is not considered a *mbommvet*, they typically answer 'That's true, but you see that's because *he isn't mbommvet.*' What is clearly implied by the use of the category *mbommvet* is that the people to whom the name applies are different from the rest of the Fang. In what they are different is not especially considered, but what is known for sure is that they must be different, otherwise they would not be *mbommvet*. From such data we can infer that:

1 The representation of such positions is very much a yes/no question: one is or is not a *mbommvet* (or a *h'ilol*). People might be unsure in certain cases, but that never means that one could be 'half-*mbommvet*' or '*mbommvet* to a certain extent'.[3]

2 What makes one a *beyem* or a *h'ilol* is not such observable features as playing an instrument or performing certain rituals. It is 'something more' that all members of those categories have. No one really knows what it consists of, but it has to be there; otherwise, whatever one's activities, one is not an exemplar of the category. External typical criteria are just indirect (and insufficient) evidence for the fact that people really belong to the relevant class.

The link between activities and positions is therefore not as simple as some anthropological descriptions might lead us to think. In order to link activities and positions, people must assume that the persons considered share another, hidden or undefined quality. In the following sections I will try to put forward some hypotheses about the cognitive mechanisms that make such processes of identification possible and relevant. Before turning to these general questions, however, it may be important to examine whether similar identification and categorisation problems can be found in other domains of religious symbolism.

Magical stones as sortals

Let me now take a brief example from M. Brown's (1985) account of magical practices among the Aguaruna of the Peruvian Amazon, which illustrates the role of some implicit ontological hypotheses in the representation of cultural categories. One of the Aguaruna magical activities implies the possession of special stones, used for various purposes: hunting, seduction, the fertility of gardens, etc. These objects are supposed to bring about or facilitate the effects desired by the owners. Their possession is a matter of great secrecy.

There are three main types of 'magical' stones, classified on the basis of the type of effects they are supposed to have. *Yuka* stones are meant to have a power of attraction, and are therefore used by men in both hunting and love-seeking. In order to attract game, the stone is covered with some red face-paint which is then applied to the hunter's body and to his bow. Such stones can also be used as love-charms. In that case the paint is applied to the owner's face. *Nantag* stones are primarily used by women; they are said to increase the productivity of the gardens. They are put in a bowl containing a decoction of several plants. The liquid is then poured on the cuttings of yam or taro before they are planted. A third type, *namug*, is specifically connected with war magic. Such a stone, if properly used, 'attracts' the enemy and gives an easy victory.

It must be emphasised that the stones used for such magical purposes do not necessarily belong to a certain type of minerals; nor does the distinction between *yuka*, *nantag* and *namug* map onto any observable differences. The tripartite 'classification' mentioned here is not based on any observable criteria, such as shape, colour or touch. As Brown points out (1985: 374), the fact that a stone is said to belong to a certain category is a question of identification rather than of classification (after a distinction originally emphasised by Ellen, 1979a: 341). A stone is supposed to be, for example, *yuka* and not *namug* because it has whatever makes it efficient in the relevant domain, hunting in this case, not because of external features which would make it obviously different from other, non-*yuka* stones. There does not seem to be any elaborate explanation of the stones' efficiency.

The 'identity' of a given stone is uncovered through a long process of personal experiences. The first clue is given by the circumstances of discovery. Stones found in the body of hunted animals are more likely to be *yuka*, good for hunting. When they are found in the entrails of aquatic mammals, they are associated with water-spirits, and consequently with love-charms. Subsequent experience, however, may modify these conjectures. Dreams and omens are especially important, as well as evidence of a more empirical nature, such as the owners' success in love-seeking, gardening, war or hunting.

The representation of the categories in question seems to be based on two fundamental assumptions. The first assumption is that the stones in question do belong, unambiguously, to one of the named categories or to the residual category of non-magical stones. There are no stones that belong to several of these categories, although it may be difficult to identify which category is relevant. In other words, what makes a stone *yuka* or *nantag* or *namug* was already there when it was found, but it was not directly observable. One cannot make a magical stone; this is especially important in contrast with other 'magical' objects, which are clearly conceived as artefacts, the efficacy of which implies that a precise recipe has been followed. A second important assumption is that for the Aguaruna, there is a relationship between the fact that a stone really belongs to one of these categories, on the one hand, and its causal powers, particularly on its owner, on the other. There is, however, no certainty in the reasoning that infers the identity of a stone on the basis of its effects. As Brown makes clear, finding out whether a stone belongs to any of these categories is a matter of reasoned guesses and corrigible inferences.

An important characteristic of these representations, which is relevant to our general problem, is that there does not seem to be any hypothesis about precisely what makes stones of a given type have specific effects. Although there is a definite assumption, that, for example, owning a *yuka* stone will increase one's success in love, there is no 'model' of the way such effects are achieved. This, of course, is a very common characteristic of 'magical' claims. Causal connections are often posited in the absence of any explanation, or indeed any conjecture about how and why the causal connections obtain, a point to which I will return presently.

Natural ontology and living kinds

Let me now sum up the theoretical problems posed by these religious categories. In the case of social positions, as well as that of categories designating the magical stones, people are led to entertain precise beliefs about certain 'mystical' qualities and entities (people having *evur* or *p'ih*, a stone being *namug*, etc.). However, the traditions concerned provide no explicit definition of these qualities or entities and no explanations of what makes the difference between them and other qualities or entities. It is therefore necessary to explain why and how, in the absence of precisely characterised schemata, people's beliefs converge on certain representations of these qualities or agencies.

In order to deal with this problem, it seems necessary to leave the domain of religious symbolism for a while, and examine certain general features of concept acquisition in more mundane domains. In this section I will present some important results and hypotheses of cognitive psychology. Their relevance to our anthropological problems will be examined in the rest of this chapter. The experimental study of concept acquisition shows that the ordinary use of concepts is organised by some implicit assumptions about ontological distinctions, that is, about whether a term refers to events, properties, physical objects, living things, artefacts, etc. Research into the representation of ontological distinctions was initiated by F. C. Keil (1979), applying notions derived from Sommers's study of the ontology of ordinary language (1959). Sommers's strictly philosophical argument focused on two points, which later turned out to be extremely relevant to the psychological study of ontological hypotheses. The first point is that ontological distinctions are made manifest by predicate restrictions. Not all predicates can be applied to a given term, and the applicability of a given predicate allows one to predict the applicability of others. If it is possible to say that a given X 'is breathing', then Xs might also, in certain cases, 'be furious', but could certainly not be described as 'difficult to make' or 'happening tomorrow'. The selection restrictions, in this case, reflect an ontological distinction between animate objects, artefacts and events. Sommers's second contention is that ontological categories like 'abstract object', 'living thing', 'animal', 'event', etc., are arranged in a taxonomical tree according to precise formal constraints.

Keil's experimental research (1979: Keil & Batterman 1984), which focused on the evolution of ontological distinctions in small children, tends to confirm Sommers's general hypotheses. There is good evidence for the existence of mentally represented ontological distinctions, which are arranged in a strict taxonomical manner (although the categories and their arrangement are slightly different from Sommers's tree). The formal constraints are respected even at an early stage. Children appear to make surprisingly fine-grained ontological distinctions, between, for example, living things and artefacts, and they have precise intuitions on whether a predicate can or cannot apply. The ontological 'tree' is gradually developed by branching out: for instance, a broad category like 'living thing' is gradually refined, so that after a while some predicates apply to plants only, to human beings to the exclusion of other animals and so on. The main conclusion to draw from such studies is that precisely organised ontological distinctions play a crucial role in the way people represent concepts.

The most important aspects of these studies, and a highly relevant point to anthropological models, is that ontological assumptions about what types of things there are in the world can be studied independently of the subjects' 'conceptions', 'models' or 'theories' attached to each concept. Indeed, some of Keil's experiments show that it is possible for subjects to make ontological hypotheses about some objects of which they have no model at all. Keil used stories which make a passing mention of objects called 'hyraxes' and 'throstles', which were never defined or described.

The only thing that is said about them is that the hyraxes 'are sometimes sleepy' and that the throstles 'need to be fixed'. Kindergarten children, who have never heard of those things, nevertheless infer, on the basis of such sentences, that it is possible that a hyrax might be 'hungry', and that a throstle might be 'made of metal'; on the other hand, they consistently deny that a hyrax could be 'made of metal' (Keil 1986 *passim*). While no 'theoretical knowledge', nor indeed any general information is communicated, the ontological distinction between living species and artefacts makes it possible to generate some inferences about the entities mentioned. 'Hyrax' and 'throstle' are used without explicit information about their ontological status, live being and artefact respectively. No 'theory' about them is given to the listeners. The acquisition of such notions, and the construction of some elaborate ideas about what they are likely to denote, are a consequence of the subjects' disposition to infer precise ontological hypotheses whenever a term is used in any natural context.

To sum up, three important conclusions must be drawn from Keil's seminal studies:

1 Implicit ontological categories organise the subject's application of predicates, and intuitions about what predicates can or cannot span a certain term, even when the categories are not explicitly represented. Children whose vocabulary does not include abstract terms like 'event', 'property' and 'living kind' nevertheless make distinctions between those ontological categories. Once the child has selected the ontological slot an object belongs to, on the very fragmentary basis of a single predicate used, this choice becomes a default value. This makes it possible to decide whether a new predicate may or may not be applied.

2 Ontological assumptions are distinct from factual ones, that is, propositions about the properties of the entities designated. This is the obvious point of the experiments in which imaginary terms are used. Children are given the term 'throstle' in a context which does not provide any information about whose properties, which they then decide to consider relevant to throstles.

3 Assumptions about the ontological status of a term are spontaneously inferred as a result of its use.[4] Children represent HYRAX as a type of living kind if the term is used with a predicate usually attributed to living things. The subjects do not need any explicit instruction, for example to the effect that 'hyraxes are animals'. In fact, ontological assumptions can be counted among those spontaneous conversational inferences which make utterances relevant. Like other such inferences, they are just assumptions, which can be refined or corrected in the light of subsequent utterances.

All three points are extremely important for our anthropological investigation. Let me focus, however, on the second result, which may lead to certain misunderstandings. As Keil shows, ontological assumptions can be inferred without any 'theoretical' representations about the objects. Obviously, ontological assumptions themselves could be described as some kind of 'micro-theory', but we must not get bogged down in purely terminological quibbles here. It is important not to misunderstand the relevance of Keil's experiments. The aim is not to deny the obvious fact that subjects in fact do create mental 'models' or 'micro-theories' with their concepts. The experimental evidence rather suggests that, even in conditions where such models have to be reduced to an empty hypothesis ('there is such a thing as hyraxes'), the range of predicates that can be applied to a concept is severely restricted by implicit ontological hypotheses. In other words, although there is no reason to think that people do not construct mental 'theories' about the various objects they usually deal with, the relative predictability or convergence of the beliefs they entertain about that object does not necessarily come from those mental 'theories'. They may come from spontaneous ontological assumptions, guessed on the basis of utterances which do not transmit information about these objects. This is a very important result, because it shows that the relative resemblance between several people's beliefs does not necessarily imply a shared theoretical description of the objects of these beliefs. This is a point to which I will return presently.

Let me now focus on certain regions of the ontological tree which are of special interest for our mystical categories. A good deal of philosophical literature has been devoted to *natural-kind terms*, which denote animal and botanical species as well as natural substances (iron, water, salt, for example).[5] It is impossible to define such terms, and it is very unlikely that their mental representation comprises a 'check-list' of necessary–sufficient properties (Schwarz 1979: 301). There cannot be a definition for such terms as 'giraffe' or 'oak'. The representation and use of a natural-kind term always invokes two types of general assumptions:

1 Some assumptions about the typical features of the exemplars of the kind. Although most of these features are present in most exemplars, they are neither necessary nor sufficient conditions. Thus, giraffes are supposed to be long-necked and lemons yellow. But short-necked giraffes and bluish lemons are still giraffes and lemons, so the features are not necessary. They only provide a 'stereotype' of the kind, which can be represented in various ways (as a series of features, or with the help of mental images, etc.) but never constitutes a definition.

2 The presumption of an underlying trait that is common to all exemplars of the kind. This is what makes giraffes and dogs; this essential feature is necessary to the use of natural-kind terms. Using the term 'giraffe'

implies that beyond surface resemblance, there is something common to all real giraffes, although what this common trait consists of is left undefined.

It is important to stress that the implicit assumption is about the existence of an underlying trait, not about what it consists of. Few people except biologists bother to represent what makes giraffes giraffes, although everyone does suppose that there is some such underlying trait. This implicit hypothesis is a necessary aspect of the everyday use of natural-kind terms. The idea of an undefined common essence is a powerful cognitive mechanism, universally available to human minds; together with basic principles of taxonomic ordering, it organises biological knowledge in all cultures (Berlin, Breadlove & Raven 1973).

Pseudo-natural kinds

In his study of magical stones, M. Brown insists on the differences between their identification and the classification of biological species, which is mainly based on observable resemblance and differences (1985: 382). In the domain of magical stones, there is no such constraint; any stone can belong to any type. The process of identification is not guided by observable discontinuities, as is the case with most natural categories. This is certainly pertinent, inasmuch as the relationship between observable properties and identification is concerned. I would argue, however, that the identification of stones implies ontological hypotheses very similar to what is put forward about natural categories. This point concerns the assumptions underlying the identification of living and natural kinds in general.

In the same way as natural kinds, *yuka*, *namug* and *nantag* are supposed to have some underlying features which make them different from other objects and different from each other. They can be partially identified on the basis of some external criteria (like the place where they are found), but these criteria are explicitly taken to be only typical. A stone found in an animal's bowels is usually supposed to be *yuka*, but this conjectural identification can be refuted by subsequent experience. What is then revealed is the 'essence' of the particular stone, which was there all along but might have been wrongly identified.

By deciding that a given stone is, say, *namug*, people make the assumption that it has whatever makes *namug* stones different from other objects, either of another magical type or ordinary, non-magical things and beings. This underlying trait need not be identified. What precisely makes *namug* stones different from *yuka* ones is not described. What is known is that, whatever it is, it makes them have different effects. This underlying trait is (1) undefined (no one represents what it consists of) and (2) not necessarily related to the object's external properties.

To return to our second example, it is difficult not to notice the structural similarity between the representation of categories like *beyem* or *h'ilol* and that of living-kind terms. As I mentioned above, the positions involved in tradition interaction seemed to be related to characteristics such as occupation but the latter do not constitute necessary and sufficient conditions for membership. At the same time, however, people suppose that there is some underlying feature that is common to all persons in the position. In other words, there is a presumption that persons occupying a certain position share an esssence, although what the essence consists of is left undefined. In many anthropological accounts, this is considered a puzzling feature. If people are given a certain position, there should be a mental 'definition' of what makes them different from others. This paradox is eliminated if we admit that positions in such a context are represented in the same way as living kinds. People who are *mbommvet* or *ngengang* are thus considered naturally different from others. If this difference is represented in terms of natural kinds, there is no need of a defining feature; what is necessary is just the presumption that the essential trait exists, not any hypothesis about what it consists of.

In cases like those examined here, where a position is intimately connected to religious interaction, notably to the enactment of religious performance, the represention of the position seems to be based on the extension to social differences of spontaneous assumptions which prove extremely successful in dealing with the natural world.[6] These remarks make it possible to re-interpret some data which are well known in the anthropological literature, although their consequences are not really examined. For instance, it is obvious that the terms denoting social groups are often understood, and glossed by people, in terms of differences between natural species. Members of two groups are different in much the same way as animals belonging to two different species.

The process of identifying stones as belonging to one of the 'magical' types and people as *beyem* therefore has some logical aspects in common with the identification of an exemplar of a natural kind. Although this is exceptionally clear in the examples presented here, I would argue that many cultural categories are used, either directly as natural-kind names, or as a predicate which implies the existence of a natural kind. Traditional categories are generally supposed to be used according to an implicit definition of an implicit theory. I would argue that they are, in fact, often used in the same way as natural-kind terms, which has important cognitive consequences, as regards the type of representations involved, the type of beliefs made possible and the process of concept acquisition. If a category is interpreted as a kind term, it follows that no mental definition of the term is represented. What is represented is a series of typical (non-necessary) properties, together with the assumption that some essential (and undefined) property is common to all exemplars.

The kinds thus picked up are not 'genuine' kinds in nature, but the assumptions made about them are similar to those which are made spontaneously in the presence of exemplars of any natural kind. This is why I will call the putative extension of these categories *pseudo-natural kinds*. The main contention here is that, under certain conditions, people are likely to extend to non-natural domains the assumptions which, from the earliest stages, organise their knowledge of natural phenomena. If this is the case, it may be possible to explain how certain beliefs can be entertained about 'mystical' categories (or rather about their putative reference) in the absence of proposition schemata or such cognitive models. The beliefs, in much the same way as beliefs involved in natural-kind identification, are not theory based; they are grounded in identification of certain exemplars as members of a real kind, combined with the powerful ontological assumptions that inevitably result from this identification.

Why pseudo-natural kinds are not metaphorical

It is important here not to misunderstand the exact claims made about the representation of religious categories. It is specially important to notice that there is an important difference between such 'pseudo-kind' identifications and the type of metaphorical construction described by Lakoff (1987) or Keesing (1984, 1985, this volume). At first sight, it may seem that the construction of 'pseudo-kinds' is a typical case of conventional metaphor. In this interpretation, social groups like *beyem* in my Fang example would be interpreted by subjects as 'living species' in a conventional metaphorical way. That is to say, *beyem*, for instance, would be taken as sharing something undefined, beyond surface resemblance, simply on the basis of an implicit metaphor, for example SOCIAL GROUPS ARE SPECIES, formally comparable to Lakoff & Johnson's (1980) famous examples like TIME IS A RESOURCE or INTELLECTUAL ARGUMENT IS WAR.

At first sight, this may seem plausible. After all, the explicit assimilation of social divisions to differences between 'species' is a widespread metaphor. There are many cultures where categories of people are explicitly conceived as 'different species'. The most telling example may be that of the Indian term *jati*, which denotes both 'species' in the natural domain and 'castes' in the social world. Such cases may lead one to think that 'pseudo-natural kinds' are simply the result of a very common conventional metaphor. I have some reasons, however, to reject this interpretation. In the following pages, I will try to show that the 'pseudo-kind' process I have sketched differs from conventional metaphors.

In order to show this, let me return to Fang culture. In Fang language, the concept of a genus (at the psychologically 'basic' level) is usually expressed by the term *ayong*. Thus, dogs, cats and pigs are said to be of different *ayong*. In spite of many differences, all cats belong to the same *ayong*. The term also has several metaphorical usages, among which one stands out as particularly important. The term is used to designate clans. Fang social organisation is based on a number of embedded patrilineal units. The apex of this segmentary system is constituted by the *ayong* 'clans' which are named and claim common descent from a largely mythical ancestor. Being of the same *ayong* has definite consequences on social relationships. This is made even more salient by the fact that the clans are not localised in any way. Their members are scattered in many villages and in constant interaction with members of other clans.

This, in a sense, is a very clear case of conventional metaphor. The terms designating the concept of LIVING SPECIES is used for clans. Indeed, some aspects of clan membership and inter-clanic relations seem to be conceptualised by using schemata derived from the natural domain: for instance, representations of what is common between members of the same clan could easily be taken as a transposition of resemblance between members of a species. After all, affiliation to a clan is hereditary, in the same way as an animal cannot be a giraffe unless it was born of giraffes. Also, inter-clanic feuds were rife in the area before the colonial order was imposed on Fang tribes, but intra-clanic warfare was a major prohibition, in much the same way as animals typically prey on animals of other species. Some aspects of the clanic systems could thus be given an intuitively adequate representation in this metaphorical frame.

Fang discourse, however, does not 'exploit' the natural-kind metaphor, and the double meaning of *ayong* is not the basis of any such metaphorical inferences. This is especially striking, given the obvious potential of the metaphor, which could provide notions of resemblance and difference, of shared essence, etc. Why is it so? An obvious reason is that relationships between clans just cannot be taken as similar to those obtaining between species. Fang clans, for one thing, are strictly exogamous. As a rule, all members of a clan must marry out. This, of course, makes the species metaphor particularly inadequate. While all giraffes mate with giraffes, all members of a clan are married to outsiders. The metaphor just breaks down when applied to a crucial domain of social relations, probably the most crucial one in Fang society. However, the fact that both clans and living kinds are called *ayong* is not taken as a simple case of homonymy either. Members of a clan are 'similar' in some way, like exemplars of a living kind. It is not possible, however, for Fang speakers to pursue the analogy any further.

There is an obvious difference between this phenomenon and the identification of *beyem*, described above. The *beyem* are a group of people supposed to share some undefined essence, and a number of non-necessary typical features. The assumptions made about them are clearly similar to those made about living kinds. At no point, however, are they explicitly defined as a genus or a kind (*ayong*). In the domain of kin groups, however, there are units called *ayong*; but it is impossible to take them as similar to living kinds. Clans are represented by using concepts used in another domain (living kinds), without importing any strong assumptions from that domain; a clan is just a 'kind' of living kind. So we have two symmetrical cases here:

1 The *beyem* case: these social categories are represented in the same way as a living kind, although they are never *called* one. The ontological assumptions concerning both shared essence and the possibility of inductive generalisation are exactly those applied to natural kinds.

2 The *ayong* case: clans and their properties are *explicitly described* as natural kind-like, but the underlying assumptions of natural-kind identification do not apply.

The point of these examples is to show that the cultural phenomena described here are not easily amenable to a description in terms of conventional metaphor. In fact, the opposite examples show that conventional metaphor is neither a necessary nor a sufficient condition for representing social categories as natural kinds. In the *beyem* example, the category is represented in the same way as a natural kind, but the metaphor is simply not there in the language. So the explicit metaphor is not a *necessary condition* for representing the group as a living kind. On the other hand, Fang 'clans', which are explicitly called 'species', are no doubt a case of 'conventional metaphor'; but the ontological assumptions concerning species are not applied to them. While they are supposed to have some resemblance, this is not linked to the possession of undefined underlying features. The point of the *ayong* examples is that conventional metaphor is not a *sufficient condition* for actually representing the group as a living kind.

Obviously, there are cultures where one can find categories for which both the conventional metaphor and the ontological assumptions are there, that is, social categories which are both treated as natural kinds in terms of underlying feature and surface resemblance, and explicitly treated like 'species' in the language. Our Fang example, however, shows that the metaphor is neither a necessary nor a sufficient condition for the presence of the ontological assumptions it seems to imply. It follows that a description of these cultural phenomena, expressed only in terms of conventional metaphors, is bound to remain incomplete. The description cannot capture the difference between calling some group a species and actually treating it like one. Not all metaphorical ways of speaking convey important assumptions about what sorts of things there are. Conversely, not all important ontological assumptions are expressed in metaphorical ways of speaking. Such differences, however, are crucial in an anthropological description. Differences in ontological and other underlying assumptions result in (1) differences in the range of possible beliefs that can be entertained about a specific category and (2) differences in the way these beliefs are acquired and transmitted. This, of course, is not in itself an argument against conventional metaphor theory; but it *is* an argument against its anthropological use as a global alternative to 'cultural metaphysics' in the description and explanation of traditional categories.

Inductive generalisations

Let me now turn to some consequences of the hypothesis presented here. I have argued that in many cases, the cognitive processes whereby people represent certain religious categories are similar to those involved in the identification and representation of natural kinds. Now, if this is the case, the use of these implicit assumptions should have precise consequences on the way the categories are used. My contention here is that the hypothesis makes it possible to give at least a partial answer to the general questions mentioned at the beginning of this chapter.

Instance-based generalisation is a crucial process in the domains we are dealing with. Two main limitations can be derived from the fact that natural-kind assumptions are made about the putative reference of a category. First, the limitation of 'possible' beliefs results from the fact that, as we saw above, a single use of a term results in spontaneous ontological hypotheses, which by themselves are the basis of predicate restrictions. Once some term is interpreted as 'name for a species', then it is impossible to say that the thing it denotes 'will happen' or that 'there is little of it here', etc. Second, another process is involved, which both allows to entertain some beliefs and limits their range. In order to understand this, it may be of help to return to the properties of real natural kinds. There is a fundamental difference between natural kinds and other classes of objects, in that the hypothesis that something belongs to a natural kind makes it possible to build inductive generalisations on the basis of limited evidence, whereas categories which do not denote natural kinds do not support such generalisations. As philosophers noticed long ago, the properties of natural kinds come in 'bundles'. Once one has seen one giraffe, one can make the hypothesis that many properties of that singular giraffe will in fact be properties of giraffes in general. That is to say, if I see a giraffe laying eggs or eating flowers, I will infer that these are general features of the species, not particular qualities of the exemplar I am watching. Such indicative generalisations are, of course, impossible with non-natural classes. No matter how many pets one has seen, one cannot infer what future pets will be like, except that they will be pets.

Experimental evidence shows that this difference plays a fundamental role in the mental representation of categories. Even young children are sensitive to the difference between natural-kind and property terms, and make induction from one exemplar to other cases if both are said to belong to the same natural kind. This mechanism is salient enough to override judgements based on perceptual resemblance or differences. To take but a very brief example, in one of Gelman and Markman's experiments, four-year-olds are shown pictures of dolphins and tropical fish and told how these animals breathe (above the surface and under water respectively). They are then shown some pictures of a shark, which looks more like the dolphin than like the tropical fish presented, and yet is presented to them as a type of fish. When asked how sharks breathe, they correctly infer, against the perceptual resemblance, that they must breathe in water (Gelman & Markman 1986: 203–5). Moreover, children seem to make inductive generalisations more easily if the properties chosen are 'inherent' properties of the exemplars, for example, ways of breathing and feeding. On the other hand, they do not easily extend properties like the weight of a given animal or the fact that it moves fast (Gelman & Markman 1987 *passim*).

Obviously, the fact that induction is safe does not guarantee that all its generalisations are true; indeed, many false inferences are made on the basis of such projections. Equally obviously, children who build their knowledge of natural kinds gradually combine and check inductive projection with many theory-like generalisations. The important point, however, is that the projection mechanism is fundamental in concept acquisition and that it is inevitably triggered when an object is identified as a member of a natural kind. Although this is more striking in small children, who lack later-stage theoretical capacities, this presumption of safe induction is the main mechanism that makes generalisation over natural exemplars possible. We must now evaluate the reluctance of these mechanisms in the domain of traditional categories.

To take the example of Fang categories, notions like *evur* and *beyem* are used in two main registers of discourse: 'common' discourse, which pervades ordinary conversations and exchanges; and 'expert' utterances, made by such specialists as witch-doctors and diviners. Common discourse is intrinsically vague: it says that *beyem* are involved in uncanny, anti-social activities, but also that it is impossible to say anything definite about such matters, because *evur*-related problems have 'neither back nor stomach', they are elusive, impossible to grasp. Expert utterances, on the other hand, consist of definite, supposedly true statements, which focus on singular cases. Experts, for instance, identify a particular person as a *beyem*, or specify that a certain behaviour or misfortune is caused by the person's *evur* and so on. At no point in these utterances do experts make use of 'general' principles. On the contrary, they focus on the singular aspects of the situation considered.

As a consequence, the representations Fang subjects entertain about *evur* and *beyem* are bound to be the result of a process of inductive generalisation from singular identifications. This does not apply to the interpretation only, but also concerns the production of expert utterances. One becomes an expert of *evur* by going through a series of personal experiences, notably a series of direct presentations of the world of the 'ghosts' (*bekong*) where *evur* is directly efficient. Being able to make definite statements about *evur* and having experienced such direct presentations of the ghosts' world are two qualities that seem necessarily connected. When experts make definite statements about specific cases and their relationship to *evur*, they are judging mainly on the basis of a resemblance between the situation at hand and whatever memories they have acquired in the course of their apprenticeship and 'mystical' experience.

The fact that the class of *beyem* is represented in much the same way as a natural kind is crucial, because it makes it possible to entertain beliefs based on inductive generalisations. Once *beyem* are represented as belonging to a 'species', characteristics of singular individuals can be represented as typical of a group as a whole. Then the properties of people identified as *beyem* will be extended as being probable properties of the whole class of *evur*-bearers. As I said above, this is precisely the way people's representations of *evur* are gradually constructed, taking statements and diagnoses from the 'specialised' discourse register as the basis for inductive generalisations. Such generalisations are based on the implicit idea that all *beyem* belong to a natural kind; otherwise no inductive generalisation would be possible.

I would argue that the conclusions drawn from this case may apply, *mutatis mutandis*, to many 'mystical' notions used in traditional contexts. Acquiring expert discourse, in such groups, usually implies undergoing a series of specific experiences, often described as an initiation, which cannot be described as the acquisition of a new 'definition' for the notions concerned. Such experiences do not transmit technical knowledge, although the latter may be acquired in parallel. The experiences themselves, not the knowledge, make the difference between expert discourse and the rest. What is acquired by the subjects is a series of salient memories, which are then used as guidelines, together with other types of knowledge, in the evaluation of subsequent situations. The crucial point here is that if subjects do represent cultural categories, like those denoting types of magical stones in Brown's example or the term '*beyem*' among the Fang, as natural-kind terms, this identification will inevitably result in a process of inductive generalisation on the basis of singular exemplars.

Conclusions

Let me now return to the general questions posed at the beginning of this chapter. The starting point here is the observation that the process of concept acquisition and belief fixation are bound to have some influence on the type of beliefs that people entertain about religious entities or events. The main reason why acquisition processes are important in this domain is that people's beliefs are under-determined by the material available. Subjects must build their representation of things such as *evur* or magical stones notably on the basis of other people's utterances and actions. Now it is not possible to think that people just passively absorb and reproduce the models found in that material. This is not possible because the material itself is insufficient for this purpose. From what the Fang say about *evur* or the Aguaruna about their stones, one could not build the actual representations and beliefs entertained by adult subjects without having certain principles that make it possible to go further than the material given.

Three general aspects of religious symbolism tend to suggest that acquisition is under-determined by the available material. First of all, most principles involved in religious beliefs are implicit. If they are transmitted at all, they are transmitted without being taught. This is a general feature of *traditional* contexts, where there is little explicit tuition. Second, the utterances made by people are often vague or inconsistent. The case of *evur* illustrates this point; although it may seem a rather extreme case in this respect, this type of ambiguity is a general feature of religious symbolism. A third aspect is perhaps the most important one. Even if religious symbolism was entirely explicit and consistent, it would still be insufficient to account for the acquisition process. Take, for instance, the case of the Aguaruna magical stones. As I indicated above, the beliefs concerning these stones are based on a fundamental principle, namely that any given stone belongs to one of the magical categories (or else to the residual category of non-magical stones). When a stone which was formerly identified as X is then recategorised as Y, people conclude that the stone was Y all along and that they were mistaken in thinking it was X. They do not conclude that the stone has changed categories. In other words, belonging to one of these categories is an essential property. Now this is a principle which guides Aguaruna beliefs about stones, but cannot be made explicit, except by psychologists or philosophers. In much the same way, we teach children beliefs about animals; but we do not have to teach them that animals cannot be made, or that animals cannot change species, while knives can be made and can be transformed into other utensils.

If religious symbolism is under-determined in this fundamental way, subjects must use intuitive heuristics in order to build their own representations of the entities and properties concerned from this fragmentary material. In this chapter I have described one such heuristics, which I think is crucial in many areas of religious symbolism. The heuristics consists in applying to certain domains of religious symbolism assumptions which are automatically triggered when a kind of objects is constructed as natural. Obviously, the hypothesis does not in itself provide a complete explanation of the acquisition of religious symbolism. It is certainly insufficient for the trivial reason that not all agencies or social categories are construed as 'pseudo-natural kinds'. The relative importance of concepts denoting pseudo-natural kinds, as opposed to kinds conceptualised in other ways, is, of course, an empirical question. Also, even in cases where the pseudo-natural-kind interpretation seems clearly relevant, we should give a more precise description of the factors that trigger and strengthen such implicit assumptions.

The 'pseudo-natural kinds' hypothesis is based on psychological hypotheses whose relevance is obvious in other areas of cognition. Although the precise points made here are strictly speculative, it seems necessary for an investigation of cultural knowledge to take into account such cognitive phenomena as the organisation and effects of ontological knowledge and the possibility that subjects treat certain cultural categories as though they were names for natural kinds.

NOTES

1 This section provides a summary of an argument presented in more detail in Boyer (1990: ch. 6) about the categories denoting social positions. The argument is based on data gathered in Cameroon and Equatorial Guinea in 1981 and 1985. For a general account of beliefs and ritual concerning the notion *evur*,

see Mallart Guimera (1975, 1981) and the status of *mbommvet*, epic story-tellers, is the subject-matter of Boyer (1988).

2 There is no space here to develop this point, which is discussed in detail in Boyer (1990: ch. 6 *passim*).

3 One must be careful not to confuse uncertainty about a yes/no question (e.g. whether the result of 356/46 is an integer) with uncertainty generated by vague categories (e.g. whether turquoise is blue or green).

4 It may be important to add, although Keil and other researchers do not pursue this point, that the ontological inferences are made in the context of conversations. The main result, maybe the triggering element of the ontological assumptions, is that they make the utterances pertinent.

5 The philosophical debates about natural-kind terms are mainly focused on the question of reference, that is, how it is possible actually to refer to sets of objects without representing necessary and sufficient conditions for category membership. The idea that the reference is in fact fixed by the world itself was put forward by Putnam (1975: 215–71; 1983: 71). Here, on the contrary, I focus on the psychological aspects of the question. See Schwarz (1977, 1979) for a general presentation of the psychological and philosophical literature on natural kinds and their representation, and Atran (1987a) for a more recent survey of the cognitive literature.

6 This, of course, applies, in an even clearer way, to categories of people which are *explicitly* conceived as 'different species'. The most telling example may be that of the Indian term *jati*, which denotes both 'species' in the natural domain and 'castes' in the social world. Such 'conventional metaphors' are extremely widespread. In such cases there is no definition of what makes the group different, only elaborations on the consequences of that undefined natural difference (Boyer 1982: 49–52).

Part III

Acquisition and belief fixation

Does religious symbolism correspond to a particular 'mode of thought'? In the previous contributions, most authors tried to show, against some classical models, that in terms of cognitive processes it is just not possible to maintain this hypothesis. Whatever the models adopted, the authors tried to show that the formal aspects of religious representations can be found in many other types of contexts: there is no 'domain-specificity' of religious symbolism. However, in many cultural contexts religious action and statements are, implicitly or explicitly, 'marked off' from the every-day. Statements are made in a special language, actions are clearly seen to be ritualised, etc. If such special contexts do not correspond to genuine differences in 'modes of thought' or cognitive processes, how are they represented? What features or criteria are used to separate contexts? Both contributions in this section aim to examine this question, from the particular viewpoint of acquisition and belief fixation, in the passage from everyday to ritualised situation. Non-ritual contexts are prior, both logi-cally (since rituals are considered 'special' against a residual background of unmarked contexts) and in terms of cognitive development (as children only gradually acquire the capacity to tell one type of contexts from the other). Toren focuses on the latter issue, and challenges the common assumption that 'symbolism' is entirely separate from, and therefore unconstrained by commonsense knowledge of everyday contexts. This is just not plausible from a developmental viewpoint. Toren takes as an example the way people sit 'below' or 'above' in Fijian households, depending on gender and other aspects of status. The underlying prin-ciples of this hierarchical ordering are not immediately obvious to chil-dren and are complex enough to give rise to several incompatible models. Toren documents the way children, in the course of conceptual develop-ment, gradually develop an abstract and 'symbolic' understanding of observable and recurrent features of social interaction. Her study, which combines experimental data and classical ethnography, leads her to question received oppositions of 'sign' and 'symbol'.

Severi, on the other hand, is working on an almost diametrical situation. Shamanistic ritual, among the Cuna of Panama, makes use of a 'special tongue' that is entirely opaque to non-specialists. Understanding shamanism, therefore, implies understanding the way this difference is acquired and represented. Severi stresses the fact that, although shamans use a special language, the transmission or use of esoteric information is secondary in such situations. On the other hand, the opacity of the language has definite consequences on the *conditions of enunciation* of shamanistic utterances. Severi shows that this has important consequences for the participants' representations of the central entities and processes involved in shamanistic ritual. The actors do not understand the shaman's action and position in terms of a prior 'cultural model' of the soul and of healing, as some anthropological descriptions tend to suggest. On the contrary, they gradually build a fragmentary representation of what souls are, and how pain can be interpreted, on the basis of the observable features of the seance, notably the conditions under which the shaman's utterances are produced.

These two contributions describe two complementary aspects of the differentiation of religious symbolism: on the one hand, there is a clear, often explicit set of criteria that make manifest the special nature of the situations and actions; on the other hand, however, subjects apply to the situations conceptual structures and processes derived from their understanding of other types of contexts. Both chapters show that cognitive processes of belief fixation impose strong constraints on the representation of religious matters. In Toren's study, general patterns of cognitive development inform the child's understanding of symbolic hierarchies, and constrain the type of abstract model subjects gradually construct. In Severi's chapter participants use features of everyday experience, for example of the experience of pain, to build a coherent account of otherwise opaque religious messages. In both studies, it is shown that the acquisition of such religious symbolism does not primarily consist in the acquisition and storage of new information. In the case of Fijian children, the observable features are the same all along; what changes in the course of development is the relative weighing, and the consequences, of these features. In the Cuna example, no-one ever 'learns' anything from shamanistic sessions, except a definite representation of what makes these sessions special.

7   Sign into symbol, symbol as sign: cognitive aspects of a social process

Christina Toren

This essay challenges a common anthropological assumption that we can demarcate a domain of 'the symbolic', that this domain is self-evident, located 'out there', its paradigm being given by ritual. This assumption itself rests on the conventional anthropological distinction between sign and symbol, where the sign is propositional or simply referential and the symbol is evocative of meaning beyond itself, and thus on the notion that the sign too is obvious. Here I argue that we should cease to make an *a priori* distinction between sign and symbol and that we should give up the lingering notion that to understand ritual is to analyse its meaning as a relation between metaphors. At best, such an analysis can be only the first step towards understanding the peculiar power of ritual.

I argue below that the notion that any given ritual act is 'symbolic', that is, that it 'stands for' something other than itself, is the product of a process of cognitive construction in persons over time. In other words, for young children ritual is *not* symbolic in the conventional anthropological sense. Rather, young children take ritualised behaviour for granted as part of the day-to-day material reality of their existence. So, in the Fijian case discussed here, the ritualised drinking of kava is, for children, merely what people do when drinking kava. The activity is of the same material and cognitive order as, say, house-building. By contrast, an adult under-standing of kava-drinking entails the conscious awareness that the activity is not merely an end in itself, but rather that it expresses certain intangible meanings which themselves make the ritual performance oblig-atory. This chapter charts the process by which Fijian village children come to understand ritualised behaviour as expressive of certain other-wise intangible truths. My data show that it is only with respect to older children and adults that the analyst is justified in interpreting ritualised behaviour as symbolic.

To some readers this may seem perhaps an obvious and unremarkable observation. However, it is only when we understand the process through which 'the symbolic' is cognitively constructed that we can also under-stand the coercive power of ritual. As I show below, young children may have a fairly thorough grasp of the explicit rules of ritualised behaviour, but it is the process of constructing over time the meanings of that behaviour that makes them as adults, convinced of the extrinsic necessity of those explicit rules. Moreover, in so far as one can show how this process occurs, one can also explain certain aspects of how people come to be at once products and producers of a specific, and inherently dynamic, cultural history.

The data described below were obtained during my fieldwork in the village and district of Sawaieke, on the island of Gau, central Fiji, from June 1981 to March 1983.[1] The data address the Fijian concern with status differentiation in terms of people's disposition in space. I begin with a very brief description of the ritualised behaviour in which this concern is manifest; there follows an account of the way that Fijian children construct their notions of differential status with reference to the spatial axis described by the terms *i cake* 'above' and *i ra* 'below'. As we shall see, this psychological process has to be described as constructive in its nature, but *it does not give rise to a cognitive structure whereby the meaning of above/below can be fixed.* Taken together, these data illustrate something of the way that culturally prescriptive acts at the level of the group enter into cognitive processes in particular persons. I end with some suggestions as to the implications of my analysis for our understanding of ritual.

Manifesting hierarchy

In Fiji, hierarchical relations are typically made manifest in people's relative position on the above/below axis that describes the space inside buildings, usually with reference to a single plane. This hierarchical construct is the spatial corollary of the exchange relation by which chiefs receive tribute and redistribute it to the people. By contrast, the term, *veiqaravi* ('attendance', lit. 'facing each other') refers to exchange relations of balanced reciprocity that ideally obtain between clans (*yavusa*) and is inscribed in the orientation of buildings to one another in the space of the village. However, the term *veiqaravi* also refers to attendance on chiefs in kava-drinking where peoples' disposition in space connotes hierarchy across households. I have shown elsewhere how hierarchical above/below is itself a transformation of the ambiguous notion of *veiqaravi*, and is thus simultaneously a transformation of balanced reciprocity into the hierarchical exchange relation of tribute and redistribution (Toren 1988). Across households this transformation is effected in the ritual of kava-drinking.

In kava ritual the root of the plant is presented to chiefs in its 'raw' form and under their aegis is transformed into drink and redistributed 'cooked' to the people (the root of the plant is pounded and infused in water). The ceremony of presentation or *sevusevu* is an obligatory form of tribute to chiefs, no occasion 'in the manner of the land' can take place without it; it is at once an everyday matter and the key ritual act of tribute to chiefs. So a chief becomes paramount and fully *mana* (effective) when he drinks the bowl of kava that is prepared and served under the aegis of the commoner chief who is head of that clan that 'makes the chief'. The commoner chief's own *mana* is at once realised and compromised in the act of installation, for in conferring upon another man a privileged access to the 'gods of the land' he thus creates his own ritual subordination. The chief who 'makes' a high chief accords to himself the status of one who 'listens to' and 'attends on' the other, like a young man to an elder or a woman to her husband. His act projects an image of the hierarchy of the household onto relations across households: the high chief becomes 'father of the people', who thus seem to stand to one another as ranked siblings. Nevertheless, the installing chief retains his status as chief and the reciprocal and balanced relations between clans remain intact, contained, but not denied by, the hierarchy that is given by seating positions in kava ritual and the order of the drinking.

On an everyday basis kava ritual transforms balanced exchanges across clans into 'tribute to chiefs'. In other contexts (e.g. marriage ritual) exchange is competitive, but balanced over time, the various clans 'face, or attend on each other'. In kava-drinking people are also said to be *veiqaravi* ('facing each other') but they do so in a space which is hierarchically valued where a small group of chiefs faces 'down' towards the people from whom they receive tribute and the people face 'up' towards the chiefs, whose *mana* from the ancestors and ultimately from God is the source of all prosperity. If men and women are drinking together, a small group of male chiefs is above the *tanoa*, the large circular bowl in which kava is prepared; a group of three to five or so young (unmarried) men sit behind and at the sides of the *tanoa* 'facing the chiefs', preparing and serving the kava; besides the young men and taking up the middle space around them are married men in their due order according to age and rank; below them sit young men not involved in kava preparation, and women. Women in general pay somewhat less attention to status distinctions among themselves than do men, though it is true that elderly women of chiefly rank are usually accorded a seating position that is above that of other women. Given that the form of kava-drinking itself works to constitute the above/below axis of the space where it takes place, one is always in a certain status position *vis-à-vis* all others present, and this status is confirmed by the order in which the drink is served, beginning with the highest-status person present.

The Fijian term for chief may denote any married man or, much more exclusively, the group of clan chiefs (including the high chief). It also refers to all persons (irrespective of sex) who are members by birth of the clan from which a paramount chief is chosen. Rank distinctions supposedly operate such that chiefs are above commoners; within sex, rank predominates over relative age where the rank difference is understood to be the marked term, for example, a named clan chief sits above other clan members even if he is somewhat younger than they are. However, for statuses below that of named chief, relative age is the deciding factor. So, within sex, the interaction between rank and seniority poses little difficulty for status differentiation on the above/below axis.

Gender is another matter. Male status varies as a function of age and rank; female status is always ambiguous. Where a woman is the eldest of a set of siblings she is owed the respect of her brothers who should defer to her wishes in any matters of ritual importance in her natal household. Thus she has a superior say, for instance, in the marriages of her brothers' children. However, as an in-marrying wife, this same woman owes respect and obedience to her husband, that is, to a man who is her brothers' equal.

The term *veiwekani* (kin) at its widest extension takes in all Fijians; in the behaviour prescribed for interaction between the various categories of kin, hierarchical relations are made to contain, and so prevail over, important egalitarian relations. These egalitarian relations are at once constituted and expressed in balanced exchange between cross-cousins both within and across sex; this relation typically obtains across households. By contrast, all other kind relations are hierarchical and require varying degrees of respect and avoidance; within the household hierarchical relations are at once constituted and expressed in exchange relations that are made to appear unbalanced. This appearance is constituted ritually in the course of every meal where a wife's contribution appears to take the form of tribute to her husband, and her inferior position is manifest in her seating place at the cloth at the pole below. This ritual transformation of the wife's contribution (in terms of both the foods obtained and the labour of preparing them) makes concrete the Fijian axiom that 'Every man is a chief in his own house'. The fundamentally balanced exchange relations between men and women at the level of the group are transformed in marriage into a hierarchical relation between particular husbands and wives.

This transformation begins in the betrothal and marriage ritual. Here the bride ceases to be party to a balanced and reciprocal exchange between equals (i.e. between cross-cousins) and is transformed into 'gift'.

Marilyn Strathern (1984) has shown how the 'objectification' of women in marriage rituals in societies with gift economies cannot be equated with the subject–object relation between people and things in commodity economies. Thus, because objects in Fijian ceremonial exchange always have 'people' qualities, that is, are gifts not commodities, a woman retains her subjectivity in marriage. Her rights in her natal lineage will devolve on her children who, as *vasu*, may 'take what they want without asking' from men of their mother's lineage. In respect of herself the woman's rights are greatly attentuated and while she has influence over her husband her formal status is rendered inferior to his. This inferior status is reiterated on a daily basis when she takes her place at the pole below at every meal in her husband's house.[2]

There is no neutral seating position inside a Fijian house, village hall or church. The internal space of buildings is valued according to the spatial axis given by the terms 'above' and 'below'. When people are seated together in a space, their relative positions on the above/below axis are understood *by adults* to be an expression of the status that has accrued to them outside the ritualised contexts in which that status is actually manifest. One sits in a place that is called 'above', because one *is* above others in a hierarchy that is given by an interaction between notions of rank, seniority and gender. For adults this means that older is above younger, chiefs are above commoners and men are above women. The product of this interaction gives rise to an inherent conflict between rank/seniority and gender.

Here I remind the reader that the above/below axis refers to a *single* plane. Thus in houses, village halls, churches, temporary shelters, and also when kava is drunk out of doors, one part of the space is called 'above' and the opposite pole of the space is 'below'. However, no-one is literally above or below anyone else. In kava-drinking the relative status of all persons in the community is manifest in the activity of the meal at home. The cloth is *always* laid on the floor along the given above/below axis of the house space, and household members have their places there in terms of their relative status. The significance of kava-drinking and meals for people's understanding of relative status is the subject of the rest of this chapter.

Children's construction of the significance of 'above/below'

Children's drawings of kava-drinking

The data below were gathered with the help of children who attended Sawaieke primary school and who ranged in age from 5/10 to 14/2. All sixty-seven children (the entire school roll) were asked to draw a picture of people drinking kava in a gathering in the village hall in Sawaieke; they were told that men and women, young men and girls were all present and having lots of fun. These instructions thus distinguished two possible statuses for each sex. After they had drawn their pictures, each child discussed his or her drawing with me and either spontaneously or in response to questioning told me who were the persons depicted and where they were seated. My questions distinguished a third possible status distinction for each sex, that of high chief and chiefly lady.

I have discussed in detail elsewhere the children's own drawings and their commentary on them (Toren 1987, 1991). Here I simply summarise some of the findings. Most important was the conclusion that the significance of above/below (*cake/ra*) is the product of a genuine constructive process. In spite of definite individual differences (i.e. all drawings had idiosyncratic features), reliable group differences emerged with respect to the age and sex of the children. With the exception of the very youngest child (aged 5/10), all had a knowledge of the polar extremes of above/below; both boys (median age 7/5) and girls (median age 7/8) accorded the position above to the high chief but differed with respect to the position below. Boys gave this place to females, girls to females and young men.

Age was a factor in children's ability to make fine status distinctions: younger children did not go beyond the three statuses for males suggested by myself and tended to make only one distinction for females, that of *marama* ('married women'); older children used two more distinctions for males and one more for females. For *all* age groups there was an interaction between the number of status distinctions made and the sex of the child doing the task; thus, at any age, girls made more distinctions for females than did boys while boys made more distinctions for males than did girls. However, for all children, more status distinctions were made for males than for females.

Younger children showed the high chief alone in the place above. By contrast, the oldest children depicted a small *group* of chiefs above; they also tended to make four or five status distinctions for males. However, they accorded the position below to females as a relatively undifferentiated group, even where they had made the maximum number of four status distinctions among them. Thus, they too, like the youngest children, showed females or females *and* young men below. Again, this choice was highly correlated with the child's own sex: boys showed females below, girls showed females and young men below. The oldest children's response to the matter of who sits below thus appeared to have remained unchanged; however, the data obtained from children in the middle age range of the sample make it plain that this is unlikely to have been the case.

These children produced drawings that showed a push for equality across gender and within status categories. Thus, boys (median age 11/1) and some girls (median age 11/0) showed either the high chief or a small groups of chiefs above, with below them men and women seated according to age seniority, and young men and girls together at the pole below. Others, all but one of them girls (median age 11/1), produced an even more radical representation where the high chief or a small group of chiefs were seated alongside their respective wives above. Below them married men sat with their wives or women of their own age and at the pole below young men sat with girls.

These drawings are especially noteworthy since it is only in the most exceptional circumstances that men and women sit on the same level in kava-drinking and certainly women never sit on the same level as their husbands. Thus these children in the middle age range *depicted a situation they can only rarely or never have seen*, one that makes gender largely irrelevant to the ordering of status. Indeed, a majority of the girls appeared to have constructed a principle whereby status is differentiated according to an interaction between rank and seniority alone. The girls whose drawings showed this radical 'push for equality' across gender and within status categories also showed the greatest concern for differentiating between females, making three or four status distinctions. I use the term 'principle' here to express the explicit Fijian adult notion of hierarchy as a kind of moral imperative; perhaps I should emphasise, therefore, that the precise form that the 'hierarchical principle' takes differs across particular persons as well as across groups.

The drawings of the oldest children revealed that they were more aware of the possibility of ambiguity regarding the position of the high chief when compared with other chiefs, that is, they always showed a small group of chiefs together above; but they also reconstituted a definition of below as the place of females, who were treated as a relatively undifferentiated group over against the ranks of men. In other words, these oldest children had grasped both the principle of hierarchy as manifest in a relative ranking on the above/below axis, *and* the way that gender is a complexly interacting factor that assigns the place below to women in general and tends to make status distinctions for them of lesser importance than they are for men.

The 'problem' of gender is given by the fact that the position of all females below conflicts with the notion that people of chiefly birth are above commoners and older people above younger people. This inherent conflict between three apparently separable factors appeared in the drawings of children aged around 11/0. These data, taken together with that from the youngest and the oldest children, show that the children are constructing a principle of status differentiation out of the interaction between rank, seniority and gender. No single factor may be given analytic priority over the others because, as the children's drawings show, being above is about being a chief and an elderly male while being below is about being a young man or a female, rank by birth being largely ignored.

Prepared drawings

In another task, children were asked to look at ten prepared drawings of different situations and to say who were the persons represented and where they were seated. This task was designed primarily to find out to what extent children would make use of the plane of the page to distinguish different status categories and whether there were any differences in response to the different situations. Here I confine myself to discussion of the main findings that emerged from analysis of children's responses to these drawings (see Toren 1991 for the complete data). A total of forty-seven children, ranging in age from 6/6 to 14/2, took part in this task. The drawings used were simple and schematic so that the seated figures could be said to be either male or female, young or old according to my own or the children's wish. The drawings fell into one of three categories: they showed people drinking kava, eating meals or at meetings. Specific instructions were given for the labelling of each drawing but, in general, the children were asked to label the figures so as to distinguish men, young men, women and girls; they might also be asked to label the high chief and his *matanivanua* ('herald', lit. 'face of the land') or asked to decide themselves whether the high chief was present and if so to indicate which figure represented him; they were also asked to indicate the position in which each of the figures was seated.

The responses to these drawings were analysed to discover the extent to which children made use of the plane of the page to distinguish the various status categories from one another and how consistently they did so. The prediction was that for drawings depicting meals and kava-drinking the children would be more likely to make consistent use of the plane of the page to distinguish status categories than they would for drawings depicting meetings. In other words, I expected children to establish an ordering of status on the above/below axis such that, for instance, having chosen a figure at the top or bottom of a page as 'high chief' and therefore 'above' the rest, the children would proceed to rank the other figures in order of descending status using the plane of the page as an implicit guide. The analysis of the response revealed that not only was there, over all, a high level of consistency in children's responses to the drawings, but that they fulfilled the prediction that there would be a greater consistency of response to the drawings depicting meals and kava-drinking than to those depicting meetings.

The merging of spatial and status categories

Analysis of the children's own drawings and of their responses to pre-pared drawings establishes that hierarchy and the above/below axis are merged, such that children construct their notions of the interaction between rank, seniority and gender by reference to the above/below axis; for example, to say that a man 'sits above' is to say that he is of high status. The merging of hierarchy with the spatial axis was found for children of both sexes as young as 6/3. Given that a partial merging was found for children around 6/0 one may assume that an understanding of above/below in terms of its polar extremes occurs just before school age.

Children's responses to prepared drawings confirmed the merging and produced further interesting findings. Perhaps the most illuminating but perhaps not so very surprising, is that the position of mother below is the anchor for situations within the household. So, for prepared drawings of meals, all children chose the figure below to be Mother, and this was the case whether she was taken to be at the top or bottom plane of the page. By contrast, the figure said to be above was either Father, Father's Elder Brother, Father's Father, Mother's Brother or a 'guest'.

This finding suggests that Mother is most salient in the household, and that it is her position at meals that defines the place that is below. Note that the woman who is Mother is Wife to a particular man. By contrast, children's own drawings of kava-drinking and their responses to prepared drawings of contexts other than meals show that, in the community domain, it is the high chief who is most salient and his seating position that there defines the place above.

But how does this merging of status with spatial categories come about? Piaget has always emphasised that a child's early cognitions are tied to concrete referents, a point also made by Bourdieu (1977). This is as much the case for my own data concerning a so-called 'symbolic' construct as it is for the so-called 'logical' constructs investigated by Piaget and his co-workers. What emerges most forcefully from the children's data is the crucial importance of the spatial axis given by above/below as this is made manifest in concrete form in houses, churches, at meals and in kava-drinking.

Children acknowledged the salience of 'the high chief' above for contexts across households and for 'mother' below at home before they were fully aware that differential status governs one's position on the above/below axis. For these youngest children it appears that status is concrete. In other words, the paramount is above because 'above' is the term that names that part of the room where he sits; similarly, a woman or a young man is below because this term names that part of the room where *they* sit. The fact that for kava-drinking boys give the position below to females, and girls to young men as well as females, suggests a child's own gender identification is a factor in his or her construction of the significance of above/below. Nevertheless, one can argue that the youngest children are not talking about status in the adult sense of the term when they describe the seating position of the figures in their drawings, but are rather expressing a simple awareness of the two poles of the above/below axis and the people who generally occupy them when adults gather together.

This is confirmed by the way that, when children begin to accommodate what they know about above/below with what they know about differential status, they produce drawings that distort the typical empirical situation in kava-drinking. The data suggest that it is not before age 8/5 at the earliest that children become aware that it is *relative status* that is expressed on the above/below axis. The youngest children merge status and above/below only in the crude sense that they 'know' that the high chief sits above and women, or women and young men, sit below with married men in between. An enlightened merging of the spatial axis with an awareness that status may be derived from contexts independent of it, occurs for many children at around age 11/0, when their drawings reveal a conflict between rank/seniority and gender in status differentiation. They 're-order' the empirically given image of hierarchy in kava-drinking in terms of an interaction between rank and seniority and largely ignore gender as a variable in differential status.

The children's data show that the high salience of above/below as constitutive of differential status is the foundation for complex adult notions of hierarchy with respect to kinship and political relations across clans, villages and chiefdoms (*vanua*, lit. 'countries'). Adult notions include ideas of *mana* (lit. 'effectiveness'), legitimacy, personal achievement, the significance of mythical relations between the ancestors of clans and of certain ritual observances such as the *sevusevu* (presentation of kava), kava-drinking and so on. Thus, adults never say that a man is above because he sits in that part of the room that is routinely described as above. Rather, he is accorded this position because his status makes it appropriate. For adults it is a matter of conscious awareness that social status governs a person's position above or below. For adults, in direct contrast to children, where the high chief sits is above, because the quality of being above is inherent in him as high chief, and where women sit is below 'because they are women who are seated with chiefs'.

However, it seems that the above/below axis is understood to be more constraining in some situations than others. This is clear from children's labelling of prepared drawings of people at meals, drinking kava and at meetings. From my own observation of meetings where there was no kava, people are no more likely to violate there the constraints imposed by above/below than they are when kava is in evidence. But children's responses to prepared drawings showed them to be more concerned with these constraints for the contexts of kava-drinking and meals than for meetings. In labelling drawings of meetings they were significantly less consistent in representing, for example, an elder above a married man, above a young man.

This differential response reveals a heightened salience of spatial constraints in certain contexts, and one is led to ask why it should occur. It cannot be because meals and kava-drinking have a set and regular format, this is also true of meetings. Nor can it be explained by any absence of association with ideas of transcendent power: prayers precede meetings just as they precede all meals and children's knowledge of the association between kava-drinking and *mana* (here meaning a transcendent 'effectiveness') is likely to be rather vague.

I would argue that it is adult notions of meals and kava-drinking as rule-governed activities that produce children's heightened awareness of the spatial constraints imposed by above/below. For adults, ritual practice can be, and is, expressed in terms of explicit rules.[3] These explicit rules mean that the cloth at meals has to be placed along the above/below axis of the house space and that the *tanoa* in kava-drinking must be placed so that it 'faces the chiefs'; the *tanoa* mediates between the two extremes of the above/below axis and marks out the chiefs' positions above it from the positions of those who are seated below. The cloth similarly draws attention to the disposition of people on the above/below axis. Thus the children's heightened awareness must hinge on the fact that certain concrete elements in kava-drinking and meals are always disposed in the same way and it is the disposition of these concrete objects that emphasises the above/below axis.

The significance of meals and kava-drinking is such that differential status is inscribed both in the activities themselves and in the space where they occur. A chief drinks first when kava is served, speaks first in a meeting and (every man being a chief in his own house) eats first at home. What distinguishes meetings from kava-drinking and meals in drawings labelled by children is that, aside from the figures depicted, there are no other concrete elements present, no *tanoa*, no cloth, to draw attention to the necessity for a continued and *consistent* ranking on the above/below axis of all those 'below' the figure chosen to represent 'the high chief'.

I would argue further that the salience of kava-drinking for an adult understanding of local hierarchy comes in time to outweigh that of any other situation where relative status is expressed. The heightened significance of kava-drinking for adults is no doubt connected with the following: though non-alcoholic, it is mildly intoxicating; it is drunk on all ceremonial occasions; the *sevusevu* and the drinking itself are obligatory and imbued with ideas of the transcendent power of the ancestors and the *mana* of chiefs, whose position in life is 'divinely ordained'. Primary-school children must know something of such matters, though their knowledge is probably at best only partial, but they too come to accept kava-drinking as providing the 'correct' image of the nature of local hierarchy. This conclusion is entailed by the finding that, while drawings by children around 11/0 represent a hierarchy where rank and seniority govern differential status and gender is largely irrelevant, those by the oldest children (the majority over 12/6) represent an image of hierarchy that accords with the typical empirical nature of kava-drinking.

However, it is the salience for younger children of material objects, such as the cloth at meals and the *tanoa* in kava ritual, that underlies the mature conception of above/below. The continuity between a child's and an adult's conception of the hierarchy inscribed in people's positions on the above/below axis actually rests on the *material stability* of ritual; that is, on the fact that certain highly salient material elements are always disposed in the same way. So any additional understanding of the 'meaning' of kava-drinking that accrues to adolescent or adult is inevitably articulated to an awareness of status as being more clearly manifest, more concrete, in certain ritual contexts. The very fact that the adult conception of kava-drinking is richer, more complex, more meaningful than the child's is itself dependent upon the initial and continued salience of the *tanoa*.

Thus children learn about the hierarchy manifest on the above/below axis in specific situations such as meals and kava-drinking and come to associate space with hierarchy in these situations. The learning process is one of gradual construction and it is initially tied to certain material objects such as the *tanoa*, the cloth at meals or the house itself, but these material objects are cultural artefacts; they refer not simply to themselves but to relations between people. So the fully developed adult conception of above/below inverts the child's concept: what was initially understood as material and concrete comes to be seen as an *expression* of a deeper and more abstract principle: the principle of hierarchy as derived from an interaction between rank, seniority and gender.

Sign and symbol as a continuum of meaning

The obligatory ritualised behaviours of adults provide the conditions under which children have cognitively to construct the meanings that make sense of adult behaviours. The child's effort is directed towards expressing and elaborating meanings he or she has already perforce constructed as given in a metaphysical (rather than purely material) sense. What is constitutive for children is, for adults, expressive. In other words, above/below for younger children is what is called a 'sign', that is, a 'signifier' whose 'signified' is certain relations between people in space; for adolescents and for adults, above/below has become what is called a 'symbol', one that contains the sign through a process of cognitive construction so that it comes to stand for status differentiation.

It is this finding that leads me to argue that we should drop any *a priori* distinction between sign and symbol in respect of the analysis of ritual. For, where we anthropologists, along with Fijian adults, take above/ below in reference to a single plane to be symbolic and so implicitly metaphorical, the youngest Fijian children take it to be propositional. In the simplest possible terms this means that, for children, ritual refers to nothing other than itself: 'kava-drinking is about kava' and 'eating a meal is about eating'. The activities are not symbolic in the conventional anthropological sense (which is not to deny that for any given child they have specific significant associations, etc.).

It is because we, as adults and anthropologists, have privileged our own notions over those of children that we have taken it for granted that for everyone ritual must stand for something other than itself and that this something is carried by the material symbols, the behaviour (including the language used, etc.) that are prescribed for a given ritual act. My data show that the notion of ritual as symbolic in this sense is an artefact of a developmental process whose eventual outcome inevitably conceals the nature of the process itself from those in whom it is instantiated. This is because the process itself entails that any previous awareness of the conflict between rank/seniority and gender is denied at the point where a mature understanding is achieved. It is only thus that each person can come to make an apparently coherent whole out of parts that are inevitably in conflict. And it is only at this point that above/below becomes fully symbolic for older children, whereas it is propositional for younger ones.

If, as I argue, ritual comes to stand for something other than itself as the outcome of a developmental process, this implies that our received anthropological notion of the symbolic inevitably distorts our analysis of 'the meaning' of ritual. For such meaning as is ascribed to any given ritualised behaviour by ourselves and others lies not only in the ritual process itself, but in the very developmental process through which persons make meaning out of ritual. *This is a process which in its nature is always unfinished, for meaning is always capable of further elaboration.*

The data here also suggest that cognitive construction of 'the symbolic' should not, as Bloch (1985) proposes, be distinguished from the construction of so-called logical relations, for example conservation of volume. In childhood, cognition is initially tied to concrete referents but a mature understanding requires that 'appearances' be in some sense disavowed. So, for example, differential status is freed of its connection to properties of the environment that are at once material and symbolic (the house, the *tanoa*), just as the volume of a liquid is disconnected from the shape of the container that holds it. Vygotsky, Bruner and other psychologists have shown that Piaget under-estimated the child's cognitive capabilities; indeed, work on the earliest cognitions of infants suggests that the ability to make certain basic conceptual discriminations is innate. However, the cognitive processes that govern, for example, conservation of volume or quantity of a linear construct of time do seem to be constructed over time. The products of these processes are derived from an interaction between the child's cognitive abilities at any given time and the nature of the experience/information on which those abilities are brought to bear.

A principle of status differentiation given by an interaction between rank, seniority and gender is constituted by children via reference to material factors given by people's disposition in space in relation to the *tanoa* in kava-drinking, the cloth at meals, the space inside houses, churches, etc. These material factors are reproduced by adults as necessary, that is, rule-governed, manifestations of that principle of hierarchy. So certain adult behaviour is rationalised in discourse by reference to this principle: it becomes traditional to arrange the space inside buildings and to make *tanoa* to accord with the proper expression of God-given hierarchical relations between kin. Thus adults can say that the chief sits 'above' the *tanoa* and is 'faced' by his people because this 'shows our respect for the chief', a chief who has all their ancestors 'at his back'.

Here Vygotsky's account of the way language mediates cognitive development is crucial for, as he shows, 'learning to direct one's own mental processes with the aid of words or signs is an integral part of the process of concept formation' (1986: 108). I would argue that the naming of the above/below axis itself forces children ultimately to make 'aboveness' and 'belowness' attributes of persons as a mark of differential status; that is to say, the way that the terms 'above' (*i cake*) and 'below' (*i ra*) are used by their seniors forces children to place a status construction on their growing awareness that the terms cannot merely name spaces or positions in space. The notion of ritual as rule-governed behaviour (Lewis 1980: 21) is important here. It is the interplay between rule and practice, practice and principle that allows above/below simultaneously in part to constitute hierarchy and to express it, and it is in this interplay that ritual takes on its coercive power in its claim to represent another reality, one that is immanent rather than grossly material, accessible only through tropes.

Roy Wagner has described what he calls 'the obviation model of trope expansion' (1986: 96); here 'core symbols' are made, synchronically in a ritual process or over time in an historical process, to play against one another. So, for example, a ritual sequence may take its meaning against the ground provided by kinship, exchange relations, marriage; when it is kinship that is in focus, the relation is reversed and the ritual sequence becomes the ground and kinship the figure whose 'meaning' is posited in ritual terms. This type of 'figure–ground reversal' is central to Wagner's 'obviations', the process by which a core symbol comes to be at once proposition and resolution, to 'stand for itself'. I would argue that, in so far as Wagner has described the process by which people make meaning, this process is itself likely to be predicated on one such as that described in this chapter.

Data from the youngest children can be understood to demonstrate a fusion between 'figure' and 'ground' with respect to the meaning of kava ritual: the material fact of kava-drinking is its own *raison d'être* and a high chief is 'above' because 'above' is where he sits. To find in kava-drinking what adults find there, children have to realise what they see as concrete to be also figurative in a specific way: they have to realise kava-drinking as being 'about' status differentiation as well as 'about' drinking. Further, if they are to arrive at an adult construct in which kava-drinking is, quite explicitly, understood as a core symbol of Fijian culture, they must come to see kava-drinking as an activity in which the figurative, the 'meaning' aspect of kava ritual, is its only valid justification.

This is a type of figure–ground reversal in which the adult notion of ritual as symbolic is the ground against which children are confronted with ritual as intransigent and material fact. Adults insist on children observing the explicit rules of ritualised behaviour because they hold these rules to express a metaphysical principle whereby differential status is given by God. So, to behave appropriately as adults children have to make the material fact of ritual merely the symbol of its significance, rather than its own justification.

Given that my data show that a 'core symbol' has to be constructed by persons out of their experience over time, it follows that neither cognition nor knowledge can, as in Bloch's model, be divided into the ideological and the non-ideological; nor can the meaning of what we often call 'the symbolic' be located, as in Sperber's (1980) model, in the activity of a symbolic mechanism in the mind. The process of coming to understand the 'meaning' of a complex notion such as Fijian above/below is a developmental one and thus distinct from the 'on-line' process by which people derive meaning from novel metaphors. This is not to suggest that metaphor is irrelevant, but rather that it is here a constitutive element in a developmental process. Indeed, I have suggested above that, for example, kava ceremonies become increasingly significant for adults in so far as they assimilate to 'the meaning of kava' all the many subtle suggestions of differentiated power that it can evoke. This raises the question of how notions of the self enter into the cognitive processes of the 'knowing subject', a question I cannot pursue here, though I note in passing Ricœur's (1978) provocative observation that 'we are assimilated, that is, made similar, to what is seen as similar ... self-assimilation is part of the commitment proper to the "illocutionary" force of the metaphor ... [we] feel *like* what we see *like*' (1978: 156). In this connection, the child's experience until well after puberty is that he or she is literally below (i.e. smaller than) others to whom obedience and respect are owed, and above (i.e. taller than) yet others who may justifiably be ordered about. In other words, the earliest understanding of above/below is actually inscribed in the child's own body. The inferential projection of this experience onto others is a crucial part of the process by which a mature understanding of hierarchical relations is reached (Johnson 1987).

It follows too from my data that cultural categories are not, as Sahlins (1985: 145) maintains, received 'ready made' and then 'risked in practice'; nor are they, as Bourdieu (1977: 87–8) argues, merely reproduced as 'practice' for which consciousness and discourse are largely irrelevant. Rather, complex features of cultural practice and the discourse that provides for its reproduction are the product of a genuinely constitutive process, a process that suggests that cultural heterodoxy is inevitable and not, as Bourdieu maintains and Sahlins implies, contingent. This constitutive process has its cognitive focus in ritual. Given that, in the specific case discussed in this chapter, a conflict between rank/seniority and gender is inherent in the principle that effects status differentiation, it is predictable that across sex, people will have somewhat different ideas about the nature of that principle (see Toren 1991 for an account of Fijian notions of personhood and gender). So it may be argued that heterodoxy is an inevitable product of the cognitive process by which that principle is constituted. This heterodoxy (to say nothing of more subtle individual differences) further implies firstly, that the conflict will emerge in discourse and secondly, that it will shape the nature of historical transformation.

I have noted elsewhere that the apprehension of meaning is, cognitively speaking, in itself a rational process, whatever its products look like (Toren 1984). Here I suggest further that all cognitions inevitably have a symbolic dimension, if only because, in being brought into being, any given concept is made to reference both predictable and unpredictable aspects of experience by virtue of people's continuing construction of meaning over time, aspects of experience that may or may not be made explicit. Further, where any new elaboration of meaning *is* made explicit and enters into others' understanding, there we find the process by which meaning may be understood as the product of a specific cultural history. Thus any 'concept', a term I have largely avoided throughout because of its connotations of boundedness, of being finished, has to be described in terms of a continuum of meaning whose dimensions may be made to manifest as either 'sign' or 'symbol' but which, from an analytical point of view, can only be understood as always both.

Meaning can be constrained but it cannot be fixed; thus Volosinov argued as long ago as 1929 that understanding language 'amounts to understanding its novelty and not to recognizing its identity' (1986: 68). This observation holds, true, I suggest, for understanding ritual. As the product of human cognitive processes, 'meaning' cannot be located anywhere outside the minds of human subjects, for it is only momentarily instantiated in the product of their interactions. This is not to imply, absurdly, that meaning is so labile as to preclude communication and the continuity of communication, but rather that it is always in the process of 'becoming'. That this is indeed so is, I suggest, borne out by my Fijian data, which show how a diversity of personal notions of the meaning of ritual may yet allow for unanimity in respect of the explicit rules of ritual practice, and so work to fix as apparently unchanging an historically specific form of social order that is nevertheless changing in everyday practice.

NOTES

1 Gau is the fifth largest of the 332 islands of Fiji. It is about 140 square kilometres in area and in 1981–3 had a population of around 3,000. The population of Sawaieke village was 260; this was among the largest of the eight villages of Sawaieke country (*vanua*) which had a population of about 1,250. Research was supported by a grant from the Social Science Research Council.
2 This consideration of kava-drinking and household meals is not meant to

suggest an opposition between a public and a private domain. Meals are a kind of public activity in that they are taken in full view of passers-by, all doors of the house being open, and passers-by are always invited to join those who are seated at the cloth. The fact that conventionally one politely refuses the invitation does not negate the general kinship obligation that is inherent in the invitation.

3 This notion of ritual as rule-governed appears to clash with that of tradition (*cakacaka vakavanua*, under which 'ritual' is subsumed) as processual, a notion I have explored elsewhere (Toren 1988). As I showed in that paper, it is the very fact of being made explicit that 'fixes' what is done, thus history is understood as unchanging and tradition as flexible, processual. In other words, what is not explicit in ritual, or about ritual, is allowed to change; what is explicit is held to be immutable.

8 Talking about souls: the pragmatic construction of meaning in Cuna ritual language

Carlo Severi

> Instinctively we use language rightly; but to the intellect this use is a puzzle.
>
> (Wittgenstein 1930[1980]: 1)

The anthropological study of ritual symbolism has payed little attention to the transformations of meaning that the ritual use of language can bring about. In this chapter, I will study the case of the Cuna[1] society, where a complex religious category, usually translated as 'soul' or 'spiritual presence', may seem almost meaningless in ordinary talk, and yet plays a crucial role in the shamanistic representation of the human experience. My claim will be that such a situation is caused by a complex web of relationships between the ritual chanter, the ill person, the auxiliary spirits and the shamanistic chant. These *pragmatic*[2] conditions both constrain the semantic field of the notion and generate the principles of its use. Although the performative aspect of ritual language has been clearly recognised in the literature (Bloch 1974; Tambiah 1985), anthropologists generally lay stress on the ontological or cosmological aspects of ritual discourse. A good example of this situation is the stance taken by Tambiah, who introduced the 'performative' approach in the study of ritual. Although Tambiah believes that ritual is 'a medium for . . . creating and bringing to life' (1985: 129) what he calls the 'cosmological scheme' of a culture, he still relegates the pragmatic aspects of ritual to the restricted, secondary function of producing 'indexical meanings' (*ibid.*, 165) about the social context of ritual action. A pragmatic analysis of a ceremonial language, thus, can only refer to the rank, or social status, of the ritual actors. For Tambiah, ritual is a process of construction of social reality in which the semantic content, that is, the 'cosmological scheme' of the culture, remains logically prior to any formal aspect of communication. In this perspective, the *form* of a ceremony – that is, 'the pattern of presentation of the ritual language, the physical gestures and the manipulation of substances which accompany it' – is the mere 'arrangement of its contents' (1985: 143). As a consequence, the pragmatic aspects of ritual are either secondary for the analysis of the symbolism, or even, in extreme cases, completely dissociated from its meaning.[3] His conclusion, thus, is that 'one should guard against attributing to all ritual the priority of functional pragmatics over semantics' (*ibid.*, 165). I think that this conception of the ritual use of language is misleading, in that it implies a reification of the 'cosmological scheme' which is supposed to be the intellectual core of a culture. If we recognise, on the contrary, that some fundamental features of a tradition are *produced* within ritual contexts (and often have no existence elsewhere), then the study of the principles of language use becomes crucial in order to understand them.

I will therefore try to show that in the Cuna case, rules about the ceremonial use of language (reflecting a specific categorisation of ritual speakers and of their addressees) play an essential role in the generation of ritual symbolism, and suggest a new approach, focused on the pragmatic construction of meaning.

The Cuna call 'talking about souls' (*purpa namakke*) the ritual recitation of therapeutic chants (*ikala*), which apply to a wide range of mental and somatic diseases. An *ikala* generally is the narration of a journey during which the auxiliary spirits of a shaman travel in the underworld, searching for the lost or kidnapped *purpa* of an ill person. In Cuna terms, to be ill is in some way 'to lack *purpa*'. This absence is always described by shamans as a *transformation* of the 'inner body' of the ill person, caused by the intervention of evil spirits. The first aim of a therapeutic chant is to represent this transformation of the *purpalet* dimension of someone's body.

In order to describe the implications of the use of this concept, I will try to show the following:

1 How ordinary, non-initiated people represent the notion of *purpa* and what the logical aspects of this representation are.
2 How shamanistic tradition constructs a pragmatic context for this category.
3 How we can derive, from an analysis of this context, a general interpretation of the use and logical status of religious categories in traditional discourse.

Talking about *purpa* in everyday life

Cuna Indians currently speak about three spiritual principles presiding over the perceivable existence of every living body: *nika, purpa* and *kurkin*. According to Erland Nordenskiöld (1938), the pioneer of Cuna ethnology *nika* relates to the idea of physical force, *purpa* to the immaterial double, or replica, *kurkin* to the more abstract ideas of 'character', 'talent' and 'personality'.[4] In Nordenskiöld's interpretation, long accepted by most scholars (see e.g. Lévi-Strauss 1958 or, more recently, Kramer 1981: 115) *purpa* appears to be roughly similar to the Western concept of 'soul'. Some of his early examples seem to confirm this point: *purpa* is a man's shadow, the echo of an animal's cry in the forest, even the mirror image of someone. Moreover, this notion is closely associated with the idea of life: a body without *nika* is a weak body; a body without *purpa* is lifeless (Nordenskiöld 1938).

Although *purpa* is said to leave the body after death, this notion never applies to the human body as a whole. Every part of it (hair, eyes, nails, hands, etc.) is thought to possess its own *purpa*. The combination of them gives to the body its *kurkin*. This word, which literally means 'hat', refers to a complex set of *purpa*, seen as a whole. It designates, then, any 'spiritual power' as opposed to physical force. For instance, a diviner (*nele*) is typically endowed with a powerful *kurkin*, while a good hunter, or peasant, has only a great *nika*. Sexual seduction is a typical example of using *kurkin* to influence someone, and the shamanistic chants often describe the power of the spirits as a result of a 'battle with hats' (*kurkin*).[5]

This interpretation, however, does not account for all the contexts where the notion of *purpa* appears. *Purpa* is present in stones as well as in every living animal, trees or men. Rocks, clouds, stars and the depths of the sea are, due to the presence of *purpa*, as alive as human beings. Every living thing owes its perceivable appearance (its *wakar* 'face') to the invisible presence of *purpa*. The metaphors used to describe it (a shadow, a far-away cry, the dim depths of the sea) show that, unlike the Platonic idea of the soul, *purpa* does not refer to an image of the person. In this perspective, the body is not purified of its matter and then duplicated in some far-away invisible world. Rather, *purpa* describes the combination of different invisible properties inherent in every living body: 'the sun's heat is *purpa*. Seated by the fire, you can feel its *purpa*. If you hear an unseen hunter shoot his gun in the forest, you have heard *purpa*. The sound of thunder is *malpurpa*. The notes of a flute are its *purpa*. The hiss of the wind is *purpa*. Even the voice of a man is called *purpa*' (Nordenskiöld 1938).

These examples may give us a better understanding of the notion. In fact, regardless to the contexts in which it appears, *purpa* seems to designate only what one can hear, feel or perceive *other than by sight*. The Cuna language itself distinguishes between 'to hear-and-see' (*ittoe*) and 'to hear-without-seeing' (*tuloenai*).

Moreover, it is remarkable that one meaning of the word *nikapurpalele*, which combines *purpa* with the idea of physical strength (*nika*) is 'foetus'. Before acquiring the 'face' (*wakar*) of a human being, the invisible living body inside the mother's womb, perceivable only by the sense of touch, is the most precise incarnation of the concept of *purpa* (see Severi 1987a, b).

At first glance, we may recognise in this concept a typical example of what Boyer (this volume) calls a 'pseudo-natural-kind' term. It is true that, from an ontological point of view, *purpa*, like the magical stones studied by Brown among the Aguaruna (Brown 1985), has the two defining properties that, according to Boyer, define a pseudo-natural kind. Indeed, anything called *purpalet* (lit. '*purpa*-like') has typical, but not necessary features (which means that it might be recognised, but not defined) and yet is thought to possess some 'underlying, though undefined properties'. None the less, it is worth noting that the content of this concept is never fully understood, or represented by people. This is why semantic analysis, and *a fortiori* etymological speculations are of little use here. When speaking of *purpalet* properties of the world, people seem to know very well what they have in mind, but regularly show themselves unable to define it in a positive or consistent way. Paradoxically enough, they seem to know better what this term *does not* mean than what it actually means.

A good example of this situation is the use of the classifier *so-*.[6] This classifier, usually applied to situations involving a relation between two actors (a fight, for instance) or to 'double faced', Janus-like objects (a pencil sharpened at both ends, or a statuette carved on two sides, etc.) designates any occurrence of *purpa*, and therefore refers to the general domain of shamanistic activity. Talking about an illness that needs the intervention of a chanter, people will currently say that they suffer from a *sokwen ailikkusa*, a 'double wound', caused by a *sokwen poni* a 'double evil spirit'. This means that their state transcends the context of ordinary experience, since it is related to the presence of invisible, vaguely defined beings.

We may conclude that, at least from a logical point of view, the only *general* feature of anything called *purpa* (or designated through the classifier *so-*) is to be always defined in negative terms. *Purpa*, then, is *something one cannot see*. Its presence transforms an object, a natural phenomenon, a state of the body, in a *so-* thing: something related to the unseen. In these terms, 'to be *purpalet*' (that is, to belong to a dimension that only diviners can see) means only 'to be different' from ordinary things. Everyone knows what a stone or a fire are. Only shamans, however, can interpret the *purpa* aspects of reality as signs of the presence of the spirits. In order to represent them, ordinary language only provides negative clues. This is the reason why, in Cuna terms, shamans must master another language, if they are to establish an effective relationship with the *purpalet* aspects of the world.

This somewhat paradoxical property of being defined only as 'different' does not necessarily imply that a special ontological category is posited. I would argue that this logical status is generated by *any* negative representation: to say that something is *not* to be identified with something else is to describe a relational, contrastive aspect of it which leaves the definition almost empty. Moreover, when an object, or a property are defined *only* in this way we can say that they are represented negatively even if the logical form of the statements produced about them is apparently positive. From this point of view, 'the heat is the *purpa* of fire' means only 'heat is a property of fire which I cannot see'. Thus, we can say that, as far as ordinary talk is concerned, *any* statement about a category like *purpa* is only apparently positive.

These statements share another important property: they make manifest the speaker's uncertainty about their veracity. At least in everyday life, their truth-value is always undecidable. Everyone knows what a stone or a fire is. But no-one of them may be certain of what a *purpa*-property or a magical stone really stand for. In order to represent them, current language provides only for negative clues.

Speaking differently

The notion of *purpa*, as we have described it, seems to refer to a context-less, almost meaningless idea of a mysterious presence. The question that naturally arises here is: how can people make use of such a term, which lacks any consistent semantic field, and potentially applies to any object, being, or phenomenon? Should we see in this concept the foundations of some exotic 'cultural metaphysics' or an illustration of a 'different' (i.e. primitive) mode of thought? I will try to show how, in Cuna tradition, the notion of *purpa* can find an empirical domain of application. So far, we have only described the usage of *purpa* in ordinary speech; but how can a *purpa-namakke*, in other words, a 'way of speaking', as J. Sherzer puts it (1987), be defined by the presence of *purpa*?

In his books on Cuna socio-linguistics (1983, 1987), Sherzer has provided a first answer to this question. *Purpa-namakke* is a variety of the Cuna language, which is not understood by common people. Also called 'the language of the auxiliary spirits of the shaman' (*swarmimmikaya'* literally 'the trees' sons' tongue'), *purpa-namakke* has its own morphological, semantic and syntactic properties.

As one of the four major Cuna linguistic varieties, the language of the auxiliary spirits is mainly characterised by lexical differentiation. If we compare its vocabulary to the common Cuna, we can distinguish three aspects of this lexical differentiation: (1) words of the common language are metaphorically used in ceremonial songs as in 'flower' for vagina, or 'young deer' for child; (2) special prefixes or suffixes (such as *olo-*, *esa-*,

-*kachi* or -*appi*) are adjoined to common words; (3) a same meaning is designated by distinct lexical items as for water: *tii* in common Cuna and *wiasali* in the language of the spirits. From a Cuna point of view, this lexical differentiation has a metaphysical significance: in the universe described by the chants every ordinary thing is called by its true name, virtually unknown by common people. Using his secret language, the shaman both uncovers the hidden nature of ordinary objects and shows his power over them.

Purpa-namakke, then, is not only 'talking about invisible things'; it is also 'to speak the tongue of the trees' sons', the auxiliary spirits, themselves called 'diviners' or *nelekan*, who help the shaman in his attempt to cure the ill person. This ceremonial language differs from common language in three ways: (1) it designates 'invisible' things; (2) it has a different linguistic morphology, which makes it incomprehensible; and (3) it is described as the language spoken by supernatural beings. When a shaman recites a chant, he is supposed to speak *their* language. In order to understand *purpa-namakke*, we will have to analyse these three aspects. For the moment, let us make clear who, in Cuna society, learns and speaks it.

The Cuna shamanistic tradition distinguishes two different kinds of knowledge, innate and acquired. The possessors of innate knowledge, which, at least in principle, leads to the 'vision of the invisible', without any learning of the chants are called *nele*, diviners or seers. A child is recognised as a *nele* when, during delivering, he comes out with his mother's placenta on his head. People will say that the child 'is born with a hat on his head' – the 'hat' (*kurkin*) being here the visible sign of the presence of a spiritual power – because, during sexual intercourse, the sexual *purpa* of his father and mother 'slipped' in the body of the child. For this reason, his parents' life depends on the health of the child, since his body contains their *purpa*.

However, this sign is only a necessary condition for being recognised as a seer. In the subsequent behaviour of the child, people constantly look for other signs of an extraordinary nature, praising, for instance, his brilliant mind, the strength of his memory, the vividness of his wit, etc. Once recognised as a *nele*, his initiation will consist mainly in a series of ritual immersions in a solution of medicinal plants, which are supposed to build a magical protection around his body.

The chanters, who learn the songs during a long apprenticeship, are, on the contrary, the possessors of acquired knowledge. They are simply called *inatuleti* ('medicine men') and no particular faculty of vision is attributed to them. They become therapists by learning a chant from a master. This apprenticeship, which, in several cases, can last for years, often leads to a political career in the village. A chanter is, however, always thought to be less intimate with spirits than a *nele*. Using his knowledge, he can increase his political influence, not his control of invisible beings. In fact, the therapeutic intervention of a chanter is always preceded by a diagnosis made by the seer. In his vision, the latter will tell the former what 'path' has been taken by evil spirits for coming to attack the ill person, and therefore what chant has to be performed. In this situation, he is the guide of the therapist, who follows his instructions.[7]

In this context, the notion of *purpa* (which is neither given a new name nor used metaphorically in the ceremonial language) takes on a special meaning. In order to understand this point, let us consider the case of a short shamanistic song published by Sherzer (1981), the *naipe ikar* ('the snake chant'), which is thought to enable its possessor to grab safely a snake and raise it in the air.

Like most Cuna *ikala*,[8] this chant describes a verbal duel between a shaman and an evil spirit. The chant opens with the setting of the scene. The man-who-knows (specialist) (the *wisit*, in Cuna) is working in his jungle farm, as the snake appears:

> The specialist is at the edge of his field
> The specialist is surveying his farm
> . . .
> When the sun is half way up in the sky
> The specialist is sharpening his little knife
> . . .
> As he is cutting small bushes
> As he is clearing small bushes
> Machi Oloaktikunappi *nele* [the snake's spirit name] is present

After a brief description of the snake ('His chin seems white under the grass cuttings', 'he sticks out the point of its tongue', 'the point of its tongue salivates'; *ibid.*: 310) the snake, as Sherzer rightly states, 'verbally challenges the man':

> [the snake] calls
> 'How well do you know the abode of my origin?'
> At this, the man responds to the challenge declaring:
> Indeed I know the abode of your origin
> I have come to play in the abode of your origin!
> and then, displaying his powerful knowledge:
> The specialist knows well your *purpa* [soul]
> the specialist is saying
> He captures your *purpa*
> The specialist is saying
> Indeed how your lips were placed on
> the specialist knows well

the specialist is saying
How your chin was put in place
How your lower chin was formed
The specialist knows well
The specialist is saying
. . .

Having thus claimed his knowledge of every part of the snake's body, the possessor of the formula can show his magical power on the animal, uttering the performative formula: '"Simply I raise you" I am saying' and the snake, as Sherzer writes, 'admits defeat'. In this text Sherzer, like Nordenskiöld, translates everywhere *purpa* by 'soul'. In some cases, we may accept this as an unusual, approximate translation of the ordinary sense of it, as for instance, in a statement like:

Indeed the specialist fortifies his *purpa*
Indeed he augments his *purpa*
He gives *nika* to his hand.

(Sherzer 1981: 311)

However, there are cases where this translation becomes meaningless. Consider the line: 'the specialist knows well your *purpa* [soul]'. What could this statement mean? A first answer is given by the text itself, which qualifies in these terms the knowledge of the shaman:

The specialist knows well . . .
how your chin was put in place
how your pupils were formed
how the point of your tongue was put in place
how your golden arrow was put in place
how your spinal cord was put in place
how your spinal cord was made flexible

How could the concept of *purpa*, defined only as an 'invisible presence perceived by all senses other then sight', justify this description, which refers to the origin of the snake's body? In fact, when applied to shamanistic knowledge, *purpa* assumes a special meaning, and implies the idea of a secret. Every *ikala* (a word which means both 'path, way' and 'shamanistic song') is always accompanied by a second text. This text, which the Indians call *secreto* in Spanish and *ikala-purpa* in Cuna ('the soul of the chant', but also 'the invisible part of the path') generally describes the mythical coitus during which a spirit (evil or benevolent, but always himself a *nele*) has been conceived. In fact, if we refer to the *purpa* of the *naipe ikar* that I could record and translate during fieldwork in a Cuna village, we can have a better understanding of the nature of the knowledge the shaman proudly displays here, facing his enemy:

When God Olopiler wished to give birth to snakes, he took a hair from the pubes of the First Woman [*Tionuchunana*], masturbated, and put a drop of his semen on the hair. Then he put the hair in the woman's vagina.
'This is how you were born, snake, I know your *purpa*.'

An *ikala-purpa*, as we have seen, always contains a definition of the nature of a spirit. However, for a Cuna shaman, the importance of this text goes far beyond the knowledge of the origin of the form of the snake's body (which is here conceived as recalling the form of the hair taken from the pubes of the First Woman). To him, the knowledge of this secret is the only source of the chant's effectiveness. Before ritually reciting the chant, a chanter must repeat the *purpa* silently. Were he not to evoke the secret origin of the snake, his chant would be ineffective. The knowledge of the secret establishes a kind of pact between the man and the snake. This silent agreement implies not only that the snake will do no offence to the man, but also that the possessor of the *purpa* should be on friendly terms with the snake. The final lines of *naipe ikar* mention this part of the agreement: 'How indeed could I kill you? [says the man] We have just become good friends' (Sherzer 1981: 314). Knowing the *purpa* of his enemy, the chanter is therefore able to force him, using a classical performative statement ('I raise you') to a friendly attitude.

This meaning of *purpa* makes manifest that, beyond the apparent opposition between innate and acquired knowledge, Cuna tradition seems to rely upon a unitary conception of the ritual intervention on the world. Despite the fact that they undergo different types of initiation and play different roles in therapy, seers and chanters are both defined in term of their access to *purpa*. The *nele* has a direct access to it, from his birth. The *inatuleti*, at the end of his initiation, acquires a certain power on the *purpalet* dimension of the world, by learning a secret (the *purpa* of a text, or the unknown part of a path) which concerns the origin of a spirit. As compared to the vision of the *nele*, his knowledge is indirect and incomplete. However, the silent recitation of the secret before chanting is essential in order to understand the therapeutic intervention, since the idea of a silent agreement, a sort of treatise between the shaman and the spirits – made possible by his knowledge of *purpa* – holds true for any therapeutic song. It is therefore necessary to come back to the conception of illness and summarise how the notion of *purpa* is used in this context.

Suffering and the *purpalet* world

For non-initiated Cuna, as I have already pointed out, illness is just the absence of *purpa*, whereas the cure comes by re-establishing its presence. For them, the cure is a journey in search of the lost *purpa*, and at the same time it is conceived of as an exploration leading to the knowledge of the mythical, invisible world where the evil spirits live.

The ritual formula used by shamans for establishing a diagnosis of illness seems to proceed from an altogether different point of view. This formula is *purpa-nai*, which we can translate as 'there is something invisible [though not a replica, or an image] hanging around [the person's] body'.[9] The shaman, thus, does not say that *purpa* is lost or absent from the body of an ill person. On the contrary, he literally says that *purpa is where the first signs of pain are*. A confirmation of this point is given by the fact that the Cuna language, for mentioning pain, uses the classifier *so-*: 'a sensation of pain 'is, in Cuna, a *sokwen numakke*, a 'double pain', both referring to the body and to the invisible world, 'situated beyond the horizon', which is inhabited by the spirits.

However, this *purpalet* world, which an *ikala* is supposed to describe, is not conceived as a separate realm of the universe. Rather, the songs always describe the soul's journey through the invisible world of spirits as a metaphor of the experience felt by a sick person. The shamanistic journey primarily designates that state of *perceiving without seeing* which *is* the feeling of pain (see Severi 1987: 81–4). Indeed, in this context, suffering is simultaneously described in cosmological and physiological terms: to suffer is to experience *a transformation of the universe*, involving a dramatic impairment of the natural balance between what is seen and what is perceived by other senses. This idea of a metamorphosis of the invisible aspects of experience, that the Cuna call *pinyemai*, is central to the shamanistic understanding of illness.

Let us see, as an example, how these two notions, the 'soul' and the 'transformation', are related in the *nai-ikala*, the chant devoted to the cure of madness. From the shamanistic point of view, the mentally ill person exhibits a contradiction between the visible and the invisible dimensions. What is *seen* of him is obviously a human form; but since, according to the local theory of mental illness, he 'speaks the language of the animals' what is *heard* of him, his *purpa*, is something inhuman and belongs to an invisible animal. For the shaman, the man suffers this contradiction because an evil spirit has taken possession of him, and actually lives in him. The crucial point here is that this spirit is literally defined as the reverse of the ill person: it is an animal who took an *invisible* human form, which can appear only in dreams. Its image is used as an interpretation of the inner body of the ill person: while the ill man is a man with an animal *purpa*, the spirit is an animal with a human *purpa*. The transformation of a living being, thus, necessarily implies a change in the relationship to its *purpa*. This holds true for human beings as well as for any being in the world. Rock crystals, clouds, trees and, above all, animals can transform themselves into spirits, and intervene in human affairs by *exchanging purpas* with human beings.[10]

This conception of metamorphosis as a universal exchange of *purpa* can help us understand one characteristic ambiguity of the chants. We have seen that, through the metaphor of the shamanistic journey, they describe an invisible world in order to represent the experience of the sick person. But, they also portray, conversely, a world where mountains can palpitate and rivers bleed. In other words, the experience of illness is represented through the combination of two usually separate dimensions: the physiological and the cosmological. This is clearly shown, for instance, in the sections of the *Mu Ikala* (the song supposed to facilitate delivery) where the extremely painful experience of the woman is described in the following way:

> The sick woman lies in the hammock, in front of you
> She is lying in her white clothes, her white clothes are budding like flowers
> The woman's body lies weak
> When they light along Muu's way, it drips with secretions, all like blood
> Her secretions drip from the hammock, like blood, all red like the *ikkwi* plant
> The inner white cloth extends towards the bosom of the earth
> In the middle of the woman's white garment, a human being is descending
> The woman is sitting, breathless, towards the East, legs open, secretions dripping like blood,
> Into the bosom of the Earth her secretions gather in drops like blood, all red.
>
> (Holmer & Wassen 1953: lines 80ff.)

> Into the bosom of the Earth the child is descending
> Into the bosom of a pale plantain leaf the child is descending
> It reddens the banana leaf
> Towards the East, a river breaks through the place
> A golden river breaks through, the golden calabash is drifting along
> The evil spirits are carried off by its flow, far away, towards the mouth of the river
> The evil alligators are carried off by its flow, far away, towards the mouth of the river
> The trunks of the trees are carried off by its flow, far away, towards the mouth of the river
> A silver river breaks through the place, the golden calabash is drifting along
> The evil spirits are carried off by its flow, far away, towards the mouth of the river
> The evil alligators are carried off by its flow, far away, towards the mouth of the river

> The trunks of the trees are carried off by its flow, far away, towards
>   the mouth of the river
> Towards the East, a golden fan causes a draft
> Towards the East, a silver fan causes a draft
> Towards the East, the golden wind is blowing
> The child is descending, the child has arrived
> A child is descending, a child has arrived
>
> (Holmer & Wassen 1953: lines 640ff.)

This text provides a good example of the alternation of 'realistic' and 'mythical' descriptions which characterises the Cuna chants. In fact, this representation of childbirth supposes *two* transformations. The first concerns the woman's body: magically situated at the 'centre' of the world, her vagina becomes part of an inaccessible, invisible dimension of the universe. The second concerns this mythical world, which appears to undergo a dramatic turbulence which symbolises the painful contractions of the woman's body.

It would be utterly misleading to understand this parallelism between the body and the world as a simple correspondence between an external macrocosm and an internal microcosm, since both these dimensions, from the shamanistic point of view, are *purpalet*. The physiological dimension is described as an 'inner body' that no visual perception can reach, and the cosmological one as an inaccessible world, situated 'beyond the horizon'. In this perspective, invisible properties of the world ('bleeding rivers') refer to the body of the woman, and invisible properties of her body (the pain generated by delivering) refer to the external world.

We can see now how Cuna discourse can generate meaning using a negatively defined notion: the shamanistic representation of the experience of the ill person is the result of a systematic relationship established between *two negatively defined dimensions of the universe*, an invisible landscape within the body and an external, though inaccessible, world described as an invisible body.

The contrast with the use of *purpa* in ordinary talk is striking. There *purpa* has no definite meaning, and is always surrounded by a halo of uncertainty. Here the same notion acquires a crucial position, referring both to the essential features of therapeutic intervention and to the field of its application to illness. In particular, *purpa* becomes here the key concept for a description of the experience of pain.

How is this passage realised, from a vague, contextless idea to a complex representation of experience? A first, obvious answer is that if the category of *purpa* itself is normally uncertain and contextless in ordinary talk, the ritual use of *purpa-namakke* is, on the contrary, always applied *only to one* context: the representation of the experience of pain.

Indeed, the relation established between two different dimensions of reality, which makes possible the shamanistic description of the experiences felt by the sick person, can only be established under ritual conditions. As we shall see, the representation of a *purpalet world*, is not achieved here by elaborating the content of the notion of *purpa* itself, which remains negatively defined, but rather by establishing a set of prescribed conditions on the ritual recitation itself. In order to realise the transformation of the meaning of *purpa*, Cuna tradition imposes strict and explicit constraints on the context of *purpa-namakke*. Since these conditions are constitutive of the action of ritual chanting about the *purpalet* world, the study of the generation of the meaning of *purpa* coincides with the study of the construction of this context. It is therefore necessary to examine how this context is generated in the ritual performance.

Performing *purpa-namakke*

The ceremonial language of the Cuna shaman is 'different' from ordinary speech, not just because it involves the use of an incomprehensible language or is a way of designating the esoteric knowledge of the shaman. *Purpa-namakke* is, above all, defined *as an action*. It requires – if the ritual recitation is to be effective – an elaborate set of rules concerning the behaviour of the chanter. The tradition, and in fact the chants themselves,[11] minutely describes the position of the *purpa* speaker, his alimentary and sexual prohibitions, the place and time of recitation, the ritual setting in which the shamanistic journey will be narrated. Before singing, the shaman sits for a few minutes in silence, burning cacao grains or crushing acrid-smelling red pepper pods in a small hearth. The recitation must occur in a separated, semi-darkened corner of the hut, always at night. The song is chanted in front of two rows of statuettes facing each other, beside the hammock where the patient is lying. These auxiliary spirits drink up the smoke, whose intoxicating effect opens their minds to the invisible aspect of reality, and gives them the power to heal. In this way, the spirit-helpers of the shaman, as several songs state explicitly,[12] are believed to become themselves 'diviners' (*nelekan*).

This empirical description of the performance of the chants, however, does not allow us to understand a crucial point: who is supposed to be singing to whom? It is clear that the communication between the chanter and the patient is merely apparent, since the latter, like most non-initiated Cuna, cannot understand what the shaman is saying. As a consequence, it is also difficult to describe the relationship established between what is actually formulated (the description of a progressive, invisible metamorphosis which has generated the suffering body) and the conditions imposed on the act of chanting itself.

In order to understand this point it is necessary to analyse the dynamics involved in the ritual scene, as well as the relations that the ritual action establishes between the magical vision of the diviner and the incomprehensible words of the singer.

The offering of the smoke to the auxiliary spirits is considered the only way to *generate* an effective knowledge about the experience of pain. In other words, by offering them the smoke, the shaman ritually regenerates the *kurkin*, or 'power of vision', of his statuettes. Moreover, we should not forget that by reciting the chant, he does not only describe their journey in a *purpalet* world; he also speaks both *like* them and *for* them their secret and incomprehensible tongue, and it is in this language that he finally engages in a verbal duel with the evil spirits. In this way, the shaman acquires an intermediary position between two *nele*: the human one, the diviner who has made the diagnosis of the illness (with whom he shares the knowledge of the secret), and the supernatural one, his spirit-helper. The narration of the shamanistic journey itself could be understood as the description in words of the vision of the *nele*. Performing *purpa-namakke*, the shaman-chanter identifies himself – and speaks on behalf of – a *nele*. On the other hand, the ritual conditions imposed to the act of chanting tend to identify the real shaman with the supernatural beings whose language he can speak, that is, the *nele*s represented by the carved statuettes. The latter's power results from an accumulation of therapeutic functions which remain always separate in real life. Usually, as we have seen, a human *nele* can only *see* and a chanter can only *speak*. In the ritual situation, a statuette can speak with the voice of the chanter while seeing with the penetrating eye of a *nele*.

What is said in the chant aims at building an image of the disease as the result of a relationship between two *purpalet* dimensions of the world. The ritual principles of language use tend to define the ritual chanter in the same terms: as related to the *purpalet* world, he too incarnates a contradiction between what is seen of him (a human body) and what is heard, the language of the supernatural diviners.

In order to represent, or understand the metamorphosis of the ill person, the chanter has to transform himself into (or to speak on behalf of) a literally semi-divine being: half-human, half-supernatural. This transformation, not the unrealistic idea of a therapeutic communication with the ill person, is the aim of the sequence of gestures that define *purpa-namakke*. In this context, 'to speak a different tongue' always supposes a parallel transformation of the speaker.

Thus, the performance of *purpa-namakke* relies upon a process of double identification: one associates the description of the suffering body to the presence of an animal spirit, and is achieved in the song itself; the other, which is silently realised by a sequence of actions that guarantees the effectiveness of chanting, progressively identifies the human chanter with a supernatural *nele*. From a formal point of view, then, *purpa-namakke* is an attempt to *define the nature* of the spirits, rather than an act of fictitious communication with them. When shamans speak their language, they personify them.

Purpa and symbolism

We may conclude that the complexity of a notion like *purpa* is the result of the complexity of its ritual usage. In order to define this category, it would not be enough just to uncover a network of related ideas (as 'force' or 'character' or 'personality'). We also need to uncover the pragmatic conditions that ritually define the action of chanting. In other words, knowledge is shared among the Cuna about the technique of ritual recitation that enables a shaman to cure an ill person, not about the content of the category *purpa*. Rather than elaborating a clear-cut definition of the invisible properties of the world, the shamanistic tradition conveys a complex representation of the action of *chanting about the purpalet* world.

Among the Cuna, there is no general, commonly shared mythology of illness which could influence and actually regulate a therapeutic ritual. No 'cosmological scheme', in Tambiah's terms, is transmitted in Cuna culture about the experience of suffering. What is primarily and positively encoded in Cuna tradition is a set of principles for generating a ritual context. Thus, the pragmatic dimension of the ritual recitation, that is, the study of *purpa-namakke* as a sequence of actions which define the ritual speaker and his addressee, is not only a useful tool for understanding what *purpa* can mean; the rules concerning *purpa-namakke* in fact establish and designate the conditions for generating its meaning.

This is, I am tempted to say, the feature which makes a 'simple' (or a negatively defined) category a complex one. In fact, to say that a traditional category is 'complex' may imply two very different hypotheses on the nature of tradition. The first is that a category is 'complex' only when it has a very large and elaborated semantic field. In this perspective, the analysis of traditional knowledge becomes akin to the study of a text, or a system of symbols. The second hypothesis is that people use very simple (even, as in the Cuna case, virtually meaningless) notions in very complex ways. In these terms, ritual tradition can no more be considered as an illustration of a general 'cosmological scheme'. It has to be analysed, rather, as a set of techniques leading to the generation of traditional representations. The study of the category of *purpa* in Cuna shamanistic tradition, which finds its way to complexity through the elaboration of rules about the ritual use of language, suggests that this latter hypothesis may be the right one.

NOTES

1 The Cuna Indians live today in the San Blas Archipelago of Panama. Cuna-land (Tule Neka) numbers from 27,000 to 30,000 persons, who speak a language traditionally associated with the Chibcha family (Holmer 1947, 1952). A small Cuna group, which still rejects all contact with the white man, lives in the Chucunaque region of the Darién forest, near the Colombian border. Essentially, the Cuna are tropical farmers. In his brief historical survey, Stout (1947) speculates that Cuna society, one of the first to come into contact with white men after the discovery of the American continent, was 'heavily stratified, and divided into four classes: leaders, nobles, citizens and slaves'. Political power today is held by the *onmakket*, an assembly of all the adult males in the village, supported by a varying number of elected leaders (*sailakan*). The Cuna kinship system is bilineal, uxorilocal and founded on strict group endogamy (Howe 1976).

2 For a tightly-argued discussion about the definition of the field of pragmatics, on which there is no general agreement among linguists, see Levinson (1983). For the purposes of this chapter, it is sufficient to refer to the minimal definition provided for by Carnap (1956), who calls 'pragmatics ... the study of aspects of language that *require* reference to the users of it' (quoted in Levinson 1983: 3).

3 Remarking that ritual 'oscillates in historical time between *ossification* and *revivalism*', Tambiah sees the decline of the meaning of a ceremony as the progressive revelation of its pragmatic aspects: 'cosmological ideas, because they reflect the epistemological and ontological understandings of the particular age in which they originated, and because they are subject to the constraint of remaining accurate and invariant, are condemned to become dated over time, and increasingly unable to speak to the minds and hearts of succeeding generations facing change and upheaval. During these periods of ossification, ritual may increasingly lose whatever semantic meaning they previously had and may carry primarily indexical meanings which derive from rules of use and from pragmatic or functional considerations' (Tambiah 1985: 165). For an example which shows, on the contrary, that the decline of a ritual's meaning (though not its ossification) can be caused precisely by radical modifications of the pragmatic conditions, cf. Severi 1988.

4 For a more detailed discussion of the Cuna theory of souls, see Severi (1981b, 1987).

5 In the *Mu Ikala*, the chant devoted to the therapy of difficult childbirth, the auxiliary spirits of the shaman engage in a verbal duel with the evil spirits. The declaration of hostilities is made in these terms: 'Let us play now with our golden hats! Let us play with the hats, in order to see who has the stronger

hats!' (Holmer & Wassen 1953: verses 384ff.). On this point, compare the remarks of Lévi-Strauss (1958), who, though, was working on an earlier, and incomplete, version of the text, published by the same authors in 1947.

6 A complete analysis of the Cuna classifiers is still lacking in Cuna studies. Some indications are in Holmer (1947, 1952) and Sherzer (1987: 37–44).

7 The seer and the chanter, though, can exchange roles on the occasion of an epidemical outbreak of disease. In this case, the seer falls asleep, and himself travels to the underworld in order to make peace with the spirits who attacked the village. On this occasion, it is the chanter who, singing a particular chant, 'guides' the seer in his travel (Howe 1976).

8 For further instances of this *topos* of Cuna therapeutic literature, see Holmer & Wassen (1953, 1958). The expression 'verbal duel' as applied to Cuna chants, can assume two meanings: it can be a challenge *verbally described* (and concluded by a performative statement), like in the *naipe ikar*, or a battle struggled *by means of* words, as in the *Mu Ikala*.

9 The verbal suffix *-nai* (usually applied, for instance, to necklaces), means 'hanging on'. Here *purpa* takes its general sense of *purpalet* (the invisible).

10 A detailed description of this process of metamorphosis is given in the *Nia-Ikar-kalu* – the central episode of the chant devoted to the therapy of madness (Gomez & Severi 1983). For an analysis, see Severi (1982: 56–62).

11 This is clearly shown, among many other instances, in the initial part of the *Mu Ikala*, the chant devoted to the therapy of difficult childbirth (Holmer & Wassen 1947: verses 1–64). In a communication presented at a conference on 'The Transmission of Knowledge', held at the University of Rome in 1986, I have argued that Cuna shamanistic tradition makes the conditions of chanting *transmissible* by including in every *ikala* – usually at the beginning of the text – a detailed description of the chant's ritual performance (Severi 1989).

12 The intoxicating effect of the smoke is always compared, in the chants, to the effect of the alcoholic *chicha* prepared by the Indians on the occasion of the ritual which celebrates the first menstruation of young girls. The *Mu Ikala* even describes some auxiliary spirits as 'drunk of chicha' (Holmer & Wassen 1953: verses 160ff.). It is because they are thus intoxicated that they can, as this chant letter states, 'give form to the invisible things using their powerful vision'.

Part IV

The structure of ritual action

The classical study of ritual centres on the question of the connections between features of ritual action, on the one hand, and various religious representations, on the other. The connections are supposed to go in both directions. On the one hand, rituals are described as contexts in which particular religious models are 'expressed', displayed, made manifest in actions and statements (see e.g. Beattie 1970). Conversely, it is generally accepted that participants in ritual make use of various shared cultural models to give 'meaning' to their actions. Both assumptions, however, are generally couched in such vague terms that they do not seem to have any practical implications for the study of religious ritual. The first hypothesis, which could be called the 'expressive' understanding of ritual, seems to be mostly a projection of the anthropologists' own methodologies. Because anthropologists consider rituals as a primary source of information about the religious representations of a given group, they spontaneously tend to consider that that is the way in which the participants too represent their rituals. This, however, is not really supported by the evidence. The hypothesis is all the more difficult to maintain, as the particular aspects of ritual contexts make communication and therefore 'expression' particularly awkward. As Bloch pointed out (1974 *passim*; 1985: 19–45), religious ritual makes constant use of behavioural modes (dance, special languages, stereotyped gestures) which, if anything, *reduce* the range of information that can be conveyed by their performance. In other words, rituals are remarkable in that they are particularly non-expressive, as other authors have stressed (Rappaport 1974; Staal 1979). Classical anthropological studies often describe ritual sequences as conveying particular information *despite* the constraints of ritual action, instead of focusing on what is particular about ritual action. The contributions in this section aim to go beyond this type of study, and to focus on the intrinsic properties of ritual. Lawson puts forward a general account of the structure of ritual sequences, whereas Houseman focuses on the form of interaction.

Lawson puts forward a general account of ritual action, founded on the

Chomskyan notion of competence. Lawson's aim is to describe the knowledge structures underlying the participants' intuitions about the 'well-formedness' of religious phenomena in their cultural environment. The various elements which constitute a ritual sequence are not arbitrarily juxtaposed. For Lawson, their ordering is rule-directed, and can be described as the result of the recursive application of formal rules. The rules specify the possible arrangements of abstract elements such as 'agent', 'act', 'object'. The specific *content* of each such element does not depend on these rules. In other words, the model is based on a clear-cut division between the *syntax* of ritual action and the *semantics* of religious representations. The description of the knowledge an idealised participant must have, in order to tell well-formed rituals from incorrect ones, is for Lawson the first step in the description of the actual representations entertained by participants.

Houseman, on the other hand, focuses on aspects of ritual situation that cannot be represented by the actors, because they are emergent properties of the interaction. Initiation rituals, because of the secrecy involved, constitute typical examples of situations where such emergent interactive forms are likely to be crucial. Houseman's viewpoint on secrecy is mainly inspired by Simmel (1908; 1950), following whom secrecy can be studied, not just in terms of information withdrawn, but more importantly as a patterning of social relations. In the Beti rites described by Houseman, and more generally in initiation rituals, the information shrouded in secrecy is either negligible or obscure. Contrary to what both initiates and non-initiates state explicitly, the transmission of information is not the main point of the rite. In this, as in most cases of initiation rites, secrecy involves not two but three parties (the transmitters of secrets, the recipients and the excluded party), whose different viewpoints on ritual interaction undergo significant changes as the complex ritual sequence unfolds. In terms that are not too distant from Lawson's syntactic perspective, Houseman shows that such interactive dynamics can be characterised by their *form*, which is independent of the content of the secrets withheld and transmitted.

In both studies the authors try to demonstrate that the features of religious ritual are, to a large degree, independent from the types of religious contents people associate with them. In Lawson's perspective, this is stated as the independence of ritual 'syntax' (the ordering of ritual sequences) from its 'semantics' (shared religious assumptions). Houseman wants to go further, and argues that some properties of the religious contents are actually constrained by the formal properties of interaction. Because initiates, candidates and non-initiates are involved in a particular type of interaction, they are particularly likely to associate certain types of representations with the performance of the ritual. These hypotheses constitute a critique of the common assumption mentioned at the beginning of this introduction, following which participants in a ritual apply prior 'cultural models' to otherwise arbitrary actions. Against this seemingly self-evident assumption, both Lawson and Houseman show that the properties of ritual action do not need this imposition of meaning to have a definite structure. On the contrary, the formal aspects of the ritual are likely to impose constraints on the type of representations participants associate with them. This converges with the conclusions of Severi's chapter, where a particular set of formal constraints was seen as the origin of certain common religious representations.

9 Cognitive categories, cultural forms and ritual structures

E. Thomas Lawson

Introduction

The recognition that human beings learn more than they are taught, already prefigured quite early in the Platonic literature and much later in Kant's notion of the synthetic *a priori*, continues to intrigue scholars concerned with cognitive matters, especially those with a stake in the possible impact of the cognitive sciences on culture theory. In fact, much to the dismay of empiricists, it has breathed new life into the rationalist tradition. Possessing more knowledge than instruction can account for obviously presents a puzzle worth solving.

Among cognitive theoreticians (especially in generative linguistics and cognitive anthropology) the acquisition puzzle has given rise to a range of suggested solutions. At one end of the theoretical spectrum proponents of the autonomy of cultural systems postulate the presence and operation of very subtle and hidden cultural forces silently transmitting culturally constrained cognitive knowledge from a 'cultural system' to the largely 'empty' minds of cultural participants. At the other end of the spectrum nativists proffer innate cognitive mechanisms, replete with cognitive content, as solutions to 'the discrepancy problem'. Even theorists in the middle seem willing to nudge the direction of research in one direction rather than the other.

There can be little doubt that arguments about acquisition take place in contentious territory. The issues are by no means resolved. Proof of that lies in the continuing combat between non-nativists and nativists about the significance of, and the solutions to, the noted discrepancy between the amount of cultural knowledge by explicit tuition and the actual knowledge a person in that culture possesses as well as about the most adequate explanatory models capable of accounting for the discrepancy. Various forms of cultural and biological determinism wait anxiously in the wings for the chance to enact familiar roles in new plays.

From my point of view, what is at stake in this debate about the acquisition of cultural knowledge is not only the issue about the nature and status of the mechanisms of acquisition but also about what counts as knowledge. After all, you had better have a theory of *what* it is that is acquired in such a puzzling fashion if you are going to argue about *how* what is acquired is in fact acquired. In this case at least, questions of form prove inseparable from questions of origin.

In this chapter I confront the acquisition problem in a relatively oblique manner. I argue that a theory of religious ritual action which employs the strategy of competence theorising is capable of illuminating certain aspects of the acquisition debate in the very process of laying the groundwork for an explanation of religious ritual. The theory I discuss here in outline was initially presented by Robert McCauley and me in *Rethinking Religion: Connecting Cognition and Culture* (Lawson & McCauley 1990) and can be found there in a larger framework. I intend here, therefore, only to highlight some of the key features of our theory and to address some of its consequences, especially those having to do with the acquisition problem.

In this chapter I discuss, first, agreements and disagreements among theorists about the acquisition of knowledge. Then I suggest that competence theorising provides a fruitful approach to those phenomena (such as religious ritual) which straddle the cognitive–cultural divide. Following that, I narrow the focus of the chapter by defending theorising about the representation of religious ritual action rather than religious thought. Having thus set the stage, I then present in brief compass the theory of religious ritual action which McCauley and I have developed. I show that our theory contains three elements: (1) an abstract mechanism for the generation of representations of religious ritual action; (2) a conceptual scheme which affects the operation of the mechanism; and (3) a set of universal principles which are activated by the application of the conceptual scheme to the action-representation system, and which constrain the representation of religious ritual action. Finally, I discuss the consequences of our theory for the problem of the acquisition of knowledge.

Under-determination and the acquisition of knowledge

When dealing with contentious matters, it is all too easy to miss fundamental areas of agreement among opponents. Differences are usually easier to take note of than similarities. This is especially the case with the acquisition problem. For example, few scholars would deny the fact of the obvious mastery of cultural form people exhibit in their *linguistic* traffic with each other. Talking comes naturally.[1] Nor would many investigators disagree about the ease with which people inhabit their *customary* worlds. People are remarkably adept in knowing what counts as a customary act and what particular kind of act is appropriate to the situation in question. Nor would many scholars raise serious doubts about the dexterity cultural participants display in their judgements about well-formedness in *symbolic* systems. The data produced by anthropological fieldwork would be uninteresting were it to lack the expertise which all members of a culture possess and which they display whenever anthropologists elicit judgements about the form and content of their social and cultural life. In fact, respect for, and attention to, the judgements informants make about their symbolic behaviour is a necessary condition for engaging in fieldwork.

With regard to linguistic, customary and symbolic matters, therefore, most cultural theorists would readily acknowledge that people daily demonstrate their cultural competence. People know what to think about their cultural world, and, for the most part, how to act in it. The problem lies in explaining such mastery. It is here that disagreements emerge most sharply. Indeed, these disagreements extend beyond the *fact* of mastery to questions about which *mechanisms* are capable of accounting for it.

Competence theorising about cultural phenomena arose as a method for dealing with such problems in the specific field of linguistic theory. And it has had considerable success. (In fact, some theoreticians argue that it is the only game in town.) Its success in the study of language suggests its considerable promise in the analysis of other cultural phenomena, especially the domain of religious ritual.

Competence theories

Competence theorists employ a thoroughly psychological strategy for dealing with cultural phenomena. They demonstrate the viability of cognitive categories for the analysis of cultural forms. While methodological solipsism is not a necessary condition for competence theorising, competence theorists do not hesitate to hold in abeyance judgements about the physical realisation of the principles they propose. They are, however, unwilling to assume that cultures are autonomous systems which unproblematically transmit cultural information through mysterious channels to cultural participants. Their cognitivist tactics require no precipitous leaps either to cultural systems or biological structures, although they are willing to consider significant roles for biological and cultural systems at later stages of analysis.

From a competence point of view, cultural systems are not simply producers of knowledge, they are also products of cognitive mechanisms and structures. Of particular interest to competence theorists are the judgements people make about cultural forms. These judgements provide a readily available source of data capable of considerable theoretical manipulation.

Competence theorists are particularly eager to avoid cultural tourism. They are not convinced that mere exposure to alien cultural spheres with their vast array of cultural facts will ensure access to a cultural 'system' underlying the welter of cultural detail. Competence theorists prefer instead to start at the cognitive level by identifying the mastery that cultural participants possess of the culture in which 'they live and move and have their being'. Such a move sets competence theorising apart from classical anthropology, which has often seemed content to assume that mere exposure to cultural phenomena is a sufficient condition for the generation of knowledge about such phenomena.

The competence approach involves constructing testable and more realistic models of what is 'in the heads' of cultural participants than empty slates or general learning mechanisms. Their view is that competence models provide, albeit quite abstractly, a more adequate way of viewing cognitive transactions among people in their traffic with their cultural context. The models also provide access to a level of psychological systematicity that is empirically tractable.

A more adequate view involves showing that, in order for people to participate in an efficient and unimpeded manner in social life, they require cultural competence (whether or not they are aware of possessing such knowledge). 'Participating in an efficient and unimpeded manner in social life' means (1) having the ability to form adequate judgements about the *well-formedness* of cultural practices, (2) possessing the capacity to make judgements about the *relationships* among practices, and (3) being able to understand the relationship of particular sets of practices to the larger aggregate of practices characteristic of a cultural form as a whole.

I think that whatever systematicity exists at the level of culture itself is already contained and reflected in the cognitive structures theoretically available to the investigator at the psychological level of analysis. The point here is that rather than culture providing the explanatory categories for human behaviour culture is itself at least partially in need of explanation by non-cultural, that is cognitive, categories. This cognitivist view has been reinforced by a long tradition in the philosophy of social science critical of the ability of the concept of culture to bear the explanatory weight that some social scientists have attempted to accord it.

In the move from exclusively cultural to predominantly cognitive categories, competence theory adopts the standard scientific strategy of idealisation in the explanation of cultural phenomena (McCauley & Lawson 1991). Such a manoeuvre involves focusing upon abstracted general properties and suspending certain details in order to construct theoretical models of mind capable of representing some aspect of cultural competence.

The purpose in constructing such 'artificial minds' or 'artificial knowledge modules' lies in devising means for discovering whether the principles, processes and products defined by the model are capable of accounting for the judgements made by ideal cultural participants (who provide the subject-matter for the model) about the form and content of the cultural activity in which they participate. Ultimately, we would expect a model worth its salt to be capable of demonstrating that the products generated by the underlying principles would conform, however indirectly, to the actual judgements made by the participants – although there is many a slip between the competence cup and the performance lip.

Theorising about ritual competence

Religious rituals are instances of symbolic behaviour. Competence theorising suggests techniques for their analysis. The theoretical object of such analysis consists of representations in the minds of ideal ritual participants. Because they are *cognitive* representations and thus not directly accessible, the data employed in their analysis consist of peoples' *judgements* about ritual form. By 'symbolic' I refer to those phenomena which are culturally uncodified in the main, restricted in their use and transmission, and, though ubiquitous in social and personal representations, seldom explicitly taught (Lawson & McCauley, 1990: 2–3). Their theoretical interest lies in the fact that they are phenomena over which participants in a culture show considerable mastery without having been explicitly taught. They are instances of symbolic fluency. As such they raise questions about acquisition because in making such 'informed' judgements people demonstrate that they know more than they were taught. Ethnographers who have concerned themselves with the issue note the very haphazard, unsystematic and partial role that instruction plays in cognitive development.

What is fortunate for competence theorists interested in religious ritual representation and the issues which emerge from it, is that they do not have to start their analyses of such symbolic–cultural phenomena *de novo*. Generative linguists have already spent a considerable amount of energy in the last thirty years developing and perfecting various formal techniques for the analysis of language, the cultural 'system' *par excellence*. They have provided useful, empirically tractable methods consisting of a wide range of skilfully honed formal tools capable of analysing apparently unruly cultural phenomena in productive ways. Because the systems of rules and representations constructed by generative linguists have proved themselves to be powerful techniques in the study of language, we think that they promise to be transportable to other areas of cognitive enquiry. They have considerable heuristic value in analysing patterns of representations.

Of particular interest to those of us concerned with religious ritual is the fact that these formal strategies produced in the competence-theoretic approach to linguistic phenomena have proved remarkably successful not only in the analysis of the grammars of particular natural languages but in explanatory theorising about universal principles that underlie and constrain particular grammars. In other words, participants in competence-theoretic research have made progress in showing how a small set of universal principles is capable of constraining a larger set of formal systems.

Such techniques have great heuristic value for the study of religious ritual, especially when such study crosses cultural boundaries in search of cultural commonalities at whatever level such generality may be found. The overall competence approach provides rich resources for the study of symbolic–cultural phenomena such as ritual. These resources should not be taken lightly.

Despite the tendency of the anthropological tradition of enquiry to over-emphasise cultural *systems* from a non-cognitive perspective, the clues provided by the science of language suggest that language and ritual have much in common. Like language, ritual systems transgress cognitive and socio-cultural lines of demarcation by showing that a purely cultural analysis is never enough. In fact, it becomes clear that ritual systems straddle fences and join territories which classical approaches to cultural phenomena have insisted upon holding apart (by claiming autonomy for social and cultural systems, *à la* Durkheim). Despite such claims of autonomy (and even methodological solipsism) it has become increasingly evident that both religious ritual and language require in their explanation a reference to, and an ordering of, the relationships between socio-cultural and psychological variables. Further, it can no longer be taken at face value that cultural categories have methodological primacy in analysing cultural phenomena. In fact, significant progress is being made in the analysis of cultural phenomena by commencing with cognitive structures which then lead to questions about cultural forces and innate structures. This is what I meant by saying earlier that even those in the middle of the spectrum are willing to nudge the direction of research in one direction or the other.

Ritual action and religious thought

The competence-theoretic approach McCauley and I employ focuses upon the representation of religious *ritual action* rather than the more inclusive domain of religious *thought*, or religious *ideas*. We do so because we see a significant opportunity for explaining important features of religion by choosing a narrower focus. For one thing, analysing the representation of ritual action provides more opportunities for specifying structural elements than is possible at the more inclusive level of thought. Of course, I do not mean to imply that McCauley and I are uninterested in religious ideas. In fact, *conceptual schemes* play a significant role in our theory by providing conceptual content to the system of rules which generate abstract ritual structures in the system for the representation of action which we propose.

We have chosen, therefore, to theorise about the cognitive representation of action systems that ritual participants employ in their judgements about the form of their ritual systems rather than the more inclusive ontologies that constrain their thinking. This shift of cognitive attention from religious ideas to the representation of action in particular permits a generative strategy that is much more difficult to achieve at more inclusive levels of ideational analysis.

I do not mean to imply that religious ontologies are unconstrained. Boyer (1990) argues that religious ontologies are constrained by universal cognitive mechanisms. In fact, Boyer has shown how core ideas affect and are presupposed by religious ideas. However, I think that there lies a more structured level for analysis in religious ritual action than is available in the variability characteristic of religious thought in a particular culture. Dan Sperber, for example, has shown how 'creative' the interpretative abilities of religious participants are in their symbolic traffic with each other, with the social world they inhabit and with the fieldworker in search of cultural information (1975b). As I have already stated, then, we do not intend to ignore religious thought; in our theory we make a special place for religious conceptual schemes as providing the *content* required by ritual structures. But the pursuit of form is by no means a fruitless task.

We do wish, especially, to counteract a tendency among scholars interested in religion, *particularly philosophers of religion*, to over-emphasise the role that religious beliefs play in the interpretation and explanation of religion. Particularly troubling is their over-attentiveness to consciously entertained *beliefs* and their putative role in religious life. The literature on 'propositional attitudes' is vast. Some philosophers of religion even talk as though religious life were nothing more than a set of bizarre beliefs in need only of translation, rationalisation or refutation.

And some anthropologists have fuelled these fires. They have given comfort to, and aided and abetted these tendencies in quite specific ways. For example, intellectualists, symbolists and functionalists jointly conspire to explain away religious thought by employing concepts such as 'idiomatic difference', 'cryptic meaning' and 'social integration' rather than seeing through the apparent bizarreness of religious thought to the ordinariness of the underlying cognitive structures, especially as these are evident in the representation of religious ritual action.

While we concede that in some general sense ritual participants do have 'theories' of the world (and often more than one at the same time!) it is an intellectualist mistake to over-emphasise the role that intellectual curiosity plays in daily life. The recovery of the mundane underlying the bizarre would be a major leap forward in theoretical work. Boyer has made that leap. In his discussion of constraints upon religious thought Boyer argues that some important properties of religious ideas are the outcome of quite ordinary cognitive processes which structure everyday, non-religious aspects of experience. Among these, for example, are views of causality that do not differ remarkably in religious and non-religious contexts. I agree. What Boyer has accomplished is to show that religious thought is not nearly as bizarre as it is sometimes taken to be. Rather than contradicting Boyer's analysis, the theory of ritual action that McCauley and I propose reinforces it.

My point is that ritual participants do not only have beliefs about the world (the problem of reference), nor are they satisfied simply to categorise its levels (the problem of ontology). They also cognitively *organise* it in such a way that they can *act* in it (the problem of action). And they do so in marvellously structured ways most of which are quite tacit (Rosch *et al.* 1976). We cannot, however, be content to settle for an analysis of religion in general and religious ritual action in particular that stops with having identified the categories people employ in their traffic with their world.

One undesirable consequence of focusing upon bizarreness as the fundamental characteristic of religious beliefs is becoming embroiled by the distractions of arguments about the conditions under which apparently bizarre beliefs can be taken to be true or false, declared to be meaningless, or be justified only 'psychologically', that is, by their functions. Actually, in explanatory theorising about religious ritual behaviour very little hangs on whether religious concepts are true or false, whether they have a reference or even whether they fulfil needs of some kind or other. Rather, what counts is their cognitive availability not only for a 'naming of parts', but for providing shape and meaning to the variability of daily social life. More than classification is at stake because daily life is

filled with 'traditional repetition' (Boyer 1990). I think that what underlies such 'traditional repetition' provides a productive domain for
explanatory theorising. It *will* show us that people have both basic and
peripheral categories. It will also show us that people act in quite structured ways in their social life.

So, granting that universal cognitive mechanisms constrain religious
thought, we still have an interesting opportunity for productive analysis
at the level of the representation of ritual action. And at that level of
analysis it is the case that the representation of ritual action, rather than
being a completely anomalous sphere, is constrained by the representation of action generally. McCauley and I argue (1991: 158) that quite
ordinary assumptions about action constrain the representation of religious ritual action. No matter how unusual a religion's metaphysical
assumptions about the entities that populate the world may be, the ritual
system will provide a means for ensuring that religious ritual representations respect the general logical distinctions which inform an everyday
view of action.

A theory of the representation of religious ritual

Our theory has two goals. The first of these is to provide a clear and
efficient way for describing the cognitive representation of religious ritual
action. The second of these is to make predictions about important
features of religious rituals so represented. Our theory consists of the
following:

1 *A system for the representation of action.* This 'action-representation
   system' consists of a set of rules and categories which generate abstract
   structural descriptions for the representation of ritual form.
2 *A conceptual scheme.* This scheme, which contains semantic information, activates the set of universal principles and penetrates the
   action representation system.
3 *A set of universal principles.* These principles constrain the products of
   the action-representation system and feed back the results into the
   conceptual scheme.
I shall discuss these three aspects of our theory in turn.

The representation of ritual action

Though our theory consists of a system for the representation of religious
ritual action we wish to emphasise that the representation of religious
ritual action differs in only very minor ways from the representation of
any action.[2] In other words, the representation of religious ritual action is

just a special case of the representation of human action generally. So whatever set of rules we devise to generate descriptions of the representation of religious ritual action will differ only in minor ways from those designed to generate descriptions of ordinary actions. For example, taking a sip of wine from a glass is a case of human action capable of being cognitively represented by the concepts applicable to any standard feature of daily life, namely, the categories of agents, actions and objects. (Agents pick up glasses, open mouths and swallow liquids.)

Taking a sip of wine from a chalice held by a priest in the ritual of the mass involves *additional descriptive elements*; it does not, however, entail accessing new categories for an adequate description of the ritual beyond the initial level already available in the representation of any action. This means that ritual representation involves elements which are merely special cases of agents, actions and objects: priests filling chalices with wine, priests consecrating wine, priests and parishioners drinking consecrated wine, priests chanting sentences over wine so consecrated and, at embedded levels of description, superhuman agents ordaining priests who, in turn, consecrate wine and ritually encourage parishioners to drink it.

The presence of such semantic information (provided by the conceptual scheme) in the representation of the action enables us to distinguish between action in general and religious action in particular. Thus declaring the wine in the chalice to be the blood of Jesus Christ spilt for the ritual participant's sins, and drinking the wine so declared from a suitable chalice, involves little more than special descriptions of the agents, actions and objects involved. Maintaining one overall formal description of action discourages tampering with standard ontological assumptions that people possess in any society and which they competently employ in their representations of action. We still have agents (with some special properties) acting (in special ways) upon objects (with some special features). It also shows that there is a continuity between religious representations and representations generally. The most significant additional element present in the cognitive representation of religious ritual is the presumption of superhuman agency on the part of ritual participants. (I shall return to a discussion of superhuman agency below.)

As I have already promised above, the formalism McCauley and I employ in the representation of religious ritual action is very similar to that employed in generative linguistics (Lawson & McCauley 1990: 84–136). Our scheme for the representation of action involves two components, a formation system and an object agency filter. The formation system consists of formation rules and constituents. The constituents consist of action elements and category symbols. The formation rules generate initial structural descriptions in which the category symbols are

instantiated by action elements. The initial structural descriptions generated by the formation rules are constrained by an object agency filter,
which ensures the proper classification of agents and, in those situations
where the formal system generates objects in the role of agents, either
re-arranges the initial structural description or eliminates it. For example,
a priest is an agent, drinking is an act and wine is an object. The rules that
McCauley and I have proposed initially permit not only descriptions of
priests drinking wine (agents acting upon objects) but also permit wine to
consecrate ritual participants (objects acting as agents upon objects). In
this latter instance we clearly have a situation in which commonsense
assumptions are violated. This is an infelicitous result not only in our
ordinary understanding of action but in some sense in religious understandings as well. The object agency filter is a principle which either
eliminates such infelicitous descriptions (in which objects assume the role
of agents acting upon objects, for example wine consecrating ritual
participants) or re-arranges the description. For example, the object
agency filter permits a redescription in which a permissible agent, a
parishioner, consecrates herself *by means of* drinking consecrated wine.[3]

Such a generative scheme permits structural descriptions of an indefinitely large set of religious rituals and permits us to identify important
features of ritual systems; but the products of such a scheme by itself
would hardly hold most theoreticians interest for very long. For one thing
its abstract structures lack content. But we promise something more
interesting than a radically syntactic approach; we argue that the conceptual scheme provides the mechanism which supplies the content. The
semantic and the syntactic elements are inextricably meshed. I turn next
to a discussion of the semantic component.

The conceptual scheme and the religious conceptual scheme

The scheme that is represented in the minds of ritual participants in any
society is that set of concepts the effects of which are made manifest in
cultural phenomena such as the following:
1 narratives, either oral or written, which are always in the process of
   change, alteration, emendation and even elimination;
2 commentaries on, and interpretations of, these narratives;
3 abstract analyses and reflections, practised by special groups but
   usually accessible to everyone;
4 prescriptions and instructions about procedures to be enacted, obligations to be met, norms to be conformed to, criteria to be followed, all
   of which may be preserved in either oral or written form in narratives,
   commentaries, manuals, etc.;

4 calendrical order (what happens when);
6 spatial organisation (who does what where);
7 social relations (who does what to whom, or is permitted to do so);
8 systems of classification of the personal, social and natural worlds.

While these cultural phenomena are available to the cultural participant the conceptual scheme is not consciously accessible. In fact, the
theoretician infers it from the judgements made by the cultural participants about their ritual system. The concepts in the scheme assume
religious content at the moment that they implicate the action of superhuman agents at some level of structural description. Without such a
pivotal concept it makes little sense to think that even a vague area of
theoretical interest deserves explanatory treatment. So modified by this
pivotal notion, a conceptual scheme has a number of systematic functions
(Lawson & McCauley 1990: 157): (1) it addresses questions about the
meaning of religious rituals; (2) it contains accounts of where, how and
why rituals originated; (3) it explicates why rituals have many of the
features that they do; and (4) it provides reasons for what they intend to
accomplish. In addition, the conceptual system contains information
about eligible participants, and will even specify who qualifies as eligible
substitutes. As we shall see later, it also makes the acquisition problem
more binding.

One of the seductive features of conceptual schemes for theoreticians is
how easily analysable they sometimes appear to be. They can rather
quickly become the exclusive focus of attention. As I have already argued
against the philosophers of religion, placing an undue emphasis upon
conceptual schemes tempts the inquirer to become more interested in their
truth content than in their structural role in a religious system. Concen-
trating on conceptual schemes (to the exclusion of religious ritual action)
also places more emphasis upon what is *publicly* available than is warran-
ted: for example, when encountering polite strangers asking questions
about everyday life, people in other societies are usually quite ready to tell
a story, give directions, explicate customs, identify important dates,
describe kin relationships, clarify procedures, etc. Even when voluble
informants are not available to the polite and inquisitive strangers some
cultures have books and documents available which provide reams of
information. And in those societies which transmit their traditions orally
the various keepers of the oral tradition are often approachable (if not
always willing) to dispense the desired information to persistent and
courteous enquirers.

What is stored in public representations, however, is not necessarily
identical with the conceptual system that is actually represented in the
heads of ritual participants, especially when such a conceptual system has

very complex cognitive relationships to other cognitive systems. In fact, even the public information often presupposes hidden cognitive structures which only adequate theory can bring to light.

First, there will be much information, especially very esoteric information, in the overall public representations of a society that is not available to all ritual participants. If it is inaccessible, then it becomes problematic about showing how it has influenced individual conceptual systems. We need a special argument about the transmission of information to make any case at all. Second, there will be things going on in the heads of participants from a cognitive-theoretic point of view that can be found nowhere in the public representations. Some representation or other will always be available for the ritual participants, but the set as a whole will never be necessary for providing any particular ritual action with specific content. The reason for this is that once ritual participants have the (tacit) system in hand (or in the head!) then those ritual participants are ritually competent to make judgements about their ritual practices because they have internalised a formation system of some kind. The internalised system is doing the explanatory work.

Once the 'grammar' of ritual has been internalised, the ritual participant knows how to employ the system in daily life. There is a great deal of information in the public set of representations that is simply not necessary for such employment; for example, the ritual participant might be quite capable of making judgements about eligible participants without having to know the contents of some esoteric doctrine held by a special priesthood. Further, both the public store of information *and* the secret doctrines known only by the few sometimes lag behind the religious ritual system that is actually in place in the ritual participant's mind. We used to refer to this as 'cultural lag'. Competence theorising puts a positive twist on an acknowledged phenomenon.

The conceptual scheme (understood now not just as the cultural scheme stored in public representations but also that which is cognitively present in the individual participant's mind) fulfils two functions from a theoretical point of view: it penetrates the action-representation system; it also (as we shall see below) activates a set of universal principles of religious ritual which assess the products generated by the system of rules in the action-representation system and in virtue of such an assessment constrain the conceptual scheme.

From a cognitivist perspective the complex role of the conceptual scheme introduces a dynamic element into the system for the representation of religious ritual action. The psychological interest of the theory emerges at the point at which we attempt to ascertain the psychological reality of such an abstract description of the principles, processes and products involved. In other words, how are the conceptual scheme, action-representation system and universal principles (to be discussed next) related psychologically?

I think that the theses of the theory that McCauley and I have proposed are not only compatible with the cultural data in question; I also think that they are testable by the quite specific predictions that the theory makes about ritual participants' behaviour, where such behaviour consists of judgements uttered by ritual participants about ritual form.

The universal principles

Although a system for the representation of religious ritual action is a valuable heuristic device for locating cognitive patterns, especially when complemented by a conceptual scheme capable of providing the formal system with content, it achieves genuine theoretical significance when it is constrained by a set of universal principles. I now turn my attention to that feature of our theory of religious ritual action.

The action-representation system which we have described above is constrained by a set of universal principles. Following standard linguistic practice, we distinguish between substantive, formal and functional universals (Lawson & McCauley 1990: 121–30). Substantive universals involve the categories and elements utilised in the rules; for example, participant, agent, action, object, quality, etc. Formal universals have to do with the way the rules are organised, the order in which they are applied, etc.: for example, they might require that logically prior actions are also temporally prior.

Functional universals are the most significant for the purposes of our theory. Given our most fundamental assumption, namely the basic principle that all religious systems involve commitments to culturally postulated superhuman agents and that all religious ritual systems involve superhuman agents at some level of description (Lawson & McCauley 1990: 123–4), functional universals constrain the representation of ritual action. Two functional universal principles of religious ritual are the principle of Superhuman Agency and the principle of Superhuman Immediacy.

The principle of Superhuman Agency refers to the *character* of the superhuman agent's involvement in a ritual system as that involvement is specified in the structural description of a religious ritual. The significance of this principle of Superhuman Agency lies in its claim that where a superhuman agent functions as the *immediate* agent of an action upon an object of action there we will find a ritual that is *central* to a religious system; for example, when Jesus as superhuman agent founds the Church.

However, where a superhuman agent is the *recipient* of action by another *non*-superhuman agent there we will find a more peripheral ritual; for example, when a ritual participant sacrifices a bowl of fruit to the appropriate superhuman agent. *What rituals are assumed to effect* (the terms of which will be provided by the conceptual scheme) depends crucially upon the action of superhuman agents – from the point of view of those with a mastery of the system.

The principle of Superhuman Immediacy involves not the character but the *immediacy* of the superhuman agent's involvement in a religious ritual's structural description. The *less* enabling actions that are required in order to implicate superhuman agency the *more* fundamental the ritual; the more enabling actions that are required in order to implicate super-human agency the less fundamental the ritual will prove to be in the judgements that ritual participants make about the form and meaning of their rituals. The principle involves the notions of *ritual distance* and *ritual proximity*; for example, the act of a parishioner lighting a memorial candle requires more enabling actions than the pope installing a cardinal. An enabling action is any ritual action the prior performance of which is presupposed by the ritual under consideration.

I should add that *no particular* representation of superhuman agency in any ritual system is required, but *some representation or other* is a *sine qua non* for the motivation of religious ritual. I speak here of an identity of form but a variability of content.[4] Anyone can conceive of an agent with more abilities or different abilities than a human being possesses. Conceiving of a system that completely transcends the natural (and which does not mean 'the artificial'!) is much more problematic. Whereas super-human properties involve *matters of degree* (for example, the ability to escape detection, the ability to overwhelm a powerful human being, the ability to avoid disease), the term 'supernatural' presupposes quite specific metaphysical commitments. You must first show what it means before you can employ it. McCauley and I have no interest in entering the metaphysical wars.

Consequences of the theory

The theory of the representation of ritual action presented above has a number of consequences, some of them quite practical. Starting with the most practical, it need hardly be said that, equipped with such a theory of the representation of religious ritual action, a theory quite capable of delivering very precise descriptions of religious ritual structures (including those that are elaborately embedded), any anthropological fieldworker would be primed to ask new kinds of questions and seek new kinds of information from informants. Fieldworkers would be able to employ new formal techniques in the analysis of the materials they have gathered.

Such analyses promise interesting discoveries both about what structures are tacitly represented in the heads of the people in the culture studied, and, *mutatis mutandis*, what patterns of representation are distributed (see Sperber 1990) in the culture itself. Our theory underwrites the kinds of questions that will elicit judgements not only about what people know by tuition, but also about what they know but do not realise they know, even though they have never been taught it. For example, the anthropologists will discover that ritual participants can be asked to make judgements not only about actual but also about possible rituals (theoretical rituals), and that their responses to these questions will disclose their ritual competence. The intuitions that participants will have about possible rituals will include the ability to sort out the imaginary but well formed and the imaginary but ill formed.

Our theory presents a way of describing the structures of competence underlying such judgements. An analysis of such structures promises to disclose novel relationships that will not easily be found by analysing the conceptual scheme independently of its relationship to the action-representation system.

Other consequences of our theory include quite precise predictions about the judgements people are capable of making about ritual form (Lawson & McCauley 1990: 176). So, for example, our theory predicts (1) that ritual participants will distinguish religious ritual action from other kinds of religious action in conformity with the universal principles of the theory, (2) that ritual participants' judgements about well-formedness of rituals and relative importance of a particular ritual to the ritual system as a whole will conform to the theory, (3) that ritual participants' judgements about the necessity of ritual repetition, the substitutability of agents and objects, and the reversibility or irreversibility of a ritual action will conform to the theory and (4) that ritual participants' judgements about, and historical analyses of, religious systems' identities in times of alteration, transformation or schism (i.e. in times of radical change) will be strongly correlated with our theory of ritual types.

These are hardly insignificant predictions. They ensure that the theory that we have proposed is independently testable, and they highlight the role that competence theorising can play in dealing with cultural phenomena from a cognitivist perspective. They also raise the question of how such knowledge (understood now as tacit knowledge constraining particular judgements about particular ritual actions), was acquired. Few can seriously believe that such knowledge about well-formedness, repeatability, substitutability, reversibility and so on is taught to members of a ritual in any thorough and explicit manner, if at all.

I am confident that cross-cultural studies of instruction and indoctrination will show, at most, that societies in their instructional situations will concentrate upon certain obvious principles taken seriously in the conceptual scheme prevalent in the society. Even when the contents of sequences of rituals *are* taught to initiates, little, if any, time will be spent *ranking* the centrality and importance of rituals. It will be enough to know what everybody is supposed to know about what to believe and what to do. More time will be spent on being sure that initiates get basic beliefs right, basic obligations ingrained. In any case, this is an empirical matter and can be tested in the field. I am reasonably sure that no time at all will be spent discussing either theoretical or possible rituals. The theoretical rituals (i.e. those in which superhuman agents appear in the structural description of the ritual as agents) will simply be assumed or stated as fact.

Clearly, people who are culturally competent will know how to cognitively manipulate ritual representations in such a manner that they are capable of issuing judgements about cultural form. The question is, then, how do they do so, if explicit cultural tuition is not available as an answer? Nativists will be inclined to look to biological structures, cultural autonomists will be inclined to search for hidden cultural forces. Before we move in either direction it is worthwhile considering what is at stake. Is it the case that such discrepancies between competence and tuition is either a biological or a cultural property? Not necessarily. First of all, it obviously is a *psychological* property. As I said at the very beginning of this chapter, it is a question of *what is acquired*. We are talking here about a form of knowledge, that is, the ability to make judgements about cultural form without explicit tuition. Now, what kind of psychological property is this form of knowledge? It is the kind of cognitive property which can be formally described by a system of rules capable of generating structural descriptions. So, given semantic information provided by a conceptual scheme, all we need to acknowledge is that a system of rules and representations is capable of generating all the structural descriptions necessary for an explanation of the structure of the ritual system (as cognitively represented). So the judgements about cultural form issued by the cultural participant (judgements which are independently testable by the predictions of the theory) can be deduced from the system of rules in relationship to a conceptual scheme and constrained by the universal principles.

There are, then, two factors present. On the one hand, we have a set of inter-related abstract mechanisms (action-representation system, conceptual scheme and universal principles) and an aggregation[5] of cultural content which, *together*, are capable of accounting for the relevant properties of the phenomena in question. Obviously, however, such an argument does not account for the status of the abstract mechanisms. What are they abstractions from? One possible answer is that, given the fact that people are extraordinarily competent in recognising certain kinds of patterns (and the structural descriptions of ritual action which our system generates are certainly patterns), and given the fact that artificial minds modelled along connectionist lines are capable of being trained up to recognise novel patterns on the basis of being presented with sets of examples, then all we might need for an explanation of how a person is capable of making a judgement about well-formedness, or repeatability, etc. is to argue that our brains are so designed. In other words, our brains are excellent pattern-recognition devices. Pattern-recognition devices with a certain level of complexity in their internal structure (of a psychophysical kind and which may even include a rules-and-representations component) and trained by 'experience' are quite capable of recognising novel patterns with relative ease.

Such a connectionist view would not justify the view of a complete autonomous cultural system relentlessly transmitting information in a unidirectional manner to cultural participants. At most, it would show that human minds sufficiently trained over a long period of cognitive development in a cultural context are capable of recognising novel patterns in cultural phenomena, and, in fact, are quite capable of contributing novel cognitive direction to prevailing cultural modes of behaviour. That already would be a great leap forward in empirically accounting for cultural patterns.

But even if the connectionist picture does not sustain itself, a nativist view of such matters would in any case have to be cautious about deriving too much cultural content from innate form. Even in a principles-and-parameters approach to the acquisition of syntactic structures (Chomsky 1981), theoretical linguistics requires only that those universal principles that constrain all particular grammars be candidates for 'innatehood'. Much of the rest occurs at the psychological level, and points to a level of complexity that needs to be acknowledged. In the same way I am claiming that with a few mechanisms (a conceptual scheme, a set of action rules and the universal principles) which represent a rich and complex set of cognitive processes we can account for both the form and content of religious ritual. This is a level of theoretical description that is complex enough to engage our attention for some time to come.

NOTES

1 In fact, recent research (Pettito & Marentette 1991) seems to confirm nativist views about universal linguistic constraints by showing that deaf children commence the first stages of the acquisition of language, in this case sign language, by the age of ten months, despite not being exposed to speech. Interestingly, though, visual cues appear to be capable of acting as substitutes for phonological parameters.

2 In this chapter I do not employ the formalism that McCauley and I propose in *Rethinking Religion*. Instead, I use a qualitative description of the theory of the representation of ritual action, and present some of its results.

3 Dealing with the role played by objects in religious conceptual schemes is complicated. Internal to the description of the structure of a ritual action, the object agency filter is crucial; but it is not the only resource available in religious systems for handling problematic objects. For example, when analysing the relationships among a set of ritual actions, situations occur in which objects are ritually transformed ('this bread, on this plate . . .') into agents, which then in subsequent rituals can act as agents.

4 The term 'superhuman' is preferable to the term supernatural, as a property that ritual agents must either have or presuppose, because whereas the term superhuman requires no ontological commitment about the superhuman agent on the part of the theorist, the term 'supernatural' certainly does.

5 In my view, there is no need to assume that a culture is one system, with different aspects, all of which have an underlying unity. A culture may be nothing more than a set of cognitively generated systems which affect each other without being thoroughly integrated into an over-arching cultural unity. A culture might very well be more like a second-rate orchestra without a conductor trying to play a vaguely remembered tune. Of course, this fact about culture may also be a picture of what the mind is like.

10   The interactive basis of ritual effectiveness in a male initiation rite

Michael Houseman

From the participants' standpoint, 'effectiveness' constitutes an integral part of what ritual behaviour is about. This is particularly evident in the case of rites of passage, whose execution is explicitly held to bring about change. In as much as such transformations provide the necessary (and sometimes sufficient) grounds for legitimately undertaking certain distinctive activities, claiming certain privileged rights and responsibilities, etc., the issue of the participants' commitment to these changes is a particularly crucial one. I will be concerned here with some of the implications of this commitment, both as a constraint upon ritual form and as a competent of ritual meaning.

The material I will draw upon concerns the initiation rite *So* of the Beti of Southern Cameroon, the undertaking of which is a necessary requisite to assuming the rightful prerogatives of adult manhood in this society.[1] Following their initiation, usually several years after puberty or later (a domestic-scale circumcision rite occurs around eight years of age), young men are authorised to marry, participate (albeit as junior members) in the decisions of the adult community, engage in certain ritual activities (ancestor cult groups, subsequent *So* initiations, etc.), eat certain foods (notably fatty meats) strictly prohibited to women, children and uninitiated men (e.g. servants, 'slaves'), etc. Not only does this ritual mark a radical change for the individuals who undergo it, but also the distinction between those who have 'fallen', 'eaten' or 'known' the *So* and those who have not constitutes a recurrent discrimatory reference intervening in a variety of domains.

It is, however, remarkably difficult to define the unnamed categories INITIATED and UNINITIATED. On the one hand, they seem at once to cut across and overlap with a series of other, highly significant, distinctions (MAN/WOMAN, ADULT/CHILD, BETI/FOREIGN, etc.), remaining all the while clearly irreducible to them. Thus, although only (Beti) males become initiates, as such they are radically distinguished from all of those, male and female, child and adult, Beti and non-Beti alike, who have not 'eaten the *So*'. On the other hand, attributes apparently specific to these categories – knowing or not knowing certain things, eating or not eating certain foods, being able or not to marry certain persons (the children of men initiated together cannot marry), etc. – refer to the equally irreducible fact of having or not having undergone initiation. In this way, it would seem that ordinary experience, on its own, cannot account for the INITIATED/UNINITIATED opposition. To do so, it is necessary to consider the ritual itself.

In the development that follows, I will be concerned less with ritual symbolism *per se*, that is, with the explication of implicit significations relating to other domains (e.g. Turner 1967), than with a number of 'obvious aspects' (Rappaport 1979 *passim*) of the ritual performance itself. Specifically, I will try to show how certain organisational features of this performance, in contributing to the persuasiveness of the transformation it is supposed to effect, establish for the participants the well-foundedness of the INITIATED/UNINITIATED dichotomy. Here, the term 'participants' refers to all those who effectively intervene in its performance, as well as, in a wider sense, to those who situate themselves and are situated by others as possible actors. In the present instance, the three categories of participants envisaged (the initiators, the candidates and the uninitiated) include, at least in theory, everyone.

Initiation is treated here as a complex higher-order *form of relationship* which has three main effects:

1 It operates a change in the pattern of relationship between the initiated and the candidates.
2 It operates another, concomitant change in the relationship between the candidates and the uninitiated.
3 It reiterates the existing pattern of relationship between initiated and uninitiated. The 'performative' dimensions of ritual, accountable in terms of an implicit discursive model (e.g. Tambiah 1981), are regarded here as subordinate to this dynamic, which implies the global coordination of behavioural (and conceptual) disparities. The inspiration for this approach is mainly Batesonian (1972, 1980).

The initial section describes the different phases of the *So* ritual. A second section identifies the overall relational scheme in which the candidates' transition from the state of MALE CHILDREN to that of INITIATED MEN is acted out. A third section shows how certain key events render this enacted change undeniable. A final section briefly considers certain implications of the proposed analysis.

The phases of the *So* ritual

The *So* lasts about a year and can be broken down into four main phases associated with different spaces that correspond to varying degrees of dissimulation.[2] Events taking place in or around the village (phase I and the latter part of phase IV) are for the most part both visible and audible for the uninitiated. Those taking place in the forest (phase II) are neither visible nor audible for them. Those taking place in the intermediate area between the village and the forest, called *afie* (phase III and the former part of phase IV), are in principle audible but not visible.

Phase I

The recurrent theme of this first phase is an ostentatious display of the candidates' inherent aptitude for manhood. This is clear from the very beginning, in the opening 'presentation of the candidates' (*meyen mvondo*), during which the novices, made up and dressed in splendid costume by their mothers, dance before the crowd with ferocious expressions and slow majestic movements. It is also apparent in the sequences that follow: public scarification, military exercises in which the candidates, although initially beaten, end up beating and chasing their initiators and/or mounting a mock attack on the village, a meal of honour offered to the novices by their initiators, a collection jointly undertaken by the candidates and the initiators during which the novices are encouraged to behave in an intimidating and swaggering manner, etc. During this initial period lasting several months, the novices are made to conform to the ideal of adult virility: beautiful, courageous, aggressive, 'hard', etc. Their innate masculinity is thus publicly proclaimed as providing the grounds for the attainment of adult manhood.

At the end of this time, from the novices' (and the other uninitiated participants') point of view, the hardships of their initiation are essentially over. They eagerly await a feast of previously forbidden fatty meats as a formal confirmation of their new status. In anticipation of this feast, the novices accompany their initiators on a long hunting trip in the forest.

Phase II

During this several week long hunting trip, the candidates' hazing takes place. Naked, obliged to sleep on the bare ground, forced to imitate sexual intercourse with dead animals, to insult their mother's vagina, etc. they are repeatedly assured by their initiators that the time has come for them to die. Most of the hardships they submit to entail an ironic and painful relationship with objects or activities normally associated with adult men. Many have to do with hunting. For example a novice is told to catch a hedge-hog hiding in a ditch overlaid with branches; when the boy does so, his hand is bitten by the initiator hiding in the ditch. The candidates, invited on a wild-pig hunt, are made to run on all fours, chased by their initiators, for hours. At one point, the novices are led to a hunter's lean-to to 'rest', where they are forced to squeeze themselves into a low hut made of thorny vines and built over a bog filled with excrement. In other ordeals, novices are made to 'wash' with pepper-filled and dirty water, to pick 'kola nuts' by climbing to the top of a tree swarming with poisonous ants, to 'forge' by getting their hands crushed, etc. During these humiliating and painful ordeals, the candidates' attributes of adult manhood, so amply demonstrated during the first stage, are systematically and violently denied.

At the end of the hunting/hazing period, the candidates leave the forest to take up residence in an initiation camp which they build just outside the organisers' village. A palm-frond curtain hides the camp from the eyes of the uninitiated. During the public festival that follows, the *ndzom So* celebration, the novices dance in a frenzied and explicitly sexual fashion on a long platform (the *ndzom*) jutting out from this curtain above the heads of the spectators. They are naked and covered with red mahogany powder applied by their sponsors (called '*So* fathers'). This, they are told, is to hide the traces of their recent ordeals from the uninitiated, and above all from their mothers who, on this occasion, are publicly congratulated for having produced such obviously magnificent and unambiguously male sons.

Phase III

At dawn, a day after the *ndzom So* festival, the women and children are banished from the village. They set up a temporary camp a small distance away, where they are supposed to make noise by singing, clapping, shouting, etc. The candidates leave the initiation camp to spend the day and the night in the deserted village. During this time, the initiators prepare the sequence of the following day. They clear a narrow path leading from the initiation camp to a long tunnel which they dig in the ground. They place packets of stinging ants next to the path, and hang bunches of nettles on the tunnel's walls.

Early the next morning, the candidates are told that the time has come for them to partake in the sumptuous feast they have been waiting for, the principal component of which is '*So* fat'. The candidates line up impatiently. They are then informed that they will have nothing to eat, but will instead have to undergo new hardships. Their initiators explain what is to come. A distribution of '*So* fat' then takes place: each novice is given a spoonful of a disgusting mixture containing, among other things, rotten bananas, the organisers' dried faeces and the fat from the '*So* bag', that is, from the animals sacrificed during previous initiations.

After this distribution, the candidates are encouraged to run around the village shouting loudly and showing how they will 'kill the *So*', before plunging into the nearby forest. There, imitiating the grunts of behaviour of wild pigs (so that, they are told, the uninitiated will not realise that it is them), they cut directly through the undergrowth, tear up the women's gardens and cover themselves with mud. They then return to the initiation camp for the ritual's climactic moment, the 'death of the *So*'.

The initiators begin beating the drums and singing the initiation song. The women are told to shout and sing as well; this, they are told, is so as not to hear what is going on. After several false starts, the candidates run, one by one, down the path leading to the tunnel, while certain initiators, standing on either side of the path, shower them with packets of stinging ants. Each candidate is accompanied by his sponsor, who encourages him to be brave, and, if he can, to grab the packets of ants in order to throw them back onto the initiators. The candidates then plunge into the tunnel. Upon emerging, each novice runs back to the village crying out 'father, father, fathers ...'. All the men cheer.

Phase IV

The ritual's final phase consists in a lengthy denouement of what has proceeded. After the 'death of the *So*', the candidates split up into small groups to take up residence in secondary initiation camps on the outskirts of their respective villages. They spend their time hunting and eating game that was so far prohibited, and steal food from the villages ('to steal like a candidate' is the idiomatic expression denoting kleptomania). This period of seclusion is characterised by markedly formal and aggressive relations towards the uninitiated, and specifically towards women. The latter are prohibited from seeing the candidates, being forewarned of their coming presence by the hammering of war bells. The mothers, who bring them food every day, calling out 'Hey, candidate!' to their sons, are also answered with war bells. The candidates have the right not only to steal any food they can find, but also to wreak havoc in the village. Such acts of violence are principally aimed at women, who, obliged to look away and prohibited from eating anything a novice has touched, are incapable of defending themselves.

After a month or two, the candidates, physically transformed by their rich diet, begin visiting other initiation camps. Disguised by means of false beards, head-dresses, etc., they also begin to appear during public celebrations. They are beautiful and aggressive, starting fights whenever possible. After three to six months, they return to live in their respective villages. There, during another three months they are subject to progress-ively less stringent prohibitions.

The 'mahogany powder' (*baa*) festival marks their final re-integration into the community. The candidates assemble in the courtyard of the ritual's organisers' village. Amidst much laughter, their feminine apparel (which the candidates wear during the final phase of their initiation) is stripped away by their classificatory 'wives' (women married into their lineage groups), whose clothing is torn off as well. Afterwards, the novices dress themselves in bark-cloth, coat themselves with mahogany powder and perform a warriors' dance. Their initiation is over.

Concealed and avowed secrecy

These different sequences combine to form a framework for the candi-dates' transition from one state of being, that of uninitiated male children (exhibited in the opening 'presentation of the candidates') to another, that of initiated men (evinced in the closing 'mahogany powder' festival). This transition corresponds to a twofold change in relationship. On the one hand, with respect to their initiators, the candidates progress from being the victims of violent and degrading misrepresentations during the hazing period, to being the objects of a fairly benign deceit concerning '*So* fat', to finally, a close solidarity during the 'death of the *So*' and thereafter. On the other hand, the novices' relationship with the uninitiated, and in particular with their mothers, evolves from a state of manifest solidarity during the first phase, to one of tacit imposture during the dance on the *ndzom*, and finally, to a situation of frankly aggressive duplicity before and following the 'death of the *So*'.[3]

The present section is concerned with trying to sketch out the under-lying pattern of this dynamic relationship between relationships. The ritual can be decomposed into a succession of three stages recalling those classically associated not only with initiation but with other rites of passage as well (Van Gennep 1909). After a preliminary stage, an abrupt separation followed by a prolonged and graduated liminal period leading to a final re-integration. This tripartite design, however, obscures an essential feature of initiation, namely that the transformative scheme it enacts is a product of something akin to what Bateson (1980 *passim*) called 'double description'. It stems from the combination of several different points of view. Indeed, the initiators and the uninitiated do not perceive the ritual in the same way. From the initiators' point of view, the hazing period introduces an irreversible break in the candidates' relation-ship *vis-à-vis* the uninitiated.[4] However, for the uninitiated, who are unaware of the hazing episode as such, there exists, on the contrary, a relative continuity between the ritual's first and third phases. From their point of view, the crucial moment of change in their relationship with the candidates takes place during the 'death of the *So*' from which whey are knowingly excluded. A scheme of the Van Gennep variety is in itself incapable of accounting for this fundamental disparity.

The alternative model proposed here is founded upon a distinction between two types of secrecy, each of which constitutes a discrete three-person system of relationship.[5] In the first of these types, which I will call 'concealed secrecy', the secret's addressee, the excluded party, remains unaware of his/her exclusion, being unaware of the secret's existence. In the other type, hereafter referred to as 'avowed secrecy', the excluded party is explicitly informed of his/her exclusion and is therefore fully aware that a secret exists.

The first half of the *So* ritual is, I suggest, organised around a *concealed* secret: the period of dissimulated hazing (phase II), preceded by an initial stage (phase I) that provides the grounds both for the candidates' subsequent disillusionment and for the uninitiated's ongoing misrepresentation of the ensuing sequences. The uninitiated are led to assume, incorrectly, that the activities pursued by the candidates and their initiators (i.e. hazing), although unwitnessed, are nevertheless ordinary and self-evident ones whose nature is well known to them (hunting).

The second half of the ritual is organised around an *avowed* secret. The episodes leading up to and including the 'death of the *So*', during which the uninitiated are banished from the village area (phase III), followed by a period of reclusion (phase IV), during which the consequences of these (for the uninitiated) mysterious episodes are made manifest. The uninitiated, who witness the actions undertaken by the candidates and their initiators in an incomplete fashion (from far away, by hearing only), are led to presume, correctly, that these actions (the 'death of the *So*'), the exact nature of which they cannot comprehend, are extraordinary.

However, this overall complementarity between the uninitiated's and the initiators' points of view is but a first approximation. A more complete picture emerges when one takes into account a third perspective, namely that of the candidates themselves, whose initiation consists in the transition from one of these contrasting points of view to the other. For the candidates, this transition takes place in three steps. Each is composed of a revelation of a secret by the initiators to the candidates, followed by a dissimulation undertaken by the candidates *vis-à-vis* the uninitiated that corroborates the secret revealed to them by the initiators. These steps are:

1 the hazing period, followed by the novices' deceitful dance during the *ndzom So* festival;

2 the '*So* fat' episode, followed by the candidates' impersonation of wild animals;

3 the 'death of the *So*', followed by the period of reclusion during which the candidates engage in various subterfuges.

As this series unfolds, the candidates take on an increasingly active role. Thus, during the hazing period, they submit to the initiators in a passive fashion, and their subsequent imposture during the dance on the *ndzom* is an essentially covert one. Then, in the '*So* fat' episode, after showing how they will 'kill the *So*', the candidates charge through the forest in an imitation of wild pigs that contrasts sharply with the 'wild-pig hunt' ordeal of the hazing period. Concomitantly, their deception of the uninitiated is more openly aggressive, involving, for example, the destruction of the women's garden plots. Finally, following the 'death of the *So*', during which the novices are encouraged to turn against their initiators, they answer their mothers by means of war bells and undertake violent forays into the village to steal food or to render it inedible for the uninitiated, who stand by helpless.

In this way, the candidates gradually act out the twofold change in relationship noted earlier. There is, on the one hand, a growing identification with the initiators, whose corresponding attitude towards the novices is one of increasing solidarity among equals, and on the other hand, a progressive differentiation with respect to the uninitiated, who react to the candidates' deceptions in an increasingly passive and subordinate fashion.

Step 1. The initiators disclose a concealed secret to the candidates: the true nature of the hunting/hazing period. This disclosure entails a first modification in the novices' relationship *vis-à-vis* their initiators. During the dance on the *ndzom* that follows, the candidates corroborate this secret (and the modification of relationship it entails) by covertly dissimulating the existence of the hazing period from the uninitiated. From the candidates' point of view, this corroboration brings about a first relational change between them and the uninitiated; specifically, it introduces the relationship of concealed secrecy that they act out on this occasion.

Step 2. The initiators disclose a further concealed secret to the candidates: the unsuspected nature of '*So* fat'. Like the preceding revelation of the hazing period, it entails the abrupt disillusionment of previously encouraged false expectations (a lavish feast of forbidden meats). This further disclosure does not in itself imply an additional modification in the relationship between the candidates and their initiators. Rather, it reiterates that introduced in step 1. However, the '*So* fat' episode occurs *after* the uninitiated have been banished from the village. Consequently, unlike the preceding revelation of the hazing period, it takes place within the context of a relationship of avowed secrecy between the initiators and the uninitiated. This second instance of corroborative behaviour on the part of the candidates thus effects, for them, a second relational innovation: the introduction of a relationship of avowed secrecy in which an overt association with their initiators and an explicit disassociation from the uninitiated are inexorably conjoined.

Step 3. The initiators disclose a further avowed secret to the candidates: the 'death of the *So*'. As in the preceding revelation of the wild-pig impersonation, the initiators and the candidates together overtly dissimulate this episode from the uninitiated. For the candidates, this further disclosure does not in itself bring about additional changes, either in their relationship with the initiators or in their relationship with the uninitiated. It merely reiterates, in a more developed fashion, those introduced in step 2. However, for the uninitiated, the situation is not the same. From the uninitiated's standpoint, the relationship of avowed secrecy is dramatically acted out in the 'death of the *So*' episode, during which they are made to sing and shout loudly in order, they are told, not to hear what is going on. By participating in this fashion, the uninitiated demonstratively corroborate, as the *excluded* party, the (further) avowed secret revealed by the initiators to the candidates at this time.

It is the intermediate step of this three-part progression that underlies the transition, for the candidates, from one type of secrecy (concealed) to the other (avowed). As we have seen, step 2 reproduces the interactive pattern characteristic of step 1 (the revelation and subsequent covert dissimulation of a concealed secret) within the novel context of avowed rather than concealed secrecy. In doing so, it provides the foundations for a new interactive pattern (the revelation and subsequent overt dissimulation of an avowed secret) fully realised in step 3. In this respect, this three-part series clearly illustrates the point repeatedly made by Bateson (1972) that change in the pattern of interaction is predicated upon a change in the context of interaction.

In this way, the former and the latter halves of the *So* ritual are articulated, from the candidates' point of view, into a single process. A positive connection is established, for them, between, on the one hand, their passive submission to the ordeals undertaken by their initiators, modelled upon a violent and ironic denial of the novices' innate aptitude for adult manhood, and on the other hand, their own aggressive subterfuges *vis-à-vis* the uninitiated following the 'death of the *So*', modelled upon an equally ironic denial of the ascendency inherent in their mothers' (and more generally women's) nurturing role. Specifically, this intermediary step enables the novices to appreciate these subterfuges, in which they withhold an avowed secret from the uninitiated, as at once a necessary consequence and a formal counterpart of their own ordeals during which they acquire a concealed secret from the initiators.[6]

The identification of this global interactive structure represents a first step towards understanding how ritual events of the *rite de passage* variety, can provide the basis for modifications of behaviour: they enact the relational changes they are purported to effect. However, the problem remains of the ontological status of the relational changes actualised in the ritual's performance. For those implicated by these transmutations (the initiated, the uninitiated and the candidates) they are not contingent representations but compelling truths. How can this be? After all, acting out a change in relationship is ordinarily, in itself, insufficient grounds for presuming the kind of irreversible metamorphosis which the *So* ritual is held to bring about. What makes the present situation so different? In short, what is it about ritual experience that commits its participants to the relational changes they enact?

Irreducible enactments

The verisimilitude of the transformations depicted in the *So* initiation rite derives, I suggest, from certain key events occurring at what are, from the standpoints of the various categories of participants, critical junctures in the twofold relational change acted out during the ritual's performance. This section is concerned with describing these key events from the uninitiated's, the candidates' and the initiators' points of view.

The uninitiated's point of view

As previously mentioned, uninitiated women play an essential role in the *So*. They dress and make up the candidates for the ritual's opening festival, attend to their ostentatious displays of beauty, courage and strength during the initial phase, dance and are publicly congratulated on the occasion of the novices' appearance on the *ndzom*, provide the candidates with food during their seclusion, all the while assuming an attitude of helplessness when confronted with their formal hostility and stealthy destructiveness, and finally, during the rite's terminal festival, rip off the novices' feminine apparel, thereby heralding their return to normal life as initiated men. From the uninitiated's perspective, the decisive turning point in this involvement occurs during their visual (but not auditory) exclusion prior to and during the 'death of the *So*'. At this occasion, the positive bond linking the candidates with the uninitiated women (their mothers especially), ostentatiously displayed up to that time, gives way to a new relationship that sets the pattern for the rite's remaining sequences: systematic avoidance characterised by the candidates' open aggression and the uninitiated's studied powerlessness.

During this phase, the women and children, banished from the village, set up a temporary camp a small distance away, where they are instructed to shout and sing. This, they are told, is so as not to overhear what is going on in the sequences that follow. In a very different approach from the one developed here, Cohen has emphasised the importance in male initiation rituals in general of such an auditory link between the candidates and the uninitiated. This 'profound but empty dialogue of wails and cries' typically marks, as in the present case, the culminating point of the rite. It conveys vividly to the novices their separation from their families of origin: 'Cry and wail as they may ... their mothers and sisters answer yet are powerless to help them. This is the true climax of the initiation ceremony' (Cohen 1964: 542). Be this as it may, it is also, and, I suggest, more significantly, the key to the uninitiated's commitment to the metamorphosis this climactic sequence is held to bring about.

In the 'death of the *So*', the uninitiated are enjoined to bear witness to those events which, from their point of view, correspond to the very moment of the candidates' mysterious transformation, that is, the pivotal episode following which their relationship with the novices is irremediably altered. At the same time, however, it is essential to the success of this transformation that these critical events remain hidden from them. The problematic character of this activity (namely, how can the uninitiated testify to what they cannot perceive?) is solved by the fact that they are engaged in the somewhat puzzling activity of having to make noise so as not to hear the noise made by the candidates. The resulting situation is a highly paradoxical one, in which experiential groundedness and conceptual undecidability are indissociably combined: it is because the uninitiated are in communication with the novices (they can hear the candidates' noise) that they are not in communication with them (they make noise so as not to hear), and, reciprocally, it is because they are not in communication with the novices (they make noise so as not to hear) that they are in communication with them (the candidates hear their noise). At the same time, however, the compulsory nature of this involvement, its dialogical form and the emotional intensity it entails, constrain the uninitiated to acknowledge this mysterious sequence not as a matter of gratuitous theatrics, but as a highly significant, if essentially inexplicable, occasion.

The candidates' point of view

For the candidates, the situation relates to the ordeals they undergo before, and in the case of the '*So* fat' episode, after the *ndzom So* festival. These ordeals are organised around the fact that the candidates are associated, in a derisive and painful fashion, with objects and activities habitually identified with adult men. They correspond to a violent negation of the novices' natural aptitude for manhood. As I have argued elsewhere (Houseman 1986), it seems unlikely that the candidates learn anything in these ordeals. Indeed, as far as empirical knowledge is concerned, there is nothing to learn at all. As the mocking attitude of their initiators suggests, the novices are fully aware of the differences between a kola tree and an ant tree, between clean and dirty water, between chasing and being chased, etc. Similarly, the relative poverty of most of these episodes in so far as their potential for symbolic evocation is concerned, casts doubt upon the notion that they enable the candidates to reflect upon certain 'axiomatic' concepts of their culture (Turner 1964: 151–2). Indeed, it seems more profitable to envisage this hazing the other way round: not as providing a context for the contemplation of cultural categories, but as associating cultural categories in such a way as to create a new context.

To begin with, these ordeals juxtapose elements (ant and kola trees, cleaning oneself and dirtying oneself, accession to manhood and unmanly behaviour, delicious and revolting foods, etc.) which are either arbitrarily associated or explicitly antithetical. As a result, the equations proposed can in no way be deduced from an analysis of the elements themselves. From this point of view, they make no sense. Moreover, this hazing has the further peculiarity of being both physically and psychically painful, and so designed that the novices' very own initiatives bring about the torments they endure. As a result, these ordeals are indisputably grounded, but in such a way as to preclude an unproblematic appreciation of their apparently arbitrary or absurd basis. In other words, for those who endure these ostensibly senseless ordeals, the inherent immediacy and seriousness of the seemingly self-inflicted pain they entail, renders them at once undismissable and unintelligible in terms of a metapropositional frame of the type 'This is play'. The candidates are thus denied the means of a definite conceptual interpretation of the experiences they so unmistakably undergo.[7]

Subsequent events, however, lead the novices to envisage these experiences as being, on the contrary, highly significant. The idea that they are, in some elusive way, not as absurd as they seem, is notably substantiated by the modifications in the candidates' relationship with the uninitiated that take place in the sequences immediately following them. These modifications are, in step 1, the novices' covert occultation of the hazing period during the *ndzom So* festival, and in step 2, their overtly misleading destructive run through the forest after the '*So* fat' episode. As we have seen, from the candidates' standpoint, the relational changes acted out in these sequences are directly linked to the ordeals that precede them and the relational changes with respect to their initiators that are actualised in these ordeals. However, in so far as these mysterious events remain unintelligible in any obvious sense, to ascribe them any significance leads to imagine that there is a higher, extraordinary level of meaning at which immediate inconsistencies are transcended. This superior order of truth, indescribable in propositional terms, is accessible solely by means of these equivocal experiences themselves.

The initiators' point of view

From the standpoint of the initiators who direct these sequences, the candidates' ordeals, like the 'death of the *So*', are in no way paradoxical: they remain potentially accountable in terms of ordinary if somewhat obscure patterns of behaviour, as instances of (successful) intimidation, mystification, or even as a particularly sadistic type of 'play'. This interpretation, however, is made difficult to sustain by two events that implicate the initiators alone. The events involve the coercive manipulation, not of persons (candidates and uninitiated), but of objects.

Towards the beginning of the rite, before the hazing period, the initiators withdraw to the forest, to cut down the tree that will be made into the *ndzom*. On this occasion, the tree is said to obey the unusual instructions that the initiators collectively shout at it. In accordance with their vociferations, the tree falls in a direction contrary to the one in which it leans and without any noise. Towards the end of the rite, following the 'death of the *So*', the initiators sacrifice a castrated goat designated by the name Oyomo. A part of its fat is placed within the '*So* bags' of the rite's officiants. This fat, combined with equivalent bits of fat taken from the sacrificial animals of previous initiations, constitutes the essential component of the '*So* fat' which will be consumed by the novices in subsequent initiations. The animal is staked out in the forest during the hazing period; during the *ndzom So* festival, it is installed in the initiation cabin with the candidates, and is fattened as much as possible. Oyomo is slaughtered in a highly peculiar fashion; it is carved, or according to other accounts, torn limb from limb while still alive. If the goat cries out, the ritual is considered invalid and must be started over.

The initiators are fully aware that the seemingly miraculous behaviour of the *ndzom*-to-be and the goat Oyomo in fact results from their own artifices. Thus, the trunk of the tree is tied by creepers, and the goat's food is poisoned. The apparent absurdity inherent in this situation (the solemn execution of at once strictly prescribed, unnecessary and obviously unconvincing tricks) is belied by two considerations.

The first consists in an 'internal' circularity. It concerns the passage, mediated by these objects, from relational changes between the initiators and the candidates realised in the latter's ordeals, to the corroborative relational changes between the candidates and the uninitiated acted out in the sequences that follow them. The actualisation of these transitions incites the initiators to appreciate the mysterious simulations surrounding the fabrication of these objects as more than the spurious tricks they might appear to be, that is, to invest them with extra-ordinary meaning.

A further consideration relates to an 'external' circularity. Given that the initiator's ability to act as the agents of the candidates' initiation derives from their own initiation, their intervention constitutes a corroboration of their own transformation, brought about by a previous performance of the *So* rite. It follows that, to the degree that the procedures undertaken by them in the candidate's initiation are recognisable as similar to those undertaken for them in their own (older initiators obviously play an important role here), these operations, regardless of their partial inscrutability, may be presumed to be significant.[8]

General remarks

To sum up, at crucial junctures in the rite's development, the candidates, the uninitiated and the initiators are involved in emotionally charged, seemingly paradoxical enactments in which, in the light of subsequent developments, the demonstrable limit of their own understanding is indissociably linked with the postulate of a further, superior order of meaning or authority. For the uninitiated, these key events concern above all step 3 of the three-step progression described in the previous section, and correspond to the disclosure (by the initiators to the candidates) and dissimulation (by the candidates and the initiators) of an avowed secret. For the candidates they take place in steps 2 and 3 of this progression, and consist in the disclosure (by the initiators) and subsequent dissimulation (from the uninitiated) of concealed secrets. For the initiators, these key events concern the preparatory measures and confirmatory divination rites that frame this three-part progression, and at the same time provide the material objects that mediate the transition from concealed to avowed secrecy that this progression entails. In this way, the 'death of the *So*', the ordeals and the felling of the *ndzom* and the killing of Oyomo, take on, for the uninitiated, the candidates and the initiators respectively, a decidedly transcendental quality: they become irreducible to the actions that compose them. As such, these events irrevocably validate, for these different categories of participants, the changes of relationship realised in, and/or following from, their performance.

Conclusion

This perspective implicitly argues for an approach to ritual phenomena founded upon the recognition of dynamic relational structures intrinsic to their enactment as a whole. Such structures may be thought of as having two main characteristics:

1 They are *interactive*. In other words, they are predicated upon the complementary articulation of dissimilarities between the points of view assignable to the various categories of participants.
2 They are *complex*, that is to say, they integrate ordinarily incompatible relational patterns into novel, higher-order configurations of inter-dependency.

In the case of the *So* ritual, this complex interactive structure is founded upon the inter-dependent articulation of concealed and avowed secrecy. Specifically, it consists in the transition from a relationship of concealed secrecy to one of avowed secrecy within the overall framework of a relationship of avowed secrecy. Implicit here is the idea that this embedded configuration represents a simplified and highly formalised expression of the comprehensive relational conditions that constrain the effectiveness not only of the *So* rite, but of male initiation rituals in general.

I have also tried to show how the changes in relationship acted out in the *So* ritual are convincing not because they entail a definite conceptualisation of the terms involved, but on the contrary, because they engage the participants in experientially grounded 'traps for thought' (Smith 1979: 14) in which definite conceptualisation is rendered impossible. These key events concern what would appear to be regular features of male initiation:

1 a compulsory involvement by the uninitiated in a reciprocal auditory but not visual communication with the candidates and the initiators;
2 painful and disorienting 'senseless' ordeals undergone by the candidates;
3 simulative manipulations by the initiators of objects relating to the rite's preparation and/or to divinatory rituals held to confirm its successful accomplishment.

The conceptual undecidability that this commitment entails takes a different form depending upon the nature of the participants concerned. For the uninitiated, it corresponds to an admitted lack of information, the acknowledgement of an explicit exclusion. For the initiators, it resides in a circular relationship between the actions they undertake and their ability to undertake them. For the candidates, it consists in an irreducible arbitrariness, at once symptom and sign of the radical and irreversible break entailed by their passage from one of these points of view to the other.

To conclude, I would like briefly to consider two issues. The first concerns the marginal role played by 'symbolism' in the present account. What is the connection between the relational structure described here and the symbolic evocations invariably entailed by the actions, utterances, objects, etc., involved in its realisation? This is a difficult question requiring a distinction between two very different aspects of ritual symbolism. On the one hand, certain elements of the rite's performance may be said to designate, for the participants, the higher-order, extraordinary context (or certain aspects of it) that this performance actualises. Such collectively recognised 'emergent symbols', as they may be called (e.g. more or less anything that can be qualified as being 'of the *So*' such as '*So* fat' the '*ndzom So*', etc.) are generated by the ritual experience itself (see Houseman & Severi 1988). On the other hand, these same elements (or others) may be interpreted, more or less systematically, in terms of definite 'meanings' relating to practices and values external to the performance. To take a single, simplified example, there exists for the Beti a close connection between fat and semen. Not only are these substances recognised as physically similar, they are also held to derive from each other. However, as I have shown, the transformative capacity of the ritual enactments in which these elements intervene, does not depend upon the symbolic imagery that such elements may occasion, but upon certain formal features and relational entailments of the enactments themselves. From this point of view, 'extrinsic symbolism' of this kind (e.g. an identification of '*So* fat' with sperm) represents an optional, inherently variable phenomenon, in which conventional metaphor (Keesing, this volume), ontological presumptions (Atran, Boyer, this volume) and private interpretative schemes all play a significant role.

I am not suggesting here that ritual symbolism is unimportant, but only that it is essentially contingent in so far as ritual effectiveness is concerned. Symbolic evocations ascribable to the *So* rite are either intrinsic to the overall relational structure its performance enacts ('emergent symbols'), in which case they are auto-referential and conceptually indefinite, or they have definite referential and conceptual content ('extrinsic symbolism'), but remain subordinate to this global structural dynamic.

A second, related issue concerns the nature of the *commitment* entailed by ritual experience. Meaningful participation in the *So* rite is informed, not by definite conceptualisation of the categories it articulates (BOY, MAN, WOMAN, CHILD, ADULT, etc.), but by its absence. It follows that this commitment does not concern specific substantive features attributable to these categories. Rather, it concerns a special type of relationship between such terms that is irreducible to the sum of particular features attributable to the terms themselves.[9] An initiation ritual does not consist in such an operation of reclassification, but in a more powerful, transformative one in which the recognition of specific contrastive features is subordinate to a higher-order connection between the categories to which these features may be assigned. This higher-order dynamic relationship implies a *hierarchical* integration of human sexual identities. As Bourdieu (1981: 206) points out with regard to rites of passage in general, the candidates' transition from an uninitiated to an initiated state operates at the same time an implicit separation between the 'initiable' and the 'uninitiable', in our example, between those naturally destined to undergo the *So* (the males) and those who, by virtue of their (female) nature, are excluded from ever doing so. In other words, it consecrates the sexual dichotomy in terms of a common, discriminatory reference not to the experience of birth but to that of initiation.

The participants' commitment to this hierarchical relationship is realised, on the manifest level, as the observance of a specific set of behavioural rules. The norms these rules define relate to the performance of the *So* ritual and to prerogatives and duties connected with it: the ability or not to eat fatty meats, the right or not to marry certain people, etc., as well as the aptitude, by virtue of one's own initiation, to initiate others. They do not constitute typical features, of man-, woman-, childhood, etc., but necessary features of the initiated/uninitiated dichotomy itself.

NOTES

1 The Beti are an Ewondo-speaking population of approximately 100,000 persons, most of whom live along the paths and roads that criss-cross the equatorial rainforest of Southern Cameroon. They are patrilineal, (patri-)viri-local, polygamous hoe-agriculturalists (cocoa is cultivated as a cash-crop). Politically acephalous, they are divided into close to fifty localised exogamous clan groups. For an account of Beti ethno-history, see Laburthe-Tolra (1981); for an analysis of Beti social organization see Houseman (1982).
2 The following, highly simplified, account is based upon a synthesis of the available material on the *So* rite presented in Houseman (1976). The principal sources are Nekes (1911), Heepe (1919), Dugast (1929, of which an expanded version appears in Berteaut 1935), Atangana (1942), Stoll (1955), Tsala (1958), Azombo (1970) and Laburthe-Tolra (1985).

3 These two inverse movements are interwoven in such a way that developments in the one are conditioned by developments in the other. Thus, the novices' intense disenchantment during the hunting/hazing period is due to the public demonstrations of solidarity characteristic of the rite's initial phase. Their deception of the uninitiated during the *ndzom So* festival derives, in turn, from the shameful and coercive 'revelation', during the hazing period, of the illusory nature of these initial demonstrations, etc.

4 This interruption, unbeknownst to the uninitiated, is demonstrated during the *ndzom So* festival by the novices' silence regarding their ordeals.

5 Regarding the three-party organisation of secrecy, see Simmel (1950: 330–4). The three positions involved are described by Zempléni (1976) as the secret's *withholder*, its *depository* (to whom it is revealed) and its *addressee* (the excluded party).

6 In this perspective, it is important to emphasise the continuity that exists between the novices' domineering dissimulations following the 'death of the *So*' and the discriminating privileges they assume following the ritual's conclusion (e.g. eating fatty meats). Such prerogatives constitute a projection, into the realm of everyday interaction, of the avowed secret so amply evinced during the rite's final stages. They represent a further recognition of the relationship of avowed secrecy between the initiated and the uninitiated, in which this relationship, pushed to its logical limits, is actualised as overtly as possible: as banal features of ordinary life.

7 Bateson is surely the first anthropologist to have commented upon the absence of conceptual closure in the case of initiatory ordeals. Thus, in a regrettably short comment, he observes in passing that 'this leads us to the recognition of a more complex form of play; the game which is constructed not upon the premise "This is play" but rather around the question "Is this play?" And this type of interaction also has its ritual forms, e.g. in the hazing of initiation' (1955 [in 1972: 182]).

8 Such reasoning would seem to be intrinsic to these preparatory procedures. Consider, for example, the Oyomo goat's silence, held to be indicative of the candidates' successful initiation. In so far as the latter is ascribable to the novices' ingestion of '*So* fat' whose essential ingredient is the fat taken from the Oyomo goats of preceding initiations, this silence consecrates the meaningfulness of Oyomo's silences on these previous occasions; this consecration, in turn, authenticates the presumed meaningfulness of Oyomo's silence in the case at hand.

9 A similar point is made by T. Turner (1973), about the ritual transition from the status/role category BOY to that of MAN. These categories may be thought of as a classification constructed of combinations of features of role relationship: sex, age, as well as other, more complex features entailing linkages with other role contrasts (BACHELOR/SPOUSE, MOTHER'S CHILD/FATHER'S CHILD, etc.). It is the sum of these roles and their features that constitute the total matrix of role relations involved in the BOY/MAN constrast.

References

Abelson, R. P. 1981. Psychological status of the script concept. *American Psychologist* 36(7): 715–29.

Agar, M. 1974. Talking about doing: lexicon and event. *Language and Society* 3: 83–9.

Armstrong, S. L., L. R. Gleitman & H. Gleitman. 1983. What some concepts might not be. *Cognition* 13: 263–308.

Astington, J. W., P. Harris & D. R. Olson (eds.) 1988. *Developing theories of mind*, Cambridge: Cambridge University Press.

Atangana, C. 1942. Aken So (le rite So) chez les Yaoundé-Banés. *Anthropos* 36–50: 149–57.

Atran, S. 1986. *Fondements de l'histoire naturelle*, Brussels: Editions Complexe.

   1987a. Ordinary constraints on the semantics of living kinds: a commonsense alternative to recent treatments of natural-object terms. *Mind and Language* 2: 27–63.

   1987b. Origin of the species and genus concepts: an anthropological perspective. *Journal of the History of Biology* 20: 195–279.

   1987c. The essence of folkbiology: a response to Randall and Hunn. *American Anthropologist* 88: 149–51.

   1990. *Cognitive foundations of natural history: towards an anthropology of science*, Cambridge: Cambridge University Press.

Atran, S. & D. Sperber 1991. Learning without teaching: its place in culture. In L. Landsman (ed.) *Culture, schooling and psychological development*, Norwood: Ablex.

Azombo, S. 1970. Séquence et signification des cérémonies d'initiation So. Unpublished doctoral thesis (Thèse d'Etat), Sorbonne, Paris.

Barker, E. 1984. *The making of a Moonie*, Oxford: Blackwell.

Bartlett, F. C. 1932. *Remembering: a study in experimental and social psychology*, Cambridge: Cambridge University Press.

Bateson, G. 1955. A theory of play and fantasy. *Psychiatric Research Reports* 1: 13–23.

   1972. *Steps to an ecology of mind*, New York: Random House.

   1980. *Mind and nature: a necessary unity*, Glasgow: Fontana.

Beattie, J. 1970. On understanding ritual. In B. Wilson (ed.), *Rationality*, Oxford: Basil Blackwell.

Beaugrande, R. de, 1982. Story of a grammar and grammar of stories. *Journal of Pragmatics* 6: 383–422.

Berlin, B. 1976. The concept of rank in ethnobiological classification: some evidence from Aguaruna folk botany. *American Ethnologist* 3: 381–99.

Berlin, B. & P. Kay 1969. *Basic color terms: their universality and evolution*, Berkeley: University of California Press.

Berlin, B., D. Breedlove & P. Raven 1973. General principles of classification and nomenclature in folk biology. *American Anthropologist* 75: 214–42.

1974. *Principles of Tzeltal plant classification*, New York: Academic Press.

Berteaut, M. 1935. *Le droit coutumier des Boulous*, Paris, Domat-Montchrestient.

Bever, T. A. 1982. The non-specific bases of language. In E. Wanner & L. Gleitman (eds.), *Language acquisition: the state of the art*, Cambridge: Cambridge University Press.

Biggs, B. 1975. Proto-Polynesian wordlist, computer printout, Auckland, New Zealand: University of Auckland.

Black, M. 1963. On formal ethnographic procedures. *American Anthropologist* 65: 1347–51.

Bloch, M. 1974. Symbols, song, dance and features of articulation. Is religion an extreme form of traditional authority? *European Journal of Sociology* 15: 55–81.

1985. From cognition to ideology. In R. Fardon (ed.), *Power and knowledge: anthropological and sociological approaches*, Edinburgh: Scottish Academic Press.

1988. The concept of wisdom in Madagascar and elsewhere. Working Paper presented to the King's College Research Centre Conference on The Representation of Complex Cultural Categories, Cambridge University, 22–4 March 1988.

Bloomfield, L. 1933. *Language*, New York: Holt.

Boas, F. 1940. *Race, language and culture*, New York: Macmillan.

Boon, J. A. 1982. *Other tribes, other scribes: symbolic anthropology in the comparative study of cultures, histories, religions and texts*, Cambridge: Cambridge University Press.

Bourdieu, P. 1977. *Outline of a theory of practice*, Cambridge: Cambridge University Press.

1981. Les Rites comme actes d'institution. In P. Centlivres & J. Hainard (eds.) *Les Rites de passage aujourd'hui: actes du colloque de Neuchâtel 1981*, Lausanne: L'Age d'Homme.

Bowerman, M. 1978. The acquisition of word-meaning: an investigation into some current conflicts. In N. Waterson & C. Snow (eds.) *The development of communication*, New York: Wiley.

1982. Reorganizational process in lexical and syntactic development. In E. Wanner & L. R. Gleitman (eds.), *Language acquisition: the state of the art*, Cambridge: Cambridge University Press.

Boyer, P. 1982. Le Status des forgerons et ses justifications symboliques. *Africa* 53: 44–63.

1986. The 'empty' concepts of traditional thinking: a semantic and pragmatic description. *Man* n.s. 21: 50–64.

1988. *Barricades mysterieuses et pièges à pensée*, Paris: Société d'Ethnologie.

1990. *Tradition as truth and communication: a cognitive description of traditional discourse*, Cambridge: Cambridge University Press.

n.d. Projectibility and mana-terms. Unpublished manuscript.

Bretherton, I. 1984. Representing the social world in symbolic play: reality and fantasy. In I. Bretherton (ed.), *Symbolic play: the development of social understanding*, New York: Academic Press.

Brown, C. 1977. Folk botanical life-forms: their universality and growth. *American Anthropologists* 79: 317–42.

1979. Folk zoological life forms: their universality and growth. *American Anthropologist* 81: 791–817.

1984. *Language and living things: uniformities in folk-classification and naming*, New Brunswick, NJ: Rutgers University Press.

Brown, M. 1985. Individual experience, dreams and the identification of magical stones in an Amazonian society. In J. Dougherty [Keller] (ed.) *Directions in cognitive anthropology*, Urbana-Champaign: University of Illinois Press.

Brugman, C. 1981. Story of over. Unpublished MA thesis, University of California, Berkeley.

Burgess, D., W. Kempton & R. MacLaury 1985. Tarahumara color modifiers: individual variation and evolutionary change. In J. W. Dougherty [Keller] (ed.) *Directions in cognitive anthropology*, Urbana-Champaign: University of Illinois Press.

Burling, R. 1964. Cognition and componential analysis: God's truth or hocus-pocus? *American Anthropologist* 66: 20–8.

Capell, A. 1958. *Anthropology and linguistics of Futuna-Aniwa, New Hebrides* (Oceanic Linguistic Series Monograph 5), Sydney: University of Sydney.

Carey, S. 1978. The child as word learner. In M. Halle & G. A. Miller (eds.), *Linguistic theory and psychological reality*, Cambridge, MA: MIT Press.

1982. Semantic development: the state of the art. In E. Wanner & L. R. Gleitman (eds.), *Language acquisition: the state of the art*, Cambridge: Cambridge University Press.

1985. *Conceptual change in childhood*, Cambridge, MA: MIT Press.

1988. Conceptual differences between children and adults. *Mind and Language* 3: 167–81.

Carnap, R. 1956. The methodological character of theoretical concepts. In H. Feigl & M. Scriven (eds.), *Minnesota Studies in the Philosophy of Science*, vol. I, Minneapolis: University of Minnesota Press.

Cassirer, E. 1953 [1924]. *Philosophie der symbolischen Formen*, Darmstadt: Wissenschaftliche Buchgesellschaft.

1965. *The philosophy of symbolic forms*, trans. C. W. Hendel, New Haven, CT: Yale University Press.

Chomsky, N. 1965. *Aspects of the theory of syntax*. Cambridge, MA: MIT Press.

1975. *Reflections on language*, New York: Random House.

1980. *Rules and representations*, New York: Columbia University Press.

1981. *Lectures on government and binding*, New York: Foris.

1985. *Knowledge of language: its nature, origin and use*, New York: Praeger.

1988. *Language and problems of knowledge: the managua lectures*, Cambridge, MA: MIT Press.

Churchland, P. M. 1981. Eliminative materialism and propositional attitudes. *Journal of Philosophy* 84: 544–55.

Clark, E. V. 1973. Non-linguistic strategies and the acquisition of word-meaning. *Cognition* 2: 161–82.

Clifford, J. & G. E. Marcus (eds.) 1986. *Writing culture: the poetics and politics of ethnography*, Berkeley: University of California Press.

Codrington, R. H. 1891. *The Melanesians*, Oxford: Clarendon Press.

Cohen, M. 1964. Establishment of identity in a social nexus. *American Anthropologist* 66: 529–52.

Colby, B. 1966. Ethnographic semantics: a preliminary survey. *Current Anthropology* 7: 3–32.

Coleman, L. & P. Kay 1981. Prototype semantics: the English verb lie. *Language* 57: 26–44.

Conklin, H. 1954. The relation of Hanuno'o culture to the plant world. Ph.D. dissertation, Yale University.

1962. Lexicographical treatment of folk taxonomies. In F. Householder & S. Saporta (eds.) *Problems in lexicography*, Report of the Conference on Lexicography, 11–12 November 1960, Bloomington: Indiana University Press.

D'Andrade, R. 1987. A folk-model of the mind. In D. Holland & N. Quinn (eds.) *Cultural models in language and thought*, Cambridge: Cambridge University Press.

Darnton, R. 1984. *The great cat massacre and other episodes in French cultural history*, New York: Basic Books.

Darwin, C. 1883. *On the origins of species by means of natural selection*, 6th edn, New York: Appleton.

De Kleer, J. 1977. Multiple representations of knowledge in a mechanistic problem solver. In *Proceedings of the Fifth Conference on Artificial Intelligence*, Cambridge, MA: MIT Press.

De Kleer, J. & J. S. Brown 1983. Assumptions and ambiguities in mechanistic mental models. In D. Gentner & A. L. Stevens (eds.) *Mental models*, Hillsdale, NJ: Lawrence Erlbaum.

Demerath, N. J. & P. Hammond 1969. *Religion in a social context*, New York: Random House.

Dennett, D. 1978. *Brainstorms: philosophical essays on mind and psychology*, Hassocks, Sussex: Harvester Press.

1987. *The intentional stance*, Cambridge, MA: MIT Press.

DiSessa, A. 1988. Knowledge in pieces. In G. Forman & P. B. Pufall (eds.) *Constructivism in the computer age*, Hillsdale, NJ: Lawrence Erlbaum.

Dougherty [Keller], J. W. D. 1977. Color categorization in West Futunese: variability and change. In Mary Sanchez (ed.) *Sociocultural dimensions of language change*, New York: Academic Press.

1979. Learning names for plants and plants for names. *Anthropological Linguistics* 21: 298–315.

1983. *West-Futuna-Aniwa: an introduction to a Polynesian outlier language* (University of California Publications in Linguistics 102), Berkeley: University of California Press.

(ed.) 1985. *Directions in cognitive anthropology*, Urbana-Champaign: University of Illinois Press.

Dougherty [Keller], J. W. D. & J. W. Fernandez (eds.) 1980. *Cognition and symbolism. American Ethnologist*, (special issue) 7.

1982. *Cognition and symbolism II. American Ethnologist*, (special issue) 9.

Dougherty [Keller], J. & Keller, C. 1985. Taskonomy. In J. Dougherty (ed.)

Directions in cognitive anthropology, Urbana-Champaign: University of Illinois Press.

Douglas, M. 1970. *Natural symbols*, Harmondsworth: Penguin.

1973. Introduction. In M. Douglas (ed.) *Rules and Meanings*, Harmondsworth: Penguin.

1975. *Implicit meanings*, London: Routledge and Kegan Paul.

1982. *Essays in the sociology of perception*, London: Routledge and Kegan Paul.

Dretske, F. 1981. *Knowledge and the flow of information*, Oxford: Basil Blackwell.

Dubois R. 1978. *Olombelona; essai sur l'existence personnelle et collective à Madagascar*, Paris: L'Harmattan.

Dugast, G. 1929. *Documents recueillis en pays Beti (rituel So)*. Dossier J. chemise m IRCAM, Yaoundé.

Durkheim, E. 1964 [1915]. The elementary forms of the religious life, London: Allen and Unwin.

Durkin, K. 1987. Minds and language: social cognition, social interaction and the acquisition of language. *Mind and language* 2: 105–40.

Dwyer, P. 1976. An analysis of Rofaifo mammal taxonomy. *American Ethnologist* 3: 425–45.

Ellen, R. F. 1979a. Omniscience and ignorance: variation in Nuaulu knowledge, identification and classification of animals. *Language in Society* 8: 337–64.

1979b. Introduction, In R. Ellen and D. Reason (eds.) *Classifications in their social context*, New York: Academic Press.

1988. Fetishism, *Man (n.s.)* 23(2): 213–35.

Evans-Pritchard, E. E. 1940. *The Nuer: a description of the modes of livelihood and political institutions of a Nilotic people*, Oxford: Clarendon.

1965. *Theories of primitive religion*, Oxford: Clarendon.

Fabrega, H. & D. B. Silver 1973. *Illness and shamanistic curing in Zinacantan: an ethnomedical analysis*, Stanford: Stanford University Press.

Fentriss, J. C. 1984. The development of coordination. *Journal of Motor Behaviour* 16: 99–134.

Fernandez, J. 1977. The performance of ritual metaphors. In J. D. Sapir & J. C. Crocker (eds.) *The social use of metaphor*, Philadelphia: University of Pennsylvania Press.

1986. *Persuasions and performances: the play of tropes in culture*, Bloomington: Indiana University Press.

Fillmore, C. 1975. An alternative to checklist theories of meaning. *Proceedings of the First Annual Meeting of the Berkeley Linguistic Society*.

Firth, R. 1967. *Tikopia ritual and belief*, London: George Allen and Unwin.

Fitzgerald, J. 1986. Autobiographical memory: a developmental perspective. In D. C. Rubin (ed.) *Autobiographical memory*, Cambridge: Cambridge University Press.

Fivush, R. 1987. Scripts and categories: interrelationships in development. In U. Neisser (ed.) *Concepts and conceptual development: ecological and intellectual factors in categorization*, Cambridge: Cambridge University Press.

Fodor, J. A. 1981. *Representations: philosophical essays on the foundations of cognitive science*, Cambridge, MA: MIT Press.

1983. *The modularity of mind: an essay on faculty psychology*, Cambridge, MA: MIT Press.

1987. *Psychosemantics: the problem of meaning in cognitive science*, Cambridge, MA: MIT Press.

1990. *A theory of content and other essays*, Cambridge, MA: MIT Press.

Fogen, R. M. 1974. Selective and evolutionary aspects of animal play. *American Naturalist*, 108: 850–8.

Foucault, M. 1970. *The order of things*, London: Tavistock.

Frake, C. 1961. The diagnosis of disease among the Subanun of Mindanao. *American Anthropologist* 63: 11–32.

1962a. Cultural ecology and ethnography, *American Anthropologist* 64: 53–9.

1962b. The ethnographic study of cognitive systems. In *Anthropology and human behavior*. Washington, DC: Anthropological Society of Washington.

1964a. A structural description of Subanum religious behaviour. In W. Goodenough (ed.) *Explorations in cultural anthropology: essays in honor of G. P. Murdock*, New York: McGraw-Hill.

1964b. Notes on queries in ethnography. *American Anthropologist* 66: 132–46 (special publication).

1975. How to enter a Yakan house. In M. Sanches & B. Blount (eds.), *Socio-cultural dimensions of language use*, New York: Academic Press.

Frazer, Sir J. G. 1922. *The golden bough* (abridged version), London: Macmillan.

Geertz, C. 1973. *The interpretation of culture*, New York: Basic Books.

1983. *Local knowledge: further essays in interpretive anthropology*, New York: Basic Books.

1988. *Works and lives: the anthropologist as author*, Stanford: Stanford University Press.

Gellner, E. 1987. *Culture, identity and politics*, Cambridge: Cambridge University Press.

Gelman, R. & R. Baillargeon 1983. A revision of some Piagetian concepts. In J. H. Flavel & E. M. Markman (eds.), *Handbook of child psychology*, vol. III: *Cognitive development*, New York: Wiley.

Gelman, R., E. Spelke & E. Meck 1983. What preschoolers know about animate and inanimate objects. In D. Rogers and J. Sloboda (eds.) *The acquisition of symbolic skills*, London: Plenum.

Gelman, S. 1988. The development of induction within natural kind and artefact categories. *Cognitive Psychology* 20: 65–95.

Gelman, S. & E. Markman 1986. Categories and induction in young children. *Cognition* 23: 183–209.

1987. Young children's inductions from natural kinds: the role of categories and appearances. *Child Development* 58: 32–41.

Gentner, D. & D. R. Gentner 1983. Flowing waters or teeming crowds: mental models of electricity. In D. Gentner & A. L. Stevens (eds.), *Mental models*, Hillsdale, NJ: Lawrence Erlbaum.

Gentner, D. & A. L. Stevens (eds.) 1983. *Mental models*, Hillsdale, NJ: Lawrence Erlbaum.

Gomez, P. & C. Severi 1983. Nia Ikar Kalu. Los pueblos del camino de la locusa, Canto chamanístico de la tradición Cuna. Texto Cuna y traducción española. *Amerindia. Revue d'ethnolinguistique amérindienne* 8: 129–79.

Goodenough, W. 1951. *Property, kin and community on Truk* (Yale University publications in Anthropology 46), New Haven, CT: Yale University Press.

1956. Componential analysis and the study of meaning. *Language* 32: 195–216.

1957. Cultural anthropology and linguistics. In P. Garvin (ed.) *Report of the Seventh Annual Round Table Meeting on Linguistics and Language Study*, Washington, DC: Georgetown University Press.

1965a. Rethinking 'status' and 'role'. In M. Banton (ed.) *The Relevance of Models for Social Anthropology*, London: Tavistock.

1965b. Yankee kinship terminology: a problem in componential analysis. In Eugene A. Harnmell (ed.) *Formal semantic analysis. American Anthropologist* 67: 259–87.

Graesser, A. C., S. E. Gordon & J. D. Sawyer 1979. Recognition memory for typical and atypical actions in scripted activities: tests of a script pointer + tag hypothesis. *Journal of Verbal Learning and Verbal Behaviour* 18: 319–32.

Graesser, A. C., S. B. Woll, D. J. Kowalski & D. A. Smith 1980. Memory for typical and atypical actions in scripted activities. *Journal of Experimental Psychology (Human Learning and Memory)* 6: 503–15.

Guiart, J. 1961. The social anthropology of Aniwa (Southern New Hebrides). *Oceania* 32: 34–53.

Gunn, Rvd W. 1914. *The Gospel of Futuna*, Futuna: Futuna Mission Press.

Hage, P. 1972. Münchner beer categories. In James Spradley (ed.) *Culture and Cognition*. San Francisco: Chandler.

Hallpike, C. 1976. Is there a primitive mentality? *Man* 11: 253–70.

Handelman, D. 1979. Is Naven Ludic? *Social Analysis* 1: 177–92.

1990. *Models and mirrors: towards an anthropology of public events*, Cambridge: Cambridge University Press.

Harris, P. & P. Heelas 1979. Cognitive processes and collective representations. *European Journal of Sociology* 20: 211–41.

Hart, J., R. Berndt & A. Caramazza 1985. Category-specific naming deficit following cerebral infarction. *Nature* 112: 316–439.

Hayes, P. 1985. Ontology for liquids. In J. Hobbs & R. Moore (eds.) *Formal theories of the commonsense world*, Norwood, NJ: Ablex.

Heepe, M. 1919. Jaunde Texte von Atangana und P. Messi, *Abhandlunggen des Hamb Kol. Inst.* 24: 63–101.

Heider, E. 1972. Universals in color naming. *Journal of Experimental Psychology* 93: 10–20.

Holland, D. & N. Quinn (eds.) 1987. *Cultural models in language and thought*, Cambridge: Cambridge University Press.

Hollis, M. 1970. Reason and ritual. In B. Wilson (ed.) *Rationality*, Oxford: Basil Blackwell.

Hollis, M. & S. Lukes (eds.) 1982. *Rationality and relativism*, Oxford: Basil Blackwell.

Holmer, N. 1947. *Critical and comparative grammar of the Cuna language*, Göteborg: Etnografiska Museet.

1952. *Cuna ethnolinguistic dictionary*, Göteborg: Etnografiska Museet.

Holmer, N. & H. Wassen 1953. *The Complete Mu-Igala*, Göteborg: Etnografiska Museet.

1958. *Nia ikala; canto magico para curar la locura*, Göteborg: Etnografiska Museet.

Holy, L. & M. Stuchlik 1983. *Actions, norms and representations: foundations of anthropological inquiry*, Cambridge: Cambridge University Press.

232   *References*

Horton, R. 1982. Tradition and modernity revisited. In M. Hollis & S. Lukes (eds.) *Rationality and relativism*, Oxford: Basil Blackwell.

Houseman, M. 1976. Structure sociale et idéologie patrilinéaire: le rite d'initiation So chez les Beti du Sud-Cameroun, Maitrise d'ethnologie, Université de Paris X, Nanterre.

   1982. Structures de parenté de d'alliance dans une société Beti. Unpublished doctoral dissertation, Université de Paris X, Nanterre.

   1986. Le Mal pour le mâle: un bien initiatique. In J. Hainard & R. Kaehr (eds.) *Le Mal et la douleur*, Neuchâtel: Musée d'Ethnographie.

Houseman, M. & C. Severi 1988. Introduzione al Naven: morphologia e logica della relazione rituale. Introduction to G. Bateson, *Naven: un rituale di travestimento in Nuova Guinea*, Turin: Einaudi.

Howe, J. 1976. Smoking out the spirits: a Cuna exorcism. In P. Young & J. Howe, *Ritual and Symbol in native Central America* (University of Oregon Anthropological Papers, 9), Eugene: Oregon University Press.

Humphreys, C. B. [1926] 1978. *The Southern New Hebrides*, Cambridge: Cambridge University Press.

Hunn, E. 1975a. Cognitive processes in folk ornithology: the identification of gulls. Language-Behavior Research Laboratory, working paper no. 42, University of California, Berkeley.

   1975b. A measure of the degree of correspondence of folk to scientific biological classification. *American Ethnologist* 2: 309–27.

Hutchins, E. 1980. *Culture and inference: a Trobriand case study*, Cambridge, MA: Harvard University Press.

Jackendoff, R. 1985. *Semantics and cognition*, Cambridge, MA: MIT Press.

Jahoda, G. 1982. *Psychology and anthropology*, London: Academic Press.

Jahoda, G. & I. M. Lewis (eds.) 1987. *Acquiring culture: cross-cultural studies in child development*, London: Croom Helm.

Jeyifous [Walker], S. 1985. Ph.D. dissertation, Cornell University. Atimodemo: semantic conceptual development among the Yoruba, Ph.D. dissertation, Cornell University.

Johnson, M. 1987. *The body in the mind: the bodily basis of meaning, imagination, and reason*, Chicago: University of Chicago Press.

Johnson-Laird, P. 1980. *Mental models: towards a cognitive science of language, inference and conciousness*, Cambridge: Cambridge University Press.

Kaiser, M. K., J. Jonides & J. Alexander 1986. Intuitive reasoning about abstract and familiar physics problems. *Memory and Cognition* 14: 308–12.

Kapferer, B. 1983. *A celebration of demons: exorcisms and the aesthetics of healing in Sri Lanka*, Bloomington: Indiana University Press.

Katz, B., G. Baker & J. MacNamara 1974. What's in a name? On the child's acquisition of proper and common nouns. *Child Development* 45: 269–73.

Katz, J. J. 1981. *Language and other abstract objects*, Oxford: Basil Blackwell.

Katz, J. J. & J. Fodor 1963. The structure of a semantic theory, *Language* 39: 170–210.

Katz, R. 1982. *Boiling energy: community healing among the Kalahari Kung*, Cambridge, MA: Harvard University Press.

Kay, P. 1966. Reply to Colby. *Current Anthropology* 7: 20–3.

   1971. On taxonomy and semantic contrast. *Language* 47: 866–87.

Keesing, R. M. 1972. Simple models of complexity. In P. Reining (ed.) *Kinship studies in the Morgan centennial year*, Washington, DC: Anthropological Society of Washington.

1974. Theories of culture, *Annual Review of Anthropology* 3: 73–98.

1982a. *Kwaio religion: the living and the dead in a Solomon Islands Society*, New York: Columbia University Press.

1982b. 'Cultural rules': methodological doubts and epistemological paradoxes. *Canberra Anthropology* 5: 37–46.

1984. Rethinking *mana. Journal of Anthropological Research* 40: 137–56.

1985. Conventional metaphors and anthropological metaphysics: the problematic of cultural translation. *Journal of Anthropological Research* 41: 201–17.

1987a. African models in the Malaita Highlands. *Man* (n.s.) 22: 431–52.

1987b. Anthropology as interpretive quest. *Current Anthropology* 28: 161–76.

1987c. Models, folk and cultural. In D. Holland & N. Quinn (eds.) *Cultural models in language and thought*, Cambridge: Cambridge University Press.

1990. Exotic Readings of cultural texts. *Current Anthropology* 30: 459–77.

Keil, F. C. 1979. *Semantic and conceptual development*, Cambridge, MA: Harvard University Press.

1986. The acquisition of natural kind and artefact terms. In A. Marrar & W. Demopoulos (eds.) *Conceptual change*, Norwood, NJ: Ablex.

1987. Conceptual development and category structure. In U. Neisser (ed.) *Concepts and conceptual development: ecological and intellectual factors in categorization*, Cambridge: Cambridge University Press.

1989. *Concepts, kinds, and conceptual development*, Cambridge, MA: MIT Press.

Keil, F. C. & N. Batterman 1984. A characteristic-to-defining shift in the development of word meaning. *Journal of Verbal Learning and Verbal Behaviour* 23: 221–36.

Kempton, W. 1978. Category grading and taxonomic relations: a mug is a sort of cup. *American Ethnologist* 5: 44–65.

Kesby, J. 1979. The Rangi classification of animals and plants. In R. Ellen and D. Reason (eds.) *Classifications in their social contexts*, New York: Academic.

Kramer, F. 1981. *Verkehrte Welten: zur imaginären Ethnographie des 19. Jahrhunderts*, Frankfurt am Main: Sindikate.

Krasnor, L. R. & D. J. Pepler 1980. The study of children's play: some suggested future directions. In K. Rubin (ed.) *Children's play*, San Francisco: Josey Bass.

Kroeber, A. 1909. Classificatory systems of relationships. *The Journal of the Royal Anthropological Institute* 39: 77–84.

1963. *Anthropology: culture patterns and processes*, New York: Harcourt, Brace and World.

Kronenfeld, D. B., J. D. Armstrong & S. Wilmoth 1985. Exploring the internal structure of linguistic categories: an extension semantic view. In J. W. D. Dougherty [Keller] (ed.) *Directions in cognitive anthropology*, Urbana-Champaign: University of Illinois Press.

Laburthe-Tolra, P. 1981. *Les Seigneurs de la forêt*. Paris: Publications de la Sorbonne.

1985. *Initiations et sociétés secrètes au Cameroun*, Paris: Karthala.

La Fontaine, J. S. 1977. The power of rights. *Man* (n.s.) 12: 421–37.

    1985. *Initiation:ritual drama and secret knowledge across the world*, Harmondsworth: Penguin.

Lakoff, G. 1987. *Women, fire and dangerous things: what categories reveal about the mind*, Chicago: University of Chicago Press.

Lakoff, G. & M. Johnson 1980. *Metaphors we live by*, Chicago: University of Chicago Press.

Lakoff, G. & Z. Kövecses 1987. The cognitive model of anger inherent in American English. In D. Holland & N. Quinn (eds.) *Cultural models in language and thought*, Cambridge: Cambridge University Press.

Langer, S. K. 1942. *Philosophy in a new key*, Cambridge, MA: Harvard University Press.

Laurendau, M. & A. Pinard 1962. *Causal thinking in the child*, New York: International Universities Press.

Lave, J. 1988. *Cognition in practice*, Cambridge: Cambridge University Press.

Lawson, E. T. & R. McCauley 1990. *Rethinking religion*, Cambridge: Cambridge University Press.

Leach, E. R. 1954. *Political systems of highland Burma*, Boston, MA: Beacon Press.

    1976. *Culture and communication: the logic by which symbols are connected*, Cambridge: Cambridge University Press.

Lehman, F. K. 1978. Symbols and the computation of meaning. In D. B. Shin *et al.* (eds.), *Anthropology for the future*, Urbana: University of Illinois.

    1985. Cognition and computation: on being sufficiently abstract. In J. W. D. Dougherty [Keller] (ed.) *Directions in cognitive anthropology*, Urbana-Champaign: University of Illinois Press.

Lehman, F. K. & K. G. Witz 1974. Prolegomena to a formal theory of kinship. In Paul Ballonoff (ed.) *Genealogical mathemataics*. The Hague: Mouton.

Levinson, S. C. 1983. *Pragmatics*, Cambridge: Cambridge University Press.

Lévi-Strauss, C. 1958. L'Efficacité symbolique. In *Anthropologie Structurale*, vol. I, Paris: Plon.

    1963. The bear and the barber. *The Journal of the Royal Anthropological Institute* 93: 1–11.

    1966. *The savage mind*. Chicago: Chicago University. (Originally published in French in 1962.)

    1969a. *The elementary structures of kinship*, trans. J. Bell & J. Von Sturmer, New York: Beacon.

    1969b. *The raw and the cooked*, trans. J. Weightman & D. Weightman, New York: Harper and Row.

Lewis, G. A. 1980. *Day of shining red: an essay on understanding ritual*, Cambridge: Cambridge University Press.

Lounsbury, F. G. 1956. The semantic analysis of Pawnee kinship usage. *Language* 32: 158–94.

Lowie, R. 1920 *Primitive society*, New York: Boni and Liveright.

Lukes, S. 1973. On the social determination of thought. In R. Horton & R. Finnegan (eds.) *Modes of thought*, London: Faber and Faber.

McCauley, R. N. & E. T. Lawson 1991. Connecting the cognitive and the cultural: artificial minds as methodological devices in the study of the sociocultural. In

R. Burton (ed.) *Minds: Natural and artificial*, Albany: State University of New York.

McCloskey, M. 1983. Naive theories of motion. In D. Gentner & A. L. Stevens (eds.) *Mental models*, Hillsdale, NJ: Lawrence Erlbaum.

Malinowski, B. K. [1935] 1978. *Coral gardens and their magic*, vol. II, New York: Dover.

Mallart Guimera, L. 1975. Ni Dos ni ventre: magie, sorcellerie et religion evuzok. *L'Homme* 15: 35–65.

1977. La Classification evuzok des maladies (première partie). *Journal des Africanistes* 47: 9–51.

1981. *Ni Dos ni ventre*, Paris: Société d'Ethnographie.

Mandler, J. M. 1983. Representation. In J. H. Flavell & E. M. Markham (eds.) *Handbook of child psychology*, vol. III: *Cognitive development*, New York: Wiley.

Mandler, M. & P. Bauer 1989. The cradle of categorisation: is the basic level basic? *Cognitive Development* 4: 247–64.

Mayr, E. 1969. *Principles of systematic zoology*, New York: McGraw-Hill.

Medin, D. L. & W. D. Wattenmaker 1987. 'Category cohesiveness, theories and cognitive archaeology. In U. Neisser (ed.) *Concepts and conceptual development*, Cambridge: Cambridge University Press.

Miller, G. A. 1978. Practical and lexical knowledge. In E. Rosch & B. V. Lloyd (eds.) *Cognition and categorization*, Hillsdale, NJ: Lawrence Erlbaum.

Minsky, M. 1963. Steps towards artificial intelligence. In E. Feigenbaum & J. Feldman (eds.) *Computers and thought*, New York: McGraw-Hill.

1981. A framework for representing knowledge. In J. Haugeland (ed.) *Mind design: philosophy, psychology, artificial intelligence*, Cambridge, MA: MIT Press.

Morris, B. 1987. *Anthropological theories of religion*, Cambridge: Cambridge University Press.

Murdock, G. 1949. *Social structure*, London: Macmillan.

Murphy, G. L. & D. L. Medlin 1985. The role of theories in conceptual coherence. *Psychological Review* 92: 289–316.

Murray, M. 1921. *Witchcult in Western Europe*, Oxford: Oxford University Press.

Nakamura, G. V., A. C. Graesser, J. A. Zimmermann & J. Riha 1985. Script processing in a natural situation. *Memory and Cognition* 13: 140–4.

Needham, R. 1964. Blood, thunder and the mockery of animals. *Sociologus* 14: 136–49.

1975. Polythetic classification. *Man* 10: 349–69.

1978. *Primordial characters*, Charlottesville: University of Virginia Press.

Neisser, U. (ed.) 1976. *Cognition and reality*, San Francisco: Freeman and Cy.

1982. *Memory observed: remembering in natural contexts*, San Francisco: Freeman and Cy.

1987. *Concepts and conceptual development: ecological and intellectual factors in categorization*, Cambridge: Cambridge University Press.

Nekes, P. H. 1911. *Lehrbuch des jaunde Sprache*, Berlin: G. Reiner.

Nelson, K. & J. Gruendel 1986. Children's scripts. In K. Nelson (ed.) *Event knowledge, structure and function in development*, Hillsdale, NJ: Lawrence Erlbaum.

von Noppen, K. (ed.) 1984. *Metaphor and religion: Theolinguistics*, vol. II, Brussels:

Nordenskiöld, E. 1938. *An historical and ethnological survey of the Cuna Indians*, Goteborg: Etnografiska.

Osherson, D. & E. Smith 1981. On the adequacy of prototype theory as a theory of concepts. *Cognition* 9: 35–58.

Pap, A. 1960. Types and meaninglessness. *Mind* 69: 41–54.

Penner, H. 1985. Language, ritual and meaning. *Numen* 22: 1–16.

Pettito, L. A. & P. F. Marentette 1991. *American Association for the Advancement of Science* 251: 1397–536.

Piaget, J. & B. Inhelder 1977. *Memory and intelligence*, London: Routledge and Kegan Paul.

Putnam, H. 1975. *Mind, language and reality: philosophical papers (II)*, Cambridge: Cambridge University Press.

    1983. *Realism and reason: philosophical papers (III)*, Cambridge: Cambridge University Press.

Quine, W. V. O. 1960. *Word and object*, Cambridge, MA: Harvard University Press.

Quinn, N. 1987. Convergent evidence for a cultural model of American marriage. In D. Holland & N. Quinn (eds.) *Cultural models in language and thought*, Cambridge: Cambridge University Press.

Rabain, J. 1979. *L'Enfant du lignage: du sevrage à la classe d'âge*, Paris: Payot.

Radcliffe-Brown, A. 1935. On the concept of function in social science. *American Anthropologist* 37: 394–402.

Randall, R. & E. Hunn 1984. Do life forms evolve or do uses for life? Some doubts about Brown's universals hypothesis. *American Ethnologist* 11: 329–49.

Rappaport, R. A. 1974. The obvious aspects of ritual. *Cambridge Anthropology* 2: 3–69.

    1979. *Ecology, meaning and religion*, Chicago: Chicago University Press.

Read, D. W. 1984. An algebraic account of the American kinship terminology. *Current Anthropology* 15: 417–50.

Rey, P. 1983. Concepts and stereotypes. *Cognition* 15: 237–62.

Ricœur, P. 1978. The metaphorical process as cognition, imagination and feeling. *Critical Inquiry* 5: 143–59.

Rifkin, A. 1985. Evidence for a basic level in event taxonomies. *Memory and cognition* 13: 538–56.

Rips, L. J. 1989. Similarity, typicality and categorization. In S. Vosniadou & A. Ortony (eds.), *Similarity and analogical reasoning*, Cambridge: Cambridge University Press.

Rosch, E. 1973. On the internal structure of perceptual and semantic categories. In T. Moore (ed.) *Cognitive development and the acquisition of language*, New York: Academic Press.

    1975. Universals and cultural specifics in categorization. In R. Brislin, S. Bochner & W. Lonner (eds.) *Cross-cultural perspectives on learning*, Halstead.

    1977. Human categorization, In N. Warren (ed.) *Studies in cross-cultural psychology (I)*, London: Academic Press.

    1978. Principles of categorization. In E. Rosch & B. B. Lloyd (eds.) *Cognition and categorization*. Hillsdale, NJ: Lawrence Erlbaum.

Rosch, E. & B. B. Lloyd (eds.) 1978. *Cognition and categorization*, Hillsdale, NJ: Lawrence Erlbaum.

Rosch, E., C. Mervis, W. Gray, C. Johnson & P. Boyes-Braem 1976. Basic objects in natural categories. *Cognitive Psychology* 8: 382–439.

Roth, E. M. & E. J. Shoben 1983. The effects of context on the structure of categories. *Cognitive Psychology* 7: 573–605.

Sahlins, M. 1985. *Islands of history*, London: Tavistock.

Sapir, E. 1921. *Language*, New York: Harcourt Brace.

Sapir, J. D. & J. C. Crocker (eds.) 1977. *The social use of metaphor*, Philadelphia: University of Pennsylvania Press.

Sartori, G. & R. Job 1988. The oyster with four legs: a neuro-psychological study of the interaction of visual and semantic information. *Cognitive Neuropsychology* 5: 105–32.

Saussure, F. de 1974. *Course in general linguistics*, trans. W. Baskin, London: Peter Owen.

Schank, R. & R. Abelson 1977. *Scripts, plans, goals, and understanding: an inquiry into human knowledge structures*, Hillsdale, NJ: Lawrence Erlbaum.

Schiefflin, B. B. & E. Ochs (eds.) 1986. *Language socialization across cultures*, Cambridge: Cambridge University Press.

Schiefflin, E. L. 1985. Performance and the cultural construction of reality. *American Ethnologist* 12: 707–24.

Schneider, D. 1972. What is kinship all about? In P. Reinig (ed.) *Kinship studies in the Morgan memorial year*, Washington, DC: Anthropological Society of Washington.

Schwarz, S. P. (ed.) 1977. *Naming, necessity and natural kinds*, Ithaca, NY: Cornell University Press.

1979. Natural kind terms. *Cognition* 7: 301–15.

Severi, C. 1981a. Le Traitement chamanique de la folie chez les Indiens Cuna de San Blas. Ph.D. thesis, Ecole des Hautes Etudes en Sciences Sociales, Paris.

1981b. Le anime Cuna, *La ricerca folklorica* 4: 69–75.

1982. Le Chemin des métamorphoses – un modèle de connaissance de la folie dans un chant chamanique cuna. *Res – Anthropology and Aesthetics*, 3: 32–67.

1987. The invisible path: ritual representation of suffering in Cuna traditional thought. *Res – Anthropology and Aesthetics* 14: 66–85.

1988. L'Etranger, l'envers de soi et l'échec du symbolisme: deux représentations du Blanc dans la tradition chamanique cuna. *L'Homme* 106–7: 176–85.

1989. Cristallizzazione e dispersione della conoscenza nella tradizione cuna. In G. Cardona (ed.) *La transmissione del sapere: aspetti linguistici e antropologici* (Quaderni del Dipartimento di Studi Glotto-antropologici, University of Rome, 5) Rome: University of Rome.

Sherzer, J. 1981. The interplay of structure and function in Kuna narrative, or: how to grab a snake in the Darien. *Georgetown University Round Table*, School of Language and Linguistics, Georgetown University Press.

1987. *Linguaggio e cultura: il caso dei Cuna*, Palermo: Sellerio.

Sherzer, J. & J. Woodbury (eds.) 1987. *Native American discourse*, Cambridge: Cambridge University Press.

Simmel, G. 1908. *Soziologie: Untersuchungen über die Formen der Vergesellschaftung*, Leipzig: Duncker and Humblot.

1950. *The sociology of Georg Simmel*, ed. E. Wolff, New York: The Free Press.

Skorupski, J. 1976. *Symbol and theory: a philosophical study of theories of religion in social anthropology*, Cambridge: Cambridge University Press.

Smith, E. E. & D. L. Medin 1981. *Categories and concepts*, Cambridge, MA: Harvard University Press.

Smith, L. B., M. Sera & B. Gattuso 1988. The development of thinking. In E. E. Smith (ed.) *The psychology of human thought*, Cambridge: Cambridge University Press.

Smith, P. 1979. Aspects de l'organisation des rites. In M. Izard & P. Smith (eds.) *La Fonction symbolique*, Paris: Gallimard.

Smith, P. K. 1982. Does play matter? Functional and evolutionary aspects of animal and human play. *Behavioural and Brain Sciences* 5: 139–84.

Sommers, F. 1959. The ordinary language tree. *Mind* 68: 160–85.

Southwold, M. 1979. Religious belief. *Man* (n.s.) 14: 628–44.

Spelke, E. 1988. The origins of physical knowledge. In L. Weizkrantz (ed.) *Thought without language*, Oxford: Oxford University Press.

1990. Principles of object perception, *Cognitive Science* 14: 29–56.

Sperber, D. 1975a. Pourquoi les animaux parfaits, les hybrides et les monstres sont-ils bons à penser symboliquement? *L'Homme* 15: 5–34.

1975b. *Rethinking symbolism*, Cambridge: Cambridge University Press.

1980. Is symbolic thought pre-rational? In X. LeCron, X. Foster & X. Brandes (eds.) *Symbol as sense*, New York: Academic Press.

1985a. Anthropology and psychology: towards an epidemiology of representations. *Man* 20: 73–89.

1985b. *On anthropological knowledge*, Cambridge: Cambridge University Press.

1990. The epidemiology of beliefs. In C. Fraser & G. Gaskell (eds.) *The social psychological study of widespread beliefs*, Oxford: Clarendon.

Spradley, J. P. 1972. Adaptive strategies of urban nomads. In James P. Spradley (ed.) *Culture and cognition*, San Francisco: Chandler.

Staal, F. 1979. The meaninglessness of ritual. *Numen* 26: 2–22.

Stich, S. 1983. *From folk psychology to cognitive science: the case against belief*, Cambridge, MA: MIT Press.

Stoll, A. 1955. La Tonétique des langues bantu et semi-bantu du Cameroun. *Etudes Camerounaises* (special issue), Yaoundé.

Stout, D. B. 1947. *San Blas Cuna acculturation: an introduction*, New York: Viking Fund Publications in Anthropology.

Strathern, M. 1984. Subject or object? Women and the circulation of valuables in highland New Guinea. In R. Hirschon (ed.) *Women and property, women as property*.

Stross, B. 1969. Language acquisition by Tenejapan Tzeltal children. Ph.D. dissertation, University of California, Berkeley.

1973. Acquisition of botanical terminology by Tzeltal children. In M. Edmondson (ed.) *Meaning in Mayan languages*, The Hague: Mouton.

Sturtevant, W. 1964. Studies in ethnoscience. *American Anthropologist* 66: 99–131.

Tambiah, S. J. 1968. The magical power of words, *Man* (n.s.) 3: 175–208.

1981. A performative approach to ritual. *Proceedings of the British Academy* 65: 113–69.

1985. *Culture, thought and social action*, Cambridge, MA: Harvard University Press.

Toren, C. 1984. Thinking symbols: a critique of Sperber (1979). *Man* (n.s.) 18: 260–8.

1987. Children's perceptions of gender and hierarchy. In G. Jahoda & J. M. Lewis (eds.) *Acquiring culture*, London: Routledge.

1988. The continuity and mutability of tradition as process. *Man* (n.s.) 23: 696–717.

1991. *Making Fijian hierarchy: social and cognitive processes in the construction of culture*, London: Athlone Press.

Tsala, Th. 1958. Mœurs et coutumes des Ewondo. *Etudes Camerounaises* 56: 8–112.

Turner, T. 1973. Transformation, hierarchy and transcendence: a reformulation of Van Gennep's model of the structure of rites de passage. In S. F. Moore & B. G. Meyerhoff (eds.) *Secular ritual*, Assen: Van Gorcum.

Turner, V. 1964. Symbols in Ndembu ritual. In M. Gluckman (ed.) *Closed systems and open minds*, Chicago: Aldine.

1967. *The forest of symbols*, Ithaca, NY: Cornell University Press.

1969. *The ritual process: structure and anti-structure*, Chicago: Aldine.

Tversky, B. & K. Hemenway 1983. Categories of environmental scenes. *Cognitive Psychology* 15: 121–49.

Tyler, S. 1969. Introduction to *Cognitive anthropology*, New York: Holt, Rinehart and Winston.

Van Esterik, P. 1985. Imitating Ban Chiang pottery. In J. W. D. Dougherty [Keller] (ed.) *Directions in cognitive anthropology*, Ubana-Champaign University of Illinois Press.

Van Gennep, A. 1909. *Les Rites de passage*, Paris: Emile Noury.

Volosinov, V. N. 1986[1929]. *Marxism and the philosophy of language*, Cambridge, MA: Harvard University Press.

Vygotsky, L. S. 1978[1936]. *Mind in society*, Cambridge, MA: Harvard University Press.

1986[1934]. *Thought and language*, Cambridge, MA: MIT Press.

Wagner, R. 1986. *Symbols that stand for themselves*, Chicago: University of Chicago Press.

Wallace, A. 1962. Culture and cognition. *Science* 135: 351–7.

Warrington, E. & R. McCarthy 1983. Category-specific access dysphasia. *Brain* 106: 859–78.

Waxman, S. 1985. Hierarchies in classification and language: evidence from preschool children. Unpublished Ph.D. dissertation University of Pennsylvania.

Weathers, N. n.d. Notes towards a theory of effective relations: institution, skill, concept and causality in the representation of knowledge. Unpublished M.A. thesis, University of Illinois, Urbana-Champaign.

Wentworth, W. 1980. *Context and understanding: an inquiry into socialization theory*, New York: Elsevier.

Werner, O. 1970. Cultural knowledge, language, and world view. In P. Garvin (ed.) *Cognition: a multiple view*, New York: Macmillan.

1985. Folk knowledge without fuzz. In J. Dougherty (ed.) *Direction in cognitive anthropology*, Urbana-Champaign: University of Illinois.

Wertsch, J. V. (ed.) *Culture, communication and cognitive: Vygotskian perspectives*, Cambridge: Cambridge University Press.

Weston, J. 1920. *From ritual to romance*, Cambridge: Cambridge University Press.

Wexler, K. & P. Culicover 1980. *Formal principles of language acquisition*, Cambridge MA: MIT Press.

Whorf, B. 1956. *Language, thought and reality*, Cambridge, MA: MIT Press.

Wierzbicka, A. 1984. Apples are not a kind of fruit: the semantics of human categorization. *American Ethnologist* 11: 313–28.

1985. *Lexicography and conceptual analyses*, Ann Arbor, MI: Karoma.

Wilson, D. & D. Sperber 1986. *Relevance, communication and cognition*, New York/Oxford; Academic Press/Blackwell.

Witherspoon, G. 1977. *Language and art in the Navajo universe*, Ann Arbor, MI: University of Michigan Press.

Wittgenstein, L. 1930[1980] *Wittgenstein's lectures: Cambridge 1930* [from notes of John King and Desmond Lee] ed. Desmond Lee, 1980, Oxford: Basil Blackwell.

Witz, Klaus G. & F. K. Lehman 1979. *A formal theory of kinship: the transformational component* (Committee on Culture and Cognition, report no. 11), Urbana-Champaign: University of Illinois at Urbana-Champaign.

Zempléni, A. 1976. La chaîne du secret. *Nouvelle Revue de Psychanalyse* 14: 312–24.

Index of names

Names of ethnic and cultural groups are indicated in SMALL CAPITALS.

Abelson, R. P., 22, 38
Agar, M., 47
AGUARUNA, 125–7, 131–3, 139–40, 168
Alexander, J., 46
Aristotle, 65
Armstrong, S. L., 31, 79
Astington, J. W., 35
Atangana, C., 223
Atran, S., 19, 46, 56, 60, 65, 70, 111, 112, 116, 120, 141
Azombo, S., 223

Baillargeon, R., 35
Bartlett, F. C., 45
Baterson, G., 38, 46, 208, 212, 215, 224
Batterman, N., 114, 128
Bauer, P., 112
Beattie, J., 185
Beaugrande, R. de, 45
Berlin, B., 52, 54, 58, 69, 112, 131
Berndt, R., 70
Berteaut, M., 223
BETI, 207–24
Bever, T. A., 44
Biggs, B., 91
Black, M., 48
Bloch, M., 14–15, 34, 64, 73, 160, 162, 165, 185
Bloomfield, L., 48
Boas, F., 50
Boon, J. A., 43
Bourdieu, P. 155, 162, 223
Bowerman, M., 44
Boyer, P., 24, 47, 73, 88, 122, 140, 141, 168, 194–6, 222
Breedlove, D., 52, 58, 69, 112, 131
Bretherton, I., 46
Brown, C., 46, 59, 62, 69
Brown, M., 125–7, 131–3, 168
Brugman, C., 98
Bruner, J., 160

Burgess, D., 75
Burling, R., 56

Capell, A., 82, 86, 91
Caramazza, A., 70
Carey, S., 35, 44, 57, 62, 63, 112
Carnap, R., 180
Cassirer, E., 43, 54
Chomsky, N., 44, 48, 57, 70, 90, 186, 205
Churchland, P. M., 43
Clark, E. V., 44
Clifford, J., 43
Codrington, R. H., 81, 82
Cohen, M., 217
Colby, B., 48
Coleman, L., 79, 91
Conklin, H., 48, 51, 64, 69
Crocker, J. C., 29
Culicover, P., 44
CUNA, 165–81

D'Andrade, R., 20, 21
De Kleer, J., 22
Dennett, D., 43, 44
DiSessa, A., 46
Dougherty, *see* Keller, J.
Douglas, M., 44, 103
Dretske, F., 43
Dubois, R., 120
Dugast, G., 223
Durkheim, E., 8, 10, 13–14, 44, 193
Durkin, K., 44
Dwyer, P., 58
DYIRBAL, 98

Ellen, R. F., 23, 126
Evans-Pritchard, E. E., 43, 110, 120

Fabrega, H., 123–4
FANG, 29–30, 36–7, 121–41

241

Subject index

Terms in vernacular languages are indicated in *italics*.
Names of ethnic and cultural groups are indicated in SMALL CAPITALS.